In Civil Rights section, include
95-126
206-221
236-241

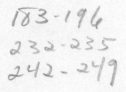

Ella Baker,
197-202

# TO REDEEM A NATION

## A History and Anthology of
the Civil Rights Movement

183-196
232-235
242-249

# TO REDEEM A NATION

## A History and Anthology of the Civil Rights Movement

**Edited by**

**Thomas R. West**    **James W. Mooney**

**BRANDYWINE PRESS** • St. James, New York

ISBN: 1-881089-20-7

1st Printing 1993

*Telephone Orders:* 1-800-345-1776

Printed in the United States of America

# TABLE OF CONTENTS

## INTRODUCTION:
### A History of the Civil Rights Movement ix

## PART 1 / PRECURSORS 1

The Fourteenth Amendment (1868) 3
*Booker T. Washington*—Atlanta Exposition Address 5
*W. E. B. Du Bois*—"Of Mr. Booker T. Washington . . ." 9
*W. E. B. Du Bois*—"The Talented Tenth" 14
The Niagara Movement—A Resolve to Seek Justice 19
*The Crisis*—Statement of Principles 23
*Marcus Garvey*—An Early Black Nationalist 24
*Langston Hughes*—The Harlem Renaissance 29

## PART 2 / INTEGRATION 33

*A. Philip Randolph*—First March on Washington Movement 35
*Ralph J. Bunche*—". . . I Like the American Way of Life" 38
Supreme Court decision in *Brown v. Board of Education
of Topeka* (1954) 41
*Mrs. Althea Simmons*—"We Sat There in Stunned Silence" 43
*Rosa Parks*—". . . I Tried Not to Think About What Might
Happen" 45
*Joseph Francis Rummel*—Segregation as Sin 47
The Southern Manifesto 49
*Elizabeth Eckford*—"Don't Let Them See You Cry" 52
*Lawrence C. Dum*—Discovering History in the Making 55
*Jimmy McDonald*—A Freedom Rider Reflects 57
*Charlayne Hunter-Gault*—A University Integrated 59
*Joanne Grant*—Youth in the Civil Rights Movement 62
*F. L. Shuttlesworth and N. H. Smith*—The Birmingham
Manifesto 66

*Whitney M. Young, Jr.*—Passion and Professionalism    69
*Slater King*—The Albany Movement    72
*John L. Perry*—A Lesson at Selma    76
*Roy Wilkins*—Standing Fast    79
*Martin Luther King, Jr.*—The Dream    82

## PART 3 / NONVIOLENCE    89

*Wilma Dykeman and James Stokely*—Greensboro and
    Beyond    91
*James Farmer*—Origins and Development of CORE    95
Statement of Purpose at the Origins of the Student Nonviolent
    Coordinating Committee, 1960    100
*Howell Raines*—Freedom Riders    101
*James Farmer*—In a Mississippi Jail    107
*Martin Luther King, Jr.*—Nonviolence and Civil
    Disobedience    111
*John Salter*—A Mississippi Demonstration    127
*Anne Moody*—Detention Center and Church    130
*Rev. Edwin King*—Christianity in Mississippi    135
*Benjamin Van Clark*—Nonviolence in Savannah, Georgia    146
*Rev. Joseph Lowery*—The Persuasive Power of
    Nonviolence    149
*Robert S. Browne*—The Civil Rights Movement and
    Vietnam    152

## PART 4 / LIBERALS    157

*Harry S Truman*—Equality in the Armed Services    159
*Robert S. McNamara*—Pressing for Equality    161
*John F. Kennedy*—Facing the Issues    164
*James Baldwin*—An Impassioned Criticism    166
*Norman Podhoretz*—Memories of a White Childhood    170
*Lyndon B. Johnson*—The Right to Vote    173
Summary of the Report of the National Advisory Commission
    on Civil Disorders, 1968    176
*Jerome Smith*—Beyond Reform    181

## PART 5 / POWER    183

*Elijah Muhammad*—The Nation of Islam    185
*Malcolm X (El Hajj Malik El Shabazz)*—A Nationalist Alternative
    to Elijah Muhammad    189

*Ella Baker*—Organization Without Dictatorship    197

*Gloria Richardson*—The Struggle for Power in Cambridge    203

*Robert Parris Moses*—Building Power and Community in Mississippi    206

Letters Home From Freedom Summer—A Summer of Discovery    213

*Septima P. Clark*—Education and Empowerment    222

*Staughton Lynd*—Education and Empowerment, Continued    225

*Jack Minnis*—Economics and Race    227

*Mrs. Fannie Lee Chaney*—Meridian Awakened    230

*Bayard Rustin*—Protest Movement and Social Movement    232

*Mrs. Fannie Lou Hamer*—Sustaining the Original Vision of SNCC    236

*Stokely Carmichael (Kwame Ture)*—Definitions of Black Power    242

*Charles Hamilton*—Another Definition    247

*James Forman*—The Black Manifesto    250

The Black Panther Manifesto    253

Black Panthers—The Rhetoric of Revolution    256

*Huey P. Newton*—Revolution as Liberation    258

**SUGGESTED READINGS    261**

Fannie Lou Hamer, grassroots Mississippi leader who played a prominent role in the Mississippi Freedom Democratic Party. *Photo: Lawrence Henry Collection, Schomburg Center for Research in Black Culture.*

# INTRODUCTION

Surely, Fannie Lou Hamer was no threat to anyone. A rural Mississippi woman, she was one of numberless black and poor Americans who from slavery times had been told to keep to their place, accept whatever slave rations or near-slave wages the white South chose to spend, and remember always to be polite and grateful. But what she did frightened the burly police, the defensive poor whites, and the genteel classes of her state. She along with others of her race attempted early in the 1960s to exercise their constitutional right to register for the vote. So frightening was this that one day she was hauled to a local police station and savagely beaten.

There was a time when the police and the power structure might have had their way—a time when Fannie Lou Hamer would not have dreamed of attempting to register, and before that a time when she would not even have had the Constitution to give her theoretical protection. But in the early 1960s, things were changing. The voter registration project went on, and at the Democratic Convention of 1964 Mrs. Hamer told her story to a nation increasingly repelled by the southern form of white racism. Simply by surviving and speaking, a woman of Mississippi's subjugated race had humiliated the police and the society that hid behind them.

Fannie Lou Hamer bled and worked for a future free of racism. She held to that faith. Later in the decade, when black militants in the rights movement turned against their white allies, cultivating a black racism in imitation of the white, she rejected their ideology. She had an integrity to match her physical courage. And that, as much as her defiance of the police thugs, makes her a symbol of a tough and enduring core of faith within the civil rights movement.

When Thurgood Marshall and other lawyers argued before the Supreme Court that segregated public schooling violates the

Constitution, they were acting in an American tradition of civil rights. And when Martin Luther King, Jr., and other ministers in their struggle against segregation argued for putting conscience above the law, they too were in a solid national tradition. Is justice, then, to be sought in the law and the Constitution, or in a call to principle outside of the law? American political and moral traditions give sanction to both claims. And so it was with Mrs. Hamer and the legions who marched with her in Mississippi in the great days of the civil rights movement. They were drawing simultaneously on the decrees of the law embedded in the Constitution, which gave them the right to vote, and on the decrees of conscience, which commanded them to fight for the destruction of white supremacy.

The major legal instrument of racial justice has been the Fourteenth Amendment, adopted in 1868. The Amendment is ambiguous in language and cautious in its attempt to prevent the southern states defeated in the Civil War from establishing something close to slavery over the freed African Americans. Its most important provisions in their bearing on race questions prohibit states from depriving "any person of life, liberty, or property, without due process of law" and from denying anyone "the equal protection of the laws."

One of the two best-known judicial renderings of the Amendment as it concerns civil rights is the Supreme Court's decision of 1896, in *Plessy v. Ferguson*, that a state could segregate by race as long as the facilities assigned to the two races were equal. The other is the Court's contrary declaration in 1954, in *Brown v. Board of Education of Topeka*, that state-imposed segregation in schooling is inherently unconstitutional discrimination against black students. This was the first and greatest of the decisions in which the Court, under Chief Justice of the United States Earl Warren, became an instrument of liberal social change. The assumption, made articulate since then, is that any other kind of racial segregation enforced by a state also violates the Fourteenth Amendment.

The Fourteenth Amendment has hastened the aims of the recent civil rights movement. But the Amendment has almost no independent power to shape the course of civil rights. Between the end of Reconstruction and President Eisenhower's decision in 1957 to enforce with federal troops the court-ordered school desegregation of Little Rock, Arkansas, the national government had little inclination to interfere with southern institutions, however unconstitutional and however unjust. In any event, much of the initiative in matters of civil rights has come from outside the government, and more particularly from African Americans themselves.

Booker T. Washington, one of the most debated figures in the history of civil rights, was born of a slave mother and educated under white patronage at Hampton Institute in Virginia. Founder in 1881 of Tuskegee Institute in Alabama for teachers, he became an advocate of a particular ethic and strategy for black Americans. He advised them to get an education, to develop habits and skills of profitable work, not to scorn the physical crafts, and to build within their communities the wealth and knowledge that, so he believed, would do them more good than a frontal assault on white supremacy. Equal justice would come slowly, in time. By early in the twentieth century Washington had accumulated wide political power within the black community. He has also won the lasting scorn of more militant figures who consider his teachings too compliant toward white supremacy. Historians have begun to discover in him a core of anger and resistance to white-racist institutions. In the final count, Washington may best be understood as applying to racial issues an American creed of work, education, and self-dependence that has radical as well as conservative implications.

It is customary and convenient to identify as the major alternative to the Tuskegee persuasion that of W. E. B. Du Bois. A brilliant record at Harvard won him its first doctorate awarded a black student. Thereafter he pursued a career of teaching and writing, meanwhile arguing for an aggressive attack on racism. He was a main founder of the Niagara Movement in 1905, which led in 1910 to the organization of the National Association for the Advancement of Colored People (NAACP), sponsored by leading black and white reformers. Du Bois and the Association together assailed white supremacy; *The Crisis* under his editorship carried the attack to the public. The demand for integration that the organization pressed in later times, most notably in the *Brown* case, earned it a reputation for radicalism until in the 1960s a new crop of militants denounced integration and the NAACP as instruments of white domination.

Beneath the contrasts between the thought of Washington and that of Du Bois and the NAACP in its first years was a common energy and a determination to improve the lives of African Americans. That energy expressed itself also in middle-class black women who early in the century were undertaking a variety of reform and welfare projects, providing playgrounds for black children, raising money to aid black women in getting a college education, and otherwise addressing the needs of a widely impoverished population. It was a time of widespread social and political activism—the progressive era, as historians now refer to it—and these women were among a growing number of female reformers who gave the age much of its character.

Then, shortly after the First World War, another burst of energy invigorated sections of the country's black population: this time, in the form of artistic creativity during the 1920s and centered in New York City's Harlem district. The Harlem artists explored the black sensibility, mingling with white intellectuals in what was perhaps the nation's first large interracial gathering of talent. Much of what the Harlem Renaissance is remembered for was literary, but Harlem also became a center for the musical experimentation that has continued among African American artists ever since.

At the same time that many black figures were demanding for their race entry into the larger society, the Jamaican immigrant Marcus Garvey was pursuing an opposite vision. He called blacks throughout the world to return to Africa, there to form a great black nation.

The Harlem Renaissance and Marcus Garvey's movement both happened at a time of heavy migration northward of black southerners. Probably largely unnoticed at the moment, it would later become recognized as providing further conditions for a massive political and social change in race relations.

An often neglected period in the growing political strength of black Americans was that of the New Deal. The Democratic party of Franklin D. Roosevelt largely succeeded in winning a black population that had previously given its allegiance to the Republican party of Abraham Lincoln. The shift in party alignment had little to do with civil rights. Liberal Democrats, notably the President's wife Eleanor Roosevelt, supported civil rights, but the party as a whole was still protecting its white southern flank, and the federal government allowed racial discrimination even in its own projects. What turned black Americans into Democrats were the same economic programs, however stingily provided to them, that also more generously aided poor or unemployed whites.

At least one incident during Roosevelt's presidency, however, hinted of the politics of later years. In 1941 the union leader A. Philip Randolph of the Brotherhood of Sleeping Car Porters planned a march on Washington calling for an end to discrimination in the military and in defense industries. The march was called off when Roosevelt began setting up a Fair Employment Practices Commission—which would prove ineffective.

The failure of the New Deal to accept black Americans as equal members of its political coalition (or its inability to do so under the political conditions of the time) was one of many things that define it as an incomplete progressive movement. At its best, the New Deal represented an attempt at fulfilling a recurrent American vision of the United States as a social democracy, a republic of workers. The alliance of the New Deal with labor unions, its projects for work relief and for the regulation of the economy, its schemes of social insurance: all were steps toward the realization of social and economic democracy. But they were halting steps. Social security, for example, did not even extend to the poorest of Americans. And so wealth would continue to be vastly maldistributed, much of the economy would remain under the control of the wealthiest classes, and African Americans though they made some gains under New Deal programs were prevented from attaining the full political rights of citizenship and the full social status of workers.

In Detroit and the city of Winston-Salem, North Carolina, during the 1940s black workers were active members of unions belonging to the powerful Congress of Industrial Organizations, a part of the liberal Democratic coalition. And during his presidency Harry Truman began the desegregation of the armed forces, called for an anti-lynching measure, and otherwise urged the extension of civil rights. Though only mildly liberal on questions of rights, Truman so antagonized southern Democratic white supremacists that in 1948 they fielded Strom Thurmond of South Carolina as the presidential candidate of the States' Rights or Dixiecrat party. The Dixiecrats were unsuccessfully attempting to draw off enough normally Democratic southern voters to wreck Truman in that year's presidential election. Truman's policies further validated his party's claim to be the party of civil rights.

Still, it is not in conventional politics that the struggle for civil rights has won its most impressive victories. The rights actions best remembered independently defied white-supremacist law or custom. To step up to a whites-only section of a lunch counter, to sit in a forbidden part of a bus, to join with white demonstrators in violating a segregated space: such acts meant that the whole system of white dominance and black acquiescence was losing its social and psychological force.

The best known of these events, a boycott in Montgomery, Alabama, followed the arrest of Rosa Parks on December 1, 1955, for refusing to yield her seat on a city bus to a white passenger. The city had a complicated rule requiring blacks to sit at the back of the bus and whites at the front and giving the drivers power to arrange seating in a middle section. Mrs. Parks was already an NAACP member and an activist, and the city's black leadership had been intending for some time an organized protest against the bus ordinance. Among the early leaders in planning the action were a local college teacher, Jo Ann Robinson, and E. D. Nixon, local head of the NAACP and the Brotherhood of Sleeping Car Porters. Soon after the start of the protest, leadership fell to Martin Luther King, Jr., a powerful speaker and the pastor of a prominent black Baptist congregation. When the city refused to consider a minimal change in the bus policy, the movement turned into the boycott—over a year long—that won through economic pressure and a suit in the federal courts an end to segregated bus seating. A bus boycott in Harlem in 1941 had successfully demanded the hiring of black drivers, and a short boycott action in Baton Rouge, Louisiana, in 1953 won a modification of discriminatory seating.

The organization and conduct of the Montgomery boycott were as significant for the future of the civil rights movement as was the result. Refusing to ride the city buses, black workers walked or organized car pools. In face of official hostility along with that of white racist thugs, King and the activists settled on a strategy of nonviolent resistance. It was inspired by the ideas of Mahatma Gandhi, who had rallied millions to the peaceful overthrow of British rule in India, and urged by the white minister Glenn Smiley and by Bayard Rustin, a black antiwar and civil rights activist. A form of resistance involving self-discipline and in some instances training, it requires protesters to confront their violent or threatening opponents without either retreating or responding with violence. The absolute self-possession that it embodies has been, as much as any other tactic, a psychological victory over white racism, which required postures of subordination on the part of American blacks. In years to come, it would be employed not only in racial actions but in resistance to the Vietnam war, to abortion clinics, and to other institutions that protesters define as doing violence.

The practice of nonviolence also has Christian roots, and added to the ministerial leadership of the Montgomery boycott it pointed to another feature of the civil rights movement in the 1950s and sixties: the major presence there of congregations from black churches and their preachers. In time, these would be joined by white ministers, priests, rabbis, and worshippers both Christian and Jewish. Within a short time after the boycott black ministers under the leadership of King organized themselves into the Southern Christian Leadership Conference (SCLC), committed to challenging white-supremacist practices and laws.

The civil rights movement in the wake of Montgomery increasingly appealed at once to law and to justice and conscience beyond the law. The *Brown* and later court decisions made it clear that any attempt on the part of a local or state government to impose segregation violated the Constitution. A protester defying a segregation ordinance was to that extent not a lawbreaker. The ordinance was itself unconstitutional, and the protester like a good law-abiding American was merely making sure that the illegal rule would be overthrown. Yet when southern police and state or city officials acted to stop civil rights activists, the protesters were in the position of pitting their consciences against people with billy-clubs and guns claiming to be enforcers of the law. For participation in the civil rights protests that followed Montgomery, demonstrators could be arrested for doing whatever the local police could define at the moment as warranting an arrest. In the rights actions of the next few years, conscience and the Constitution therefore made up a dual principle of resistance to unjust authority.

In 1954 the Supreme Court had spoken in the *Brown* decision, and not long afterwards the black citizens of Montgomery made their more personal rejection of white supremacy. Congress enacted and President Dwight D. Eisenhower signed in 1957 a bill containing some civil rights provisions. But the President had earlier withdrawn support from a section of the bill that would have allowed the attorney general to bring suits to desegregate schools without a request from local authorities.

Yet this President who had shown little liking for the *Brown* ruling used federal troops to compel the city of Little Rock, Arkansas, in the 1957–1958 school year to desegregate its public schools. The Little Rock school board had approved an integration plan. A state court blocked it, claiming that it would endanger the public peace. Thereupon a federal court ordered desegregation. The state's governor Orville Faubus, citing the risk of violence, set Arkansas national guard troops to preventing black students from entering previously all-white school grounds. Eisenhower then put the guard under federal command, as the Constitution permitted him, told it to protect rather than hinder desegregation, and sent paratroopers to stand off white racist mobs and enforce the federal court order. After some eighty years of neglect, the federal government had at last acted to make a southern state respect constitutionally guaranteed rights of African Americans. Henceforth, rights activists could hope that they might call for aid from Washington.

By the late 1950s, civil rights organizations were in place in much of the South, drawing strength from the churches and from motivated students. NAACP chapters stretched through the region. Public transportation in some cities surrendered to the demand for desegregation. Here and there were sit-ins, as they are called. A group of black southerners would literally sit in, or perhaps stand, at a segregated establishment or section of a private business, testing the willingness of whites to abandon an increasingly discredited practice of discrimination. In the semi-southern federal city of Washington, blacks had succeeded in this tactic in the early 1950s. Little if any of this received the notice of newspapers outside the South. Then, on February 1, 1960, began an action that gave the struggle against segregation a renewed national prominence; and again, the initiative came not from the government or white liberals but from ordinary black citizens.

On that day Ezell Blair, Jr., David Richmond, Franklin McCain, and Joseph McNeil, four students from the black North Carolina Agricultural and Technical College, went up to the segregated section of a lunch counter at Woolworth's in Greensboro, North Carolina. After remaining at the counter without being served, the demonstrators went outside and prayed on the sidewalk. The next day more showed up, including a few white women from a neighboring school. Similar actions had been taking place elsewhere throughout the South, but now the time had ripened for the country to take notice. Demonstrations, relentless in their mild persuasiveness, spread to distant southern communities. That meant that segregation was finished, for it had lost that power to command black deference that had been its point and meaning. In Greensboro, meanwhile, persistence brought an end to segregation at the disputed lunch counter.

For some time, a number of groups dissenting from American institutions and practices other than white supremacy had been sympathetic to the cause of civil rights. Besides antiwar organizations such as the Fellowship of Reconciliation and the War Resisters League, rights activists could look to the Highlander Folk School in east Tennessee. Highlander ran workshops at which poor people or others dedicated to changing the conditions around them could gather to discuss methods of social reconstruction. Some time before the Montgomery boycott, Rosa Parks had attended Highlander, and later King visited the institution. Highlander sponsored informal schools elsewhere in the South designed to teach blacks the skills necessary for acquiring political power. The Fellowship of Reconciliation, moreover, at the initiative of James Farmer had spawned in 1942 a northern group, the racially mixed Congress of Racial Equality (CORE), which conducted sit-ins in the North. Now, in the energetic days following Greensboro, that organization became increasingly visible and active.

Under the directorship of Farmer, CORE sent through the South racially integrated busloads of freedom riders to test the presence of discrimination in interstate bus terminals. As early as 1947 an interracial CORE group had ridden through the upper South to measure compliance with a Supreme Court civil rights ruling, a rarity before *Brown*, against discrimination on interstate buses. The action had gone largely unnoticed. Not so in 1961. When freedom riders were attacked by mobs, and some beaten, the press was on hand. The administration of John F. Kennedy, at least moderately liberal on racial matters, was nervous about the situation, and the president's brother Attorney General Robert F. Kennedy tried to discourage the riders from continuing. But toward the end of their project he gave them some protection by federal marshals. He also requested the Interstate Commerce Commission to ban segregation in bus terminals serving interstate passengers.

In the autumn of 1961 the movement began putting much of its effort into support of a civil rights campaign that was taking place in Albany, Georgia. King was at Albany, trying to move the black population with a series of demonstrations and acts of civil disobedience—a variety of nonviolent resistance in which the demonstrator violates a local ordinance or a command of a police officer and then peacefully acquiesces in arrest. The police chief Laurie Pritchett, shrewder and perhaps more humane than some others of his rank, refused to countenance or engage in the kinds of pointless viciousness that had already disgraced the remnants of white supremacy. Joining demonstrators in prayer before arresting them was among the gestures that distinguished him from his ham-handed colleagues in other localities. Federal prosecution of some of the activists in connection with what the government considered to be illegal picketing was an early incident among many that would in time turn much of the rights movement distrustful of Washington.

In 1961 two black students, Hamilton Holman and Charlayne Hunter—now the journalist Charlayne Hunter-Gault—integrated the University of Georgia in an intricate legal battle punctuated by a white racist riot on the campus. The act had as a precedent Autherine Lucy's earlier battle to integrate the University of Alabama: entering in February 1956 under a court order requiring the university to admit her, she had almost immediately been expelled on the grounds that her presence was causing turmoil. In September 1962 James Meredith attempted to enroll in the University of Mississippi as the institution's first black student. Since Ole Miss was an institution directly run by the state government, segregation there was now recognizably unconstitutional. The state's governor Ross Barnett tried to prevent Meredith's enrollment. After fruitless bargaining with the governor, President Kennedy sent federal marshals, national guardsmen, and federal troops to the campus to protect Meredith against a mob. In the riot that ensued, two reporters were killed, while 375 people were injured and two hundred arrested; but Meredith was able to enter the university.

In the spring of 1963, Vivian Malone enrolled at the University of Alabama. It was the occasion for Governor George Wallace's act of standing in the doorway of a campus building in symbolic defiance of integration (pure stage drama: he was not blocking anyone). That, along with an address in which he proclaimed, "Segregation now, segregation tomorrow, segregation forever," gave him a prominence that was to launch him into his strong showing in the Democratic presidential primaries of 1964 and his separate-party presidential candidacy in 1968. Later this basically genial demagogue would attempt to make his peace with African Americans. But in 1963 there occurred in his state one of the most violent of the white racist attempts to impede the progress of integration.

It happened in Birmingham. There the Reverend Fred Shuttlesworth was leading a movement demanding desegregation of businesses. In the confrontations that followed, King came to the city to help rally the movement. Facing him was Police Commissioner Bull Connor, whose tactics belonged to primitive racism rather than to the more sophisticated maneuverings of Albany's Laurie Pritchett. From a Birmingham jail, King wrote to his fellow clergymen a memorable letter that articulated both the reasons for the demonstrations and the meaning of nonviolent civil disobedience.

King's letter caught the mind of the nation; the behavior of the police and the more loutish of the city's whites enraged the country's conscience. As though perversely determined to reveal what racism and white supremacy were all about, police used cattle prods against demonstrators and attack dogs against children. In September a bomb explosion killed four black children in a Sunday school.

During the many civil rights actions preceding Birmingham, the Kennedy administration had been sympathetic to demonstrators yet cautious about offending Democratic voters who might not care for the rights movement. But Birmingham was too much. In a nationally broadcast address on June 11, 1963, Kennedy called for racial justice and harmony and proposed a bill that would include the banning of segregation in establishments of public accommodation such as restaurants. Under its constitutional power to regulate interstate commerce, Congress could pass such a law and apply it to all but the smallest businesses, for even restaurants, hotels, and motels serving a largely local trade may be perceived as part of a flow of commerce that runs across state lines. In Birmingham, meanwhile, the white business community was coming to see that having a peaceful city enjoying its share of respect in the rest of the nation would be financially advantageous, and businesses began to adopt some of the demands of the rights protesters.

As demonstrations, arrests and violence, and northern sympathy for the rights movement interacted to hasten the end of official white supremacy, national television with its vivid renderings of happenings in the South contributed to what was becoming a single ongoing event as experienced in the collective American mind. In this as in so many other ways, the movement belonged to its times. This was an era that especially later in the days of Vietnam and campus protests, of hippies and communes, possessed a peculiarly public quality. It came to seem, in those angry, hopeful days, as though what the media reported of some event in a distant city was simultaneously taking place on the streets just outside, and within the consciousness of whoever listened, or watched, or imagined.

That summer of Birmingham, another event gave the movement the look of commanding the future that it was increasingly acquiring. On August 28, some 250,000 black and white Americans gathered in Washington, D.C., in support of civil rights. A main figure in the event was A. Philip Randolph, who had planned the unexecuted march on Washington of 1941. The 1963 march, unlike earlier civil rights events, had wide endorsement from establishment liberals. Its high moment was King's delivery of a version of the speech known as "I Have a Dream"—a dream of future community of blacks and whites.

The momentum of the rights movement was now unstoppable, and the previously hesitant federal government was acting on its behalf. After the assassination of Kennedy in November 1963, Vice President Lyndon Johnson became President. A southerner from Texas, Johnson nevertheless agreed with the aims of the rights activists. Johnson energetically supported a bill that would enact the civil rights program Kennedy had imagined. Senators and Representatives were pressured by religious leaders, always influential in the national legislature. The Republican Senator Everett Dirksen of Illinois, a leader of the conservative opposition to the Democratic administration, nevertheless became a major supporter of the bill. It passed both houses: the Senate in a notable departure from the past voted to cut off a southern filibuster intended to stave off passage of a rights measure. The Civil Rights Act of 1964 required the integration of public accommodations. It permitted the attorney general to file suits to force desegregation of schools. It provided for the withdrawal of federal funds from projects practicing discrimination. The law banned discrimination in employment in all businesses hiring more than twenty-five people, and set up an Equal Employment Opportunity Commission that could investigate complaints of discrimination. In 1965 Johnson signed the Voting Rights Act preventing interference with that right. The federal government now had a formidable arsenal of laws against whatever remained of state or institutional white supremacy.

The civil rights movement had its internal distinctions, the NAACP being perceived as committing itself to careful judicial procedures while the Southern Christian Leadership Conference spoke with the voice and acted with the passion of evangelical Christianity. The movement as a whole, however, went by its compound ethic: against unjust law and custom, set your conscience; when law is just, demand obedience.

Much of the same applies as well to the Student Nonviolent Coordinating Committee (SNCC), a group that did some of the toughest rights work of the times. Yet from the beginning SNCC had an edge of anger and rebellion that set it apart.

A founder of SNCC was Ella Baker, a critic of the Southern Christian Leadership Conference for what she thought to be its heavyhanded domination of the movement. She wanted a thoroughly democratic movement, and SNCC, formed soon after Greensboro and never having a membership of more than a few hundred, was designed to operate not through conventional leadership but through continuous democratic participation on the part of all members. SNCC was active in the freedom rides. Its most notable work was in Mississippi during the early 1960s.

There, facing the constant possibility of violence from white thugs and police and subject to arrest at the whim of local officials, SNCC activists encouraged black Mississippians to register for the vote. The purpose was not only to increase registration but to awaken among black people an awareness of their latent power and independence. It was difficult to persuade the black community that the gain was worth the risk; and beyond the fear of physical retaliation was the recognition that officials were going to find excuses to reject registrants anyway. A powerful force in the movement was Bob Moses of New York, an introspective young black intellectual who, in keeping with his own personality as well as SNCC's commitment to democracy, refused to act the part of a commander and instead encouraged those around him to make decisions.

In time the project decided to hold a separate unofficial primary vote nominating candidates for state positions, while the rights workers also continued their efforts to open up the official registration process. The candidates so chosen would have no chance in the real contest, and at any rate the procedure brought the threat of harassment by police, who did not like to see black Mississippians doing anything that suggested political activity. But the unofficial registration would not be in the hands of local officials determined to reject black applicants. And the participation of black Mississippians could increase their self-confidence, at the same time showing the rest of the country their determination to become politically empowered. In 1963 their Freedom Vote nominated Aaron Henry of the NAACP for governor. For lieutenant governor they chose Edwin King, a white minister and veteran of civil rights actions who would maintain the integrationist faith into a future in which others had forsaken it.

Then, in 1964, the Mississippi project carried out the idea of bringing in northerners, most of whom would be white, to help voter registration. Some hostility to the recruitment of northern whites foreshadowed the future of the organization. But SNCC recognized both that the extra volunteers would be a material help and that the presence of comparatively affluent young whites was sure to draw national attention. During Freedom Summer of 1964, some thousand volunteers came south: the typical volunteer was a northern white college student. The murder of three SNCC workers—Michael Schwerner, Andrew Goodman, and their black companion James Chaney—dramatized for people outside the southern states the condition of Mississippi.

That summer the project sent to the Democratic National Convention at Atlantic City delegates chosen in another unofficial tally, this time drawing from eighty to ninety thousand black votes. These dissidents called themselves the Mississippi Freedom

Democratic Party (MFDP). The delegates claimed that as representatives of a vote more democratic than that which had chosen the
official Mississippi slate, they were more fit to receive acceptance
at Atlantic City as the true Mississippi delegation. Fannie Lou
Hamer was one of them, and she gave an eloquent speech before
the credentials committee at the Convention, recounting her arrest
and beating for having tried to register. Part of it was televised.
But Lyndon Johnson, who upon the assassination of John Kennedy
had succeeded to the presidency and was certain to receive at the
Convention the Democratic nomination for the coming presidential election, held a live news conference and thereby managed to
preempt the television channels before Mrs. Hamer had finished
speaking. Johnson and other organizers of the Convention, liberal
but fearful of antagonizing white voters in the South, wanted the
MFDP to have as little visibility at Atlantic City as possible, and
offered the Freedom Democrats nothing immediate beyond token
compromise. Lyndon Johnson was nominated overwhelmingly as
the party's presidential candidate. He went on to win the national
election by a large margin against the Republican candidate Barry
Goldwater, and as President he worked impressively for civil
rights. But the memory of the treatment his political handlers at
Atlantic City had accorded the MFDP continued to embitter SNCC
along with others in the civil rights movement, and was instrumental in bringing about a material change in its character.

That change included a rejection of established political liberalism. Relations between liberals and civil rights activists had
been tenuous anyway. Washington had shown itself to be sympathetic to the movement but uncomfortable with actions that it considered politically dangerous to the Democratic party. Perhaps it
was unreasonable of the rights forces not to understand that a government and a political party have many considerations to balance and can rarely make a complete commitment to any one goal.
But resentment was a natural reaction to the frustrating caution of
establishment liberals. The party's handling of the MFDP at Atlantic City was bad. By every political measure, Lyndon Johnson was
sure to be the winner in November, and the liberals could have
afforded the very small risk that would have come with granting
substantial recognition at the Convention to one of the most spir-
ited and politically deserving efforts of the time. Instead, it turned
a difficult ally into an enemy.

SNCC went further. Rejecting political liberalism, it became
increasingly distant from whites in general, liberal and radical as
well as conservative. Not adopting an explicitly racist language

against whites, militants were claiming that whites were incapable of understanding the black experience, that blacks must concentrate on cultivating their own racial pride and power. SNCC during the time of the Mississippi project itself intended to nurture black communal power and self-dependence. Now self-dependence was turning into self-enclosure.

One last major civil rights episode remained bringing together blacks and whites, committed activists and well-wishing liberals. Early in 1965 the movement waged in Selma, Alabama, a campaign for registration of black voters. In a nearby town a state trooper shot and killed Jimmy Lee Jackson, a young black church deacon. His death and funeral contributed to public outrage—now a frequent national response to the behavior of southern racism under siege. A protest march set out from Selma to the state capital of Montgomery. At Pettus Bridge along the way, police attacked the marchers with clubs and tear gas. John Lewis, chairman of SNCC, was among the victims of the police riot. Again, the defenders of white supremacy had managed to draw disgusted nationwide attention to themselves. President Johnson sent troops and helicopters to protect the highway to Montgomery, and a five-day march beginning on Sunday, March 21, included thousands of people from outside the South. Celebrities and northern liberals joined with southern black marchers. After the arrival at Montgomery, King delivered one of his powerful speeches: the repeated "How long? Not long ...." gave it cadence. That night Viola Liuzzo, a northerner and mother who had come to the demonstration, was shot to death by a Ku Klux Klansman as she was driving on an Alabama highway with a black passenger. She, and earlier in Selma the Reverend James Reeb, were among a number of white civil rights activists who fell victim to a violence that was more usually visited upon African Americans.

Shortly after the march, Johnson presented to Congress the bill that became the Voting Rights Act of 1965. During the previous year the Twenty-Fourth Amendment to the Constitution had won ratification. It outlawed the poll tax as a qualification for voting in federal elections.

The march to Montgomery was the culmination of a rights movement that had reached out to white society and included liberal participants as well as supporters. The march also provides a convenient date for the demise of that spirit. Interracial demonstrations would continue to occur. They still do. But the turn that black militancy had taken after the 1964 Democratic Convention and even earlier was now clearly going to qualify or complicate rights activities for some years to come. The next large rights action, in Mississippi in June 1966, made that clear.

After James Meredith was shot on a lonely walk across Mississippi in the cause of racial equality, a march called by King and other rights leaders crossed the state demanding that federal marshals be assigned to the protection of black voter registration. King's intention was to unify the movement. But militants, most notably Stokely Carmichael of SNCC, brought to the march their determination to draw a line between blacks and even the most committed of white supporters. Some hostility among black marchers was directed not at Mississippi racism but at the whites among them. A film of the event records a moment of nonviolent self-containment on the part of a white woman demonstrator who walks resolutely onward while a black youth beside her chants his rejection of whites.

Besides King, a core of seasoned rights figures remained to keep alive the vision of an interracial society and to concentrate on concrete social, economic, and political problems. They included Whitney Young of the Urban League, King's associate in the Southern Christian Leadership Conference Ralph Abernathy, the young Jesse Jackson, and Roy Wilkins of the NAACP. Wilkins was to be a persistent critic of the direction black militancy was taking. But SNCC made a decisive break. Calling itself the Atlanta Project, a group within the organization was proclaiming white people to be incapable of understanding the struggle of blacks and urged the expulsion of whites from SNCC. Fannie Lou Hamer was repelled at the hostility toward whites she discovered in SNCC, which in 1967 voted by a narrow margin to expel all whites, the measure to become effective the following year. By this time as well, the organization was abandoning its ethic of nonviolence.

Among a number of phrases soon to be in confused and at times interchangeable use among black militants and observers of them is "black militant" itself, a term that could cover just about anyone who is black and militant on the racial issue. We employ it here, somewhat unsatisfactorily, to apply to blacks who stress not so much an end to racial division as the development of black unity and action. "Black consciousness" and "black pride" are among the most elusive of the other terms. They do not have to point to anything more than the degree of self-awareness to be expected within any ethnic group, and could look back, for example, to the Harlem Renaissance. In this usage they suggest another term current in the sixties: "black culture." Or "black consciousness" could represent a belief that deep within their collective psyche blacks share a consciousness, an experience inaccessible to outsiders—a belief that comes close to denying to the individual black man or woman an individual mind and will and a personal identity freely constructed.

"Black power," again, has possible contrary meanings, referring to no more than the building of a power base of a kind desirable to any group, or to no less than the acquisition of power to be wielded defensively or aggressively against the rest of society. "Black separatism" is clear enough: it designates the intent to withdraw as far as possible from the white world. It is near in signification to the slightly softer "black nationalism," referring to a phenomenon going back at least as far as to Marcus Garvey.

That the word "black" itself has become prominent in recent usage in place of the once-common "Negro" or "colored" is probably attributable mostly to insistence on the part of the black power movement. Employment of the word was intended as a strong and clear statement of the distinctiveness of black Americans. Still more recent, at least as a term in wide usage, is "African American," designating an ancestry and ethnicity as does "Irish American" or "Polish American."

In its more antiwhite meanings, black power had a predecessor in Elijah Muhammad's Nation of Islam, a group popularly called the Black Muslims. The sect had preached a doctrine combining a few scraps of the actual Moslem faith with a bizarre and fanciful mythology purporting to demonstrate that the white race is a devilish and degenerate offspring of black ancestors. Elijah Muhammad's followers were to prepare for the day when whites would be destroyed and blacks would inherit the earth. The organization practiced a stern code in sexual matters, personal hygiene, and the avoidance of drugs and alcohol. Its most famous leader was Malcolm X (he had rejected his family name "Little": believers held that in time blacks would learn their true names). He was a former hustler who after conversion to the teachings of the Nation of Islam demonstrated power in oratory and debate. After a break with Elijah Muhammad early in the 1960s and in the course of a trip to Mecca, as is expected of Moslems, Malcolm X encountered the true Islamic religion and discovered there an ethic of interracial harmony. For the short period that remained to him, he presented a radical modification of his old convictions, urging separate economic and political development among black Americans but insisting that they could live at peace with whites of good will. In 1965 he was assassinated. Followers of the Nation of Islam were convicted of the murder.

The newer crop of militants who for one reason or another rejected the mainline civil rights movement were widely varied in belief and practice. The Black Panthers, active particularly in California in the late sixties and counting among their leaders Huey Newton, Bobby Seale, and Fred Hampton, were distinctive particularly for a semi-military mode of conduct and for hostility to the police. The Panthers were recognizable for a style of dress: black jackets and black berets. Differences in tone and emphasis racked SNCC. Agreeing that blacks must be the vanguard of revolution and whites at best followers, James Forman insisted that white racism was ultimately a function of class rather than of skin color. Under black leadership in the United States and that of other colored peoples throughout the world, Forman argued, a revolution including enlightened whites could win a future free of class oppression, imperialism, and racism.

Even in the absence of such incidents as that of the backhanded treatment accorded the Mississippi Freedom Democratic Party at the 1964 Convention, an eventual end would have been inevitable for the spirit of the Montgomery boycott and the Greensboro sit-ins. Nonviolent action, accompanied when necessary by civil disobedience, was effective against specific offensive white-supremacist laws and practices. It was almost useless when the problem was to address some stubborn social or economic condition having racist roots but requiring complex measures of law and bargaining.

From as far back as the time of Booker T. Washington, civil rights had been about more than the elimination of the explicit and insulting symbols of white racism. The *Brown* decision forecast not only the end to an insult but an improvement in the education available to black children and hence to their community. Both the Kennedy administration and Lyndon Johnson's Great Society knew that projects providing jobs or other benefits to the poor were especially important to African Americans. In the politics that attended the design and adoption of such programs questions of race mingled with general economic issues. The Economic Opportunity Act of 1964, providing funds to be distributed by local communities and setting up a Job Corps offering vocational education and temporary jobs for the young, had racial minorities especially in mind. A law forbidding discrimination in employment is both a law against racism and a measure for economic opportunity. A program of job training saying nothing explicit about discrimination may have above all the intention of injecting into black communities skills and opportunities that discriminatory practices had kept from them.

Issues of this kind, moreover, directed the energies of the civil rights movement northward. There white workers began to fear competition for their jobs. Informally segregated neighborhoods now felt besieged. Taxpayers recoiled from the cost of programs attacking poverty. And a racism previously less self-aware and articulate than that of the white South began to find an expression at times evasively worded, and at others primitively direct. Even northerners having little social conscience could feel the appropriate anger at the brainless brutality of mobs and police in the South, and applaud the measures of a federal government increasingly determined to combat southern white supremacy. Accepting the tangible economic and social costs of eliminating not only racism but its many indirect results was another matter, and Lyndon Johnson's War on Poverty made it clear that there would be a price tag.

In 1966 King attempted to open up Chicago. The city under the Democratic mayor Richard Daley grossly discriminated against blacks. The city government worked out complex residential formulas to ensure that schools would remain effectively segregated. Employing the methods of demonstrations that came most naturally to his temper and eloquence, King attempted to win from the city more favorable treatment of blacks, and he and his followers marched against neighborhood segregation. In segments of Chicago's white population, fury was palpable. While King addressed civil rights marchers in Marquette Park, police held back a white mob estimated to be four thousand in number.

By now, the whole issue of race was clearly centering in the cities. Black urban riots, notably in the Watts section of Los Angeles in 1965 and in Detroit two years later, defined it as an urban question. So the black garbage collectors of Memphis, Tennessee, whose strike King went to support in the early spring of 1968 were acting in accord with a rights activism that had come to fix itself in the economic and social problems of the cities. It was there on April 4 that an assassin took the life of the leader who had embodied the spirit of the nonviolent civil rights movement.

Black power militants who until April 4 had been trying to discredit Martin Luther King and the whole idea of integration of the races called for an uprising. Riots in a number of cities were a response to King's death that mocked the meaning of his life. Within months of his murder there lived for a moment in Washington, D.C., and then died, a scheme he had initiated that brought together the integrationist persuasion of the early rights movement and the economic and social concerns of the late sixties. It was a gathering of the poor to call for social justice. That summer poor people did assemble in the nation's capital—black, American Indian, Chicano, and whites of older European descent. The encampment of the Poor People's Campaign was known as Resurrection City. Before long the camp disbanded without clear accomplishment. Once again it was proven: demonstrations of a kind that had been effective against the visible institutions of white supremacy were less successful at prying open the nation's more complex and deep-seated economic inequalities.

One more event of the late 1960s deserves mention as illustrative of how diffuse the old rights movement had become. At Cornell University in 1969, a core of black students demanded control over a projected black-studies program, which they envisaged as an instrument of militancy and black consciousness. In the course of their confrontations they seized arms and took over a building. The administration and faculty, perhaps wisely deciding that the life of a student or two taken by a stray bullet would be too high a price, gave in to the fantasies of the rebels.

The main character of Ralph Ellison's *The Invisible Man*, published in 1952, is a southern black migrant to New York City. He is invisible in the sense that, lacking the firm social status occupied by whites, he is largely unknown, even to himself, and is seen through the stereotypes that American society has imposed on the black race. A black educator tries to turn him into the Good Negro, a white radical group attempts to define him as a hero of the Oppressed, and so on. In the course of the novel the protagonist learns to discover himself as a very private individual having his own inner knowledge: to perceive himself as an intelligence independent of the stereotypes he has taken up and passed beyond. His self-discovery is symbolized in a lonely room he occupies, lighted by electricity he has tapped from the city wires: a light clear and stark like his own mind. *The Invisible Man*, one of the most influential of all American novels, is a black writer's exploration of a longstanding problem: how were African Americans supposed to know and define themselves in the absence of the civic, social, and economic institutions available to whites? The civil rights movement, in full flower within a few short years of the publication of *The Invisible Man*, made for a public airing of the problem of identity that Ellison's character has to pursue in isolation.

The exacting and often dangerous activities of the movement made for self-discovery. In a demonstration that required facing the taunts of spectators and the anger of the police, a demonstrator might look inward and find composure and resolve. That introspective knowledge, though achieved in an activity with other demonstrators, has something in common with the identity that Ellison's protagonist wins for himself in privacy. Quite a different way to identity was that of the various black power advocacies later in the decade. Anticipated by the Nation of Islam and by Malcolm X, these invited the African American to identification by membership in a group. Two potentially conflicting means to personal definition, then, had now received clear public presentation: that of independent self-identity, independently achieved, and that of surrender to collective identity.

During the sixties, the civil rights movement had acquired connections with much that was happening outside its own province. Even the other events that began to eclipse it in the public mind, especially the resistance to the war in Vietnam, appeared to be continuing its spirit in new forms. The activism of various kinds among white university students took much of its character from the energy and example of the rights workers and demonstrators. The diverse and divided movement against the war in Vietnam defined the conflict as a war of aggression against a poor and nonwhite Third World people, an export of the nation's domestic racism. The women's movement claimed to be speaking for a group exploited and marginalized on the basis of gender, as blacks had been exploited on the basis of race. The deepest resonances, however, between the rights campaigns and other portions of the ongoing event that today is often remembered simply as "the sixties" were the ethos of nonviolence and the practice that New Leftists would term "participatory democracy."

Only part of the antiwar movement committed itself to the concept of nonviolence and the tactics of nonviolent civil disobedience. But since the protest was against the lethal violence of the war, as the protests of the rights demonstrators had been against the psychological and physical violence of white supremacy, nonviolence was a symbolically logical response. Blocking streets or entrances to buildings as an expression of resistance to the conflict in Southeast Asia and then submitting to arrest was a reenactment of the conduct of rights workers and, decades earlier, of the followers of Gandhi in India. It was peaceful defiance of an authority perceived as unjust, aimed at reaching an eventual reconciliation with the agents of injustice.

The advocates of participatory democracy conceived of breaking up society into small communities and committees in which each member would actively engage in argument, group decision, and consequent action. That was the kind of activity that

Bob Moses had wished to promote in Mississippi. Many practitioners of participatory democracy were of quite another mind than
that of the activists of nonviolence. But the self-possession and personal independence required by nonviolent action, especially the
restraint and tolerance in the face of an opponent, makes it a companion to any plan as demanding as participatory democracy. And
together with nonviolence, the idea of free and wide democratic
participation captures what the civil rights movement imagined
for the American nation: a people at cooperative peace.

# TO REDEEM A NATION

### A History and Anthology of
### the Civil Rights Movement

Booker T. Washington, founder of Tuskegee Institute
in Alabama in 1881. Some criticized his gradualist,
conciliatory approach to race relations, but he was very
much a man of action who often defied traditional racial
conventions. *(Courtesy, Library of Congress)*

# Part 1

# PRECURSORS

*The materials here reflect some of the earliest efforts to define the rights of African Americans. That such efforts even existed in times of massive social and legal barriers to equality gives them a significance beyond their specific content.*

*The Fourteenth Amendment to the Constitution is today an important protector of the rights of black Americans as well as others whose political status or fundamental freedoms are in any danger from state authorities. It was many decades, though, before the Amendment had serious employment for the protection of the rights of African Americans.*

*In Booker T. Washington's era, other leaders in the incipient civil rights struggles accused him of being too accommodating to white supremacist institutions, and over the years the impression of him as submissive to white supremacy has endured. But he was a defender of as many of the rights of black citizens as he believed he could possibly protect. His idea that the black community should cultivate its own resources, acquiring education, skills, professional knowledge, and economic strength, has something in common with the beliefs of the black power advocates of the 1960s, whose militancy was at poles from his reluctance to challenge institutions of white supremacy.*

*W. E. B. Du Bois and the National Association for the Advancement of Colored People (NAACP) were once at the forefront of black militancy, and their denunciations of white racism and its practices offered a combative alternative to the conciliatory words of Washington. But one day a portion of the African American leadership was to dismiss the NAACP as an organization of appeasers and claim that integration is submission to white society. Exponents of that way of*

1

*thinking will more easily endorse the vision of black nationalism as Marcus Garvey articulated it.*

*The Harlem Renaissance and the migration northward of black southerners were not events of immediate political significance. But they had to do with cultural and demographic changes that have since been essential to the civil rights movement.*

William Edward Burghardt Du Bois, 1869–1963.
*(Courtesy, National Portrait Gallery)*

# The Fourteenth Amendment (1868)

*Congress passed this Amendment to the Constitution to prevent the defeated South from imposing severely restrictive laws on the freed slaves. By the end of 1868 three-fourths of the states, the necessary number for ratification, had given their approval. Among those ratifying the measure were some southern states that were by then under Reconstruction governments. But only in recent decades have the courts and the national legislature begun using it seriously for the protection of civil rights. Sections 1, 2 and 5 are the portions of the Amendment most applicable to questions of civil rights; sections 3 and 4 were punitive measures against supporters of the Confederacy.*

SEC. 1. All persons born or naturalized in the United States, and subject to the jurisdiction thereof, are citizens of the United States and of the State wherein they reside. No State shall make or enforce any law which shall abridge the privileges or immunities of citizens of the United States; nor shall any State deprive any person of life, liberty, or property, without due process of law; nor deny to any person within its jurisdiction the equal protection of the laws.

SEC. 2. Representatives shall be apportioned among the several States according to their respective numbers, counting the whole number of persons in each State, excluding Indians not taxed. But when the right to vote at any election for the choice of electors for President and Vice President of the United States, Representatives in Congress, the Executive and Judicial officers of a State, or the members of the Legislature thereof, is denied to any of the male inhabitants of such State, being twenty-one years of age, and citizens of the United States, or in any way abridged, except for participation in rebellion, or other crime, the basis of representation therein shall be reduced in the proportion which the number of such male citizens shall bear to the whole number of male citizens twenty-one years of age in such State.

SEC. 3. No person shall be a Senator or Representative in Congress, or elector of President and Vice President, or hold any office, civil or military, under the United States, or under any State, who, having previously taken an oath, as a member of Congress, or as an officer of the United States, or as a member of any State legislature, or as an executive or judicial officer of any State, to support the Constitution of the United States, shall have engaged in insurrection or rebellion against the same, or given aid or comfort to the enemies thereof. But Congress may by a vote of two-thirds of each House, remove such disability.

SEC. 4. The validity of the public debt of the United States, authorized by law, including debts incurred for payment of pensions and bounties for services in suppressing insurrection or rebellion shall not be questioned. But neither the United States nor any State shall assume or pay any debt or obligation incurred in aid of insurrection or rebellion against the United States, or any claim for the loss or emancipation of any slave; but all such debts, obligations and claims shall be held illegal and void.

SEC. 5. The Congress shall have power to enforce, by appropriate legislation, the provisions of this article.

# Booker T. Washington

## Atlanta Exposition Address

*This famous address was delivered at the opening of the Cotton States Exposition in Atlanta, Georgia, in 1895. It is widely associated with Washington's conviction that the most productive course for black Americans was not to attempt directly to overthrow white racist laws or customs but instead to work at collective self-betterment through agriculture and industry. Soon afterward, the more radical black writer W. E. B. Du Bois in an essay respectful of Washington nonetheless took issue with what Du Bois termed "the Atlanta compromise."*

Mr. President and Gentlemen of the Board of Directors and Citizens: One third of the population of the South is of the Negro race. No enterprise seeking the material, civil, or moral welfare of this section can disregard this element of our population and reach the highest success. I but convey to you, Mr. President and Directors, the sentiment of the masses of my race when I say that in no way have the value and manhood of the American Negro been more fittingly and generously recognized than by the managers of this magnificent exposition at every stage of its progress. It is a recognition that will do more to cement the friendship of the two races than any occurrence since the dawn of our freedom.

Not only this, but the opportunity here afforded will awaken among us a new era of industrial progress. Ignorant and inexperienced, it is not strange that in the first years of our new life we began at the top instead of at the bottom; that a seat in Congress or the State Legislature was more sought than real estate or industrial skill; that the political convention or stump speaking had more attraction than starting a dairy farm or truck garden.

A ship lost at sea for many days suddenly sighted a friendly

*Source:* Louis R. Harlan, ed., *The Booker T. Washington Papers*, Vol. 3, *1889–95* (Urbana, Illinois: University of Illinois Press, 1974).

vessel. From the mast of the unfortunate vessel was seen a signal: "Water, water; we die of thirst!" The answer from the friendly vessel at once came back: "Cast down your bucket where you are." A second time the signal, "Water, water; send us water!" ran up from the distressed vessel, and was answered: "Cast down your bucket where you are." And a third and fourth signal for water was answered, "Cast down your bucket where you are." The captain of the distressed vessel, at last heeding the injunction, cast down his bucket, and it came up full of fresh, sparkling water from the mouth of the Amazon River. To those of my race who depend upon bettering their condition in a foreign land, or who underestimate the importance of cultivating friendly relations with the Southern white man who is their next-door neighbor, I would say: "Cast down your bucket where you are"—cast it down in making friends, in every manly way, of the people of all races by whom we are surrounded.

Cast it down in agriculture, mechanics, in commerce, in domestic service, and in the professions. And in this connection it is well to bear in mind that whatever other sins the South may be called to bear, when it comes to business, pure and simple, it is in the South that the Negro is given a man's chance in the commercial world, and in nothing is this Exposition more eloquent than in emphasizing this chance. Our greatest danger is that in the great leap from slavery to freedom we may overlook the fact that the masses of us are to live by the productions of our hands, and fail to keep in mind that we shall prosper in proportion as we learn to dignify and glorify common labor, and put brains and skill into the common occupations of life; shall prosper in proportion as we learn to draw the line between the superficial and the substantial, the ornamental gew-gaws of life and the useful. No race can prosper till it learns that there is as much dignity in tilling a field as in writing a poem. It is at the bottom of life we must begin, and not at the top. Nor should we permit our grievances to overshadow our opportunities.

To those of the white race who look to the incoming of those of foreign birth and strange tongue and habits for the prosperity of the South, were I permitted, I would repeat what I say to my own race, "Cast down your bucket where you are." Cast it down among the eight million Negroes whose habits you know, whose fidelity and love you have tested in days when to have proved treacherous meant the ruin of your firesides. Cast down your bucket among these people who have without strikes and labor wars tilled your fields, cleared your forests, builded your railroads and cities, brought forth treasures from the bowels of the earth, and helped make possible this magnificent representation of the progress of the South. Casting down your bucket among my people, helping and encouraging them as you are doing on these grounds, and, with education of head, hand, and heart, you will find that they will buy your surplus land, make blossom the waste places in your fields, and run your factories. While doing this, you can be sure in the future, as in the past, that you and your families will be sur- *personality* rounded by the most patient, faithful, law-abiding, and unresent- ful people that the world has seen. As we have proved our loyalty to you in the past, in nursing your children, watching by the sick bed of your mothers and fathers, and often following them with tear-dimmed eyes to their graves, so in the future, in our humble way, we shall stand by you with a devotion that no foreigner can approach, ready to lay down our lives, if need be, in defense of yours, interlacing our industrial, commercial, civil, and religious life with yours in a way that shall make the interests of both races one. In all things that are purely social we can be as separate as the fingers, yet one as the hand in all things essential to mutual progress.

There is no defense or security for any of us except in the highest intelligence and development of all. If anywhere there are efforts tending to curtail the fullest growth of the Negro, let these efforts be turned into stimulating, encouraging, and making him the most useful and intelligent citizen. Effort or means so invested will pay a thousand per cent interest. These efforts will be twice blessed—"Blessing him that gives and him that takes."

There is no escape through law of man or God from the in- evitable:

> "The laws of changeless justice bind
>   Oppressor with oppressed;
> And close as sin and suffering joined
>   We march to fate abreast."

Nearly sixteen millions of hands will aid you in pulling the load upward, or they will pull, against you, the load downward. We shall constitute one third and more of the ignorance and crime of the South, or one third its intelligence and progress; we shall contribute one third to the business and industrial prosperity of the South, or we shall prove a veritable body of death, stagnating, depressing, retarding every effort to advance the body politic.

Gentlemen of the Exposition, as we present to you our hum- ble effort at an exhibition of our progress, you must not expect overmuch. Starting thirty years ago with ownership here and there in a few quilts and pumpkins and chickens (gathered from miscellaneous sources), remember, the path that has led from these to the inventions and production of agricultural implements, buggies, steam engines, newspapers, books, statuary, carving, paintings, the management of drugstores and banks, has not been trodden without contact with thorns and thistles. While we take pride in what we exhibit as a result of our independent efforts, we do not for a moment forget that our part in this exhibition would fall far short of your expectations but for the constant help that has come to our educational life, not only from the Southern states, but especially from Northern philanthropists, who have made their gifts a constant stream of blessing and encouragement.

The wisest among my race understand that the agitation of questions of social equality is the extremest folly, and that progress in the enjoyment of all the privileges that will come to us must be the result of severe and constant struggle rather than of artificial forcing. No race that has anything to contribute to the markets of the world is long, in any degree, ostracized. It is important and right that all privileges of the law be ours, but it is vastly more important that we be prepared for the exercise of those privileges. The opportunity to earn a dollar in a factory just now is worth infinitely more than the opportunity to spend a dollar in an opera house.

In conclusion, may I repeat that nothing in thirty years has given us more hope and encouragement, and drawn us so near to you of the white race, as this opportunity offered by the Exposition; and here bending, as it were, over the altar that represents the results of the struggles of your race and mine, both starting practically empty-handed three decades ago, I pledge that, in your effort to work out the great and intricate problem which God has laid at the doors of the South, you shall have at all times the patient, sympathetic help of my race; only let this be constantly in mind, that while, from representations in these buildings of the product of field, of forest, of mine, of factory, letters, and art, much good will come, yet far above and beyond material benefits will be that higher good, that, let us pray God, will come in a blotting out of sectional differences and racial animosities and suspicions, in a determination to administer absolute justice, in a willing obedience among all classes to the mandates of law. This, coupled with our material prosperity, will bring into our beloved South a new heaven and a new earth.

# W. E. B. Du Bois

## "Of Mr. Booker T. Washington ..."

*This selection is from a chapter of Du Bois'* The Souls of Black Folk, *published in 1903. His comments on Washington, which include his labeling of Washington's program as "the Atlanta compromise," are an early statement of the more militant course that he would be urging upon black Americans and their white allies.*

Easily the most striking thing in the history of the American Negro since 1876 is the ascendancy of Mr. Booker T. Washington. It began at the time when war memories and ideals were rapidly passing; a day of astonishing commercial development was dawning; a sense of doubt and hesitation overtook the freedmen's sons,—then it was that his leading began. Mr. Washington came, with a simple definite programme, at the psychological moment when the nation was a little ashamed of having bestowed so much sentiment on Negroes, and was concentrating its energies on Dollars. His programme of industrial education, conciliation of the South, and submission and silence as to civil and political rights, was not wholly original; the Free Negroes from 1830 up to wartime had striven to build industrial schools, and the American Missionary Association had from the first taught various trades; and Price and others had sought a way of honorable alliance with the best of the Southerners. But Mr. Washington first indissolubly linked these things; he put enthusiasm, unlimited energy, and perfect faith into this programme, and changed it from a by-path into a veritable Way of Life. And the tale of the methods by which he did this is a fascinating study of human life.

It startled the nation to hear a Negro advocating such a programme after many decades of bitter complaint; it startled and won the applause of the South, it interested and won the admira-

*Source:* W. E. Burghardt Du Bois, *The Souls of Black Folk: Essays and Sketches* (Chicago: A. C. McClurg and Company, 1903).

tion of the North; and after a confused murmur of protest, it silenced if it did not convert the Negroes themselves.

To gain the sympathy and cooperation of the various elements comprising the white South was Mr. Washington's first task; and this, at the time Tuskegee was founded, seemed, for a black man, well-nigh impossible. And yet ten years later it was done in the word spoken at Atlanta: "In all things purely social we can be as separate as the five fingers, and yet one as the hand in all things essential to mutual progress." This "Atlanta Compromise" is by all odds the most notable thing in Mr. Washington's career. The South interpreted it in different ways: the radicals received it as a complete surrender of the demand for civil and political equality; the conservatives, as a generously conceived working basis for mutual understanding. So both approved it, and to-day its author is certainly the most distinguished Southerner since Jefferson Davis, and the one with the largest personal following.

Next to this achievement comes Mr. Washington's work in gaining place and consideration in the North. Others less shrewd and tactful had formerly essayed to sit on these two stools and had fallen between them; but as Mr. Washington knew the heart of the South from birth and training, so by singular insight he intuitively grasped the spirit of the age which was dominating the North. . . .

So Mr. Washington's cult has gained unquestioning followers, his work has wonderfully prospered, his friends are legion, and his enemies are confounded. To-day he stands as the one recognized spokesman of his ten million fellows, and one of the most notable figures in a nation of seventy millions. One hesitates, therefore, to criticise a life which, beginning with so little, has done so much. And yet the time is come when one may speak in all sincerity and utter courtesy of the mistakes and shortcomings of Mr. Washington's career, as well as of his triumphs, without being thought captious or envious, and without forgetting that it is easier to do ill than well in the world. . . .

Mr. Washington represents in Negro thought the old attitude of adjustment and submission; but adjustment at such a peculiar time as to make his programme unique. This is an age of unusual economic development, and Mr. Washington's programme naturally takes an economic cast, becoming a gospel of Work and Money to such an extent as apparently almost completely to overshadow the higher aims of life. Moreover, this is an age when the more advanced races are coming in closer contact with the less developed races, and the race-feeling is therefore intensified; and Mr. Washington's programme practically accepts the alleged inferiority of the Negro races. Again, in our own land, the reaction from the sentiment of war time has given impetus to race-prejudice against Negroes, and Mr. Washington withdraws many of the high demands of Negroes as men and American citizens. In other periods of intensified prejudice all the Negro's tendency to self-assertion has been called forth; at this period a policy of submission is advocated. In the history of nearly all other races and peoples the doctrine preached at such crises has been that manly self-respect is worth more than lands and houses, and that a people who voluntarily surrender such respect, or cease striving for it, are not worth civilizing.

In answer to this, it has been claimed that the Negro can survive only through submission. Mr. Washington distinctly asks that black people give up, at least for the present, three things, —
First, political power,
Second, insistence on civil rights,
Third, higher education of Negro youth, —
and concentrate all their energies on industrial education, the accumulation of wealth, and the conciliation of the South. This policy has been courageously and insistently advocated for over fifteen years, and has been triumphant for perhaps ten years. As a result of this tender of the palm-branch, what has been the return? In these years there have occurred:

1. The disfranchisement of the Negro.
2. The legal creation of a distinct status of civil inferiority for the Negro.
3. The steady withdrawal of aid from institutions for the higher training of the Negro.

These movements are not, to be sure, direct results of Mr. Washington's teachings; but his propaganda had, without a shadow of doubt, helped their speedier accomplishment. The question then comes: Is it possible, and probable, that nine millions of men can make effective progress in economic lines if they are deprived of political rights, made a servile caste, and allowed only the most meagre chance for developing their exceptional men? If history and reason give any distinct answer to these questions, it is an emphatic *No*. And Mr. Washington thus faces the triple paradox of his career:

1. He is striving nobly to make Negro artisans business men and property-owners; but it is utterly impossible, under modern competitive methods, for workingmen and property-owners to defend their rights and exist without the right of suffrage.
2. He insists on thrift and self-respect, but at the same time

counsels a silent submission to civic inferiority such as is bound to sap the manhood of any race in the long run.

3. He advocates common-school and industrial training, and depreciates institutions of higher learning; but neither the Negro common-schools, nor Tuskegee itself, could remain open a day were it not for teachers trained in Negro colleges, or trained by their graduates. . . .

It is wrong to encourage a man or a people in evil-doing; it is wrong to aid and abet a national crime simply because it is unpopular not to do so. The growing spirit of kindliness and reconciliation between the North and South after the frightful differences of a generation ago ought to be a source of deep congratulation to all, and especially to those whose mistreatment caused the war; but if that reconciliation is to be marked by the industrial slavery and civic death of those same black men, with permanent legislation into a position of inferiority, then those black men, if they are really men, are called upon by every consideration of patriotism and loyalty to oppose such a course by all civilized methods, even though such opposition involves disagreement with Mr. Booker T. Washington. We have no right to sit silently by while the inevitable seeds are sown for a harvest of disaster to our children, black and white. . . .

The South ought to be led, by candid and honest criticism, to assert her better self and so her full duty to the race she has cruelly wronged and is still wronging. The North—her co-partner in guilt—cannot salve her conscience by plastering it with gold. We cannot settle this problem by diplomacy and suaveness, by "policy" alone. If worse come to worst, can the moral fibre of this country survive the slow throttling and murder of nine millions of men?

The black men of America have a duty to perform, a duty stern and delicate,—a forward movement to oppose a part of the work of their greatest leader. So far as Mr. Washington preaches Thrift, Patience, and Industrial Training for the masses, we must hold up his bands and strive with him, rejoicing in his honors and glorying in the strength of this Joshua called of God and of man to lead the headless host. But so far as Mr. Washington apologizes for injustice, North or South, does not rightly value the privilege and duty of voting, belittles the emasculating effects of caste distinctions, and opposes the higher training and ambition of our brighter minds,—so far as he, the South, or the Nation, does this,—we must unceasingly and firmly oppose them. By every civilized and peaceful method we must strive for the rights which the world accords to men, clinging unwaveringly to those great words which the sons of the Fathers would fain forget: "We hold these truths to be self-evident: That all men are created equal; that they are endowed by their Creator with certain unalienable rights; that among these are life, liberty, and the pursuit of happiness."

Theodore Roosevelt with Booker T. Washington. *(Courtesy, Tuskegee Institute, Alabama)*

# W. E. B. Du Bois

## "The Talented Tenth"

*This essay, one of the author's best known, may be taken as a response to Booker T. Washington's plea that blacks concentrate on the achievement of manual skills. Du Bois' argument is for an education in higher culture that will develop fullness of character and intelligence. Here Du Bois may have been overlooking Washington's assumption that the acquisition of skills and ambition also makes for character.*

The Negro race, like all races, is going to be saved by its exceptional men. The problem of education, then, among Negroes must first of all deal with the Talented Tenth; it is the problem of developing the Best of this race that they may guide the Mass away from the contamination and death of the Worst, in their own and other races. Now the training of men is a difficult and intricate task. Its technique is a matter for educational experts, but its object is for the vision of seers. If we make money the object of man-training, we shall develop money-makers but not necessarily men; if we make technical skill the object of education, we may possess artisans but not, in nature, men. Men we shall have only as we make manhood the object of the work of the schools—intelligence, broad sympathy, knowledge of the world that was and is, and of the relation of men to it—this is the curriculum of that Higher Education which must underlie true life. On this foundation we may build bread winning, skill of hand and quickness of brain, with never a fear lest the child and man mistake the means of living for the object of life. . . .

From the very first it has been the educated and intelligent of the Negro people that have led and elevated the mass, and the sole obstacles that nullified and retarded their efforts were slavery and

*Source:* W. E. B. Du Bois, "The Talented Tenth," in *The Negro Problem: A Series of Articles by Representative American Negroes of To-Day* (New York: James Pott and Company, 1903).

race prejudice; for what is slavery but the legalized survival of the unfit and the nullification of the work of natural internal leadership? Negro leadership, therefore, sought from the first to rid the race of this awful incubus that it might make way for natural selection and the survival of the fittest. In colonial days came Phillis Wheatley and Paul Cuffe striving against the bars of prejudice; and Benjamin Banneker, the almanac maker...

Then came Dr. James Derham, who could tell even the learned Dr. Rush something of medicine, and Lemuel Haynes, to whom Middlebury College gave a honorary A.M. in 1804. These and others we may call the Revolutionary group of distinguished Negroes—they were persons of marked ability, leaders of a Talented Tenth, standing conspicuously among the best of their time. They strove by word and deed to save the color line from becoming the line between the bond and free, but all they could do was nullified by Eli Whitney and the Curse of Gold. So they passed into forgetfulness.

But their spirit did not wholly die; here and there in the early part of the century came other exceptional men....

In 1831 there met that first Negro convention in Philadelphia, at which the world gaped curiously but which bravely attacked the problems of race and slavery, crying out against persecution.... Side by side this free Negro movement, and the movement for abolition, strove until they merged into one strong stream. Too little notice has been taken of the work which the Talented Tenth among Negroes took in the great abolition crusade. From the very day that a Philadelphia colored man became the first subscriber to Garrison's "Liberator," to the day when Negro soldiers made the Emancipation Proclamation possible, black leaders worked shoulder to shoulder with white men in a movement, the success of which would have been impossible without them. There was Purvis and Remond, Pennington and Highland Garnett, Sojourner Truth and Alexander Crummell, and above all, Frederick Douglass—what would the abolition movement have been without them? They stood as living examples of the possibilities of the Negro race, their own hard experiences and well wrought culture said silently more than all the drawn periods of orators—they were the men who made American slavery impossible....

After emancipation came a new group of educated and gifted leaders: Langston, Bruce and Elliot, Greener, Williams and Payne. Through political organization, historical and polemic writing and moral regeneration, these men strove to uplift their people. It is the fashion of to-day to sneer at them and to say that with freedom

Negro leadership should have begun at the plow and not in the Senate—a foolish and mischievous lie; two hundred and fifty years that black serf toiled at the plow and yet that toiling was in vain till the Senate passed the war amendments; and two hundred and fifty years more the half-free serf of to-day may toil at his plow, but unless he have political rights and righteously guarded civic status, he will still remain the poverty-striken and ignorant plaything of rascals, that he now is. This all sane men know even if they dare not say it.

And so we come to the present—a day of cowardice and vacillation, of strident wide-voiced wrong and faint hearted compromise; of double-faced dallying with Truth and Right. Who are to-day guiding the work of the Negro people? The "exceptions" of course. And yet so sure as this Talented Tenth is pointed out, the blind worshippers of the Average cry out in alarm: "These are exceptions, look here at death, disease and crime—these are the happy rule." Of course they are the rule, because a silly nation made them the rule: Because for three long centuries this people lynched Negroes who dared to be brave, raped black women who dared to be virtuous, crushed dark-hued youth who dared to be ambitious, and encouraged and made to flourish servility and lewdness and apathy. But not even this was able to crush all manhood and chastity and aspiration from black folk. A saving remnant continually survives and persists, continually aspires, continually shows itself in thrift and ability and character. Exceptional it is to be sure, but this is its chiefest promise; it shows the capability of Negro blood, the promise of black men. Do Americans ever stop to reflect that there are in this land a million men of Negro blood, well-educated, owners of homes, against the honor of whose womanhood no breath was ever raised, whose men occupy positions of trust and usefulness, and who, judged by any standard, have reached the full measure of the best type of modern European culture? Is it fair, is it decent, is it Christian to ignore these facts of the Negro problem, to belittle such aspiration, to nullify such leadership and seek to crush these people back into the mass out of which by toil and travail, they and their fathers have raised themselves?

Can the masses of the Negro people be in any possible way more quickly raised than by the effort and example of this aristocracy of talent and character? Was there ever a nation on God's fair earth civilized from the bottom upward? Never; it is, ever was and ever will be from the top downward that culture filters. The Talented Tenth rises and pulls all that are worth the saving up to their vantage ground. This is the history of human progress; and the two historic mistakes which have hindered that progress were the thinking first that no more could ever rise save the few already risen; or second, that it would better the unrisen to pull the risen down.

How then shall the leaders of a struggling people be trained and the hands of the risen few strengthened? There can be but one answer: The best and most capable of their youth must be schooled in the colleges and universities of the land. We will not quarrel as to just what the university of the Negro should teach or how it should teach it—I willingly admit that each soul and each race-soul needs its own peculiar curriculum. But this is true: A university is a human invention for the transmission of knowledge and culture from generation to generation, through the training of quick minds and pure hearts, and for this work no other human invention will suffice, not even trade and industrial schools. . . .

The main question, so far as the Southern Negro is concerned, is: What under the present circumstance, must a system of education do in order to raise the Negro as quickly as possible in the scale of civilization? The answer to this question seems to me clear: It must strengthen the Negro's character, increase his knowledge and teach him to earn a living. Now it goes without saying, that it is hard to do all these things simultaneously or suddenly, and that at the same time it will not do to give all the attention to one and neglect the others; we could give black boys trades, but that alone will not civilize a race of ex-slaves; we might simply increase their knowledge of the world, but this would not necessarily make them wish to use this knowledge honestly; we might seek to strengthen character and purpose, but to what end if this people have nothing to eat or to wear? A system of education is not one thing, nor does it have a single definite object, nor is it a mere matter of schools. Education is that whole system of human training within and without the school house walls, which molds and develops men. If then we start out to train an ignorant and unskilled people with a heritage of bad habits, our system of training must set before itself two great aims—the one dealing with knowledge and character, the other part seeking to give the child the technical knowledge necessary for him to earn a living under the present circumstances. These objects are accomplished in part by the opening of the common schools on the one, and of the industrial schools on the other. But only in part, for there must also be trained those who are to teach these schools—men and women of knowledge and culture and technical skill who understand modern civilization, and have the training and aptitude to impart it to the children under them. There must be teachers, and teachers of teachers, and to attempt to establish any sort of a system of common and industrial school training, without *first* (and I say *first* advisedly) without *first* providing for the higher training of the very best teachers, is simply throwing your money to the winds. School houses do not teach themselves—piles of brick and mortar and machinery do not send out *men*. It is the trained, living human soul, cultivated and strengthened by long study and thought, that breathes the real breath of life into boys and girls and makes them human, whether they be black or white, Greek, Russian or American. Nothing, in these latter days, has so dampened the faith of thinking Negroes in recent educational movements, as the fact that such movements have been accompanied by ridicule and denouncement and decrying of those very institutions of higher training which made the Negro public school possible, and make Negro industrial schools thinkable. . . .

I am an earnest advocate of manual training and trade teaching for black boys, and for white boys, too. I believe that next to the founding of Negro colleges the most valuable addition to Negro education since the war, has been industrial training for black boys. Nevertheless, I insist that the object of all true education is not to make men carpenters, it is to make carpenters men; there are two means of making the carpenter a man, each equally important: the first is to give the group and community in which he works, liberally trained teachers and leaders to teach him and his family what life means; the second is to give him sufficient intelligence and technical skill to make him an efficient workman; the first object demands the Negro college and college-bred men—not a quantity of such colleges, but a few of excellent quality; not too many college-bred men, but enough to leaven the lump, to inspire the masses, to raise the Talented Tenth to leadership; the second object demands a good system of common schools, well-taught, conveniently located and properly equipped. . . .

Men of America, the problem is plain before you. Here is a race transplanted through the criminal foolishness of your fathers. Whether you like it or not the millions are here, and here they will remain. If you do not lift them up, they will pull you down. Education and work are the levers to uplift a people. Work alone will not do it unless inspired by the right ideals and guided by intelligence. Education must not simply teach work—it must teach Life. The Talented Tenth of the Negro race must be made leaders of thought and missionaries of culture among their people. No others can do this work and Negro colleges must train men for it. The Negro race, like all other races, is going to be saved by its exceptional men.

# The Niagara Movement

## A Resolve to Seek Justice

*This statement describes the purposes of the Niagara Move-
ment, the name initially given to a conference of 1905 at
the urging of Du Bois that held its first meeting on the
Canadian side of Niagara Falls. The movement, a handful
of black Americans of the more privileged classes, continued for a few years and fed into the National Association
for the Advancement of Colored People, which began its
work in 1910.*

The members of the conference, known as the Niagara Movement, assembled in annual meeting at Buffalo, July 11th, 12th
and 13th, 1905, congratulate the Negro-Americans on certain un-
doubted evidences of progress in the last decade, particularly the
increase of intelligence, the buying of property, the checking of
crime, and uplift in home life, the advance in literature and art,
and the demonstration of constructive and executive ability in the
conduct of great religious, economic and educational institutions.

At the same time, we believe that this class of American citizens should protest emphatically and continually against the curtailment of their political rights. We believe in manhood suffrage;
we believe that no man is so good, intelligent or wealthy as to be
entrusted wholly with the welfare of his neighbor.

We believe also in protest against the curtailment of our civil
rights. All American citizens have the right to equal treatment in
places of public accommodation according to their behavior and
deserts.

We especially complain against the denial of equal opportunities to us in economic life; in the rural districts of the South this
amounts to peonage and virtual slavery; all over the South it tends
to crush labor and small business enterprises; and everywhere

*Source: Washington (D.C.) Bee* (July 22, 1905).

American prejudice, helped often by iniquitous laws, is making it more difficult for Negro-Americans to earn a decent living.

Common school education should be free to all American children and compulsory. High school training should be adequately provided for all, and college training should be the monopoly of no class or race in any section of our common country. We believe that, in defense of our own institutions, the United States should aid common school education, particularly in the South, and we especially recommend concerted agitation to this end. We urge an increase in public high school facilities in the South, where Negro-Americans are almost wholly without such provisions. We favor well-equipped trade and technical schools for the training of artisans, and the need of adequate and liberal endowment for a few institutions of higher education must be patent to sincere well-wishers of the race.

We demand upright judges in courts, juries selected without discrimination on account of color and the same measure of punishment and the same efforts at reformation for black as for white offenders. We need orphanages and farm schools for dependent children, juvenile reformatories for delinquents, and the abolition of the dehumanizing convict-lease system.

We note with alarm the evident retrogression in this land of sound public opinion on the subject of manhood rights, republican government and human brotherhood, and we pray God that this nation will not degenerate into a mob of boasters and oppressors, but rather will return to the faith of the fathers, that all men were created free and equal, with certain unalienable rights.

We plead for health—for an opportunity to live in decent houses and localities, for a chance to rear our children in physical and moral cleanliness.

We hold up for public execration the conduct of two opposite classes of men: The practice among employers of importing ignorant Negro-American laborers in emergencies, and then affording them neither protection nor permanent employment; and the practice of labor unions in proscribing and boycotting and oppressing thousands of their fellow-toilers, simply because they are black. These methods have accentuated and will accentuate the war of labor and capital, and they are disgraceful to both sides.

We refuse to allow the impression to remain that the Negro-American assents to inferiority, is submissive under oppression and apologetic before insults. Through helplessness we may submit, but the voice of protest of ten million Americans must never cease to assail the ears of their fellows, so long as America is unjust.

Any discrimination based simply on race or color is barbarous, we care not how hallowed it be by custom, expediency, or prejudice. Differences made on account of ignorance, immorality, or disease are legitimate methods of fighting evil, and against them we have no word of protest; but discrimination based simply and solely on physical peculiarities, place of birth, color of skin, are relics of that unreasoning human savagery of which the world is and ought to be thoroughly ashamed.

We protest against the "Jim Crow" car, since its effect is and must be, to make us pay first-class fare for third-class accommodations, render us open to insults and discomfort and to crucify wantonly our manhood, womanhood and self-respect.

We regret that this nation has never seen fit adequately to reward the black soldiers who, in its five wars, have defended their country with their blood, and yet have been systematically denied the promotions which their abilities deserve. And we regard as unjust, the exclusion of black boys from the military and navy training schools.

We urge upon Congress the enactment of appropriate legislation for securing the proper enforcement of those articles of freedom, the thirteenth, fourteenth and fifteenth amendments of the Constitution of the United States.

We repudiate the monstrous doctrine that the oppressor should be the sole authority as to the rights of the oppressed.

The Negro race in America, stolen, ravished and degraded, struggling up through difficulties and oppression, needs sympathy and receives criticism; needs help and is given hindrance, needs protection and is given mob-violence, needs justice and is given charity, needs leadership and is given cowardice and apology, needs bread and is given a stone. This nation will never stand justified before God until these things are changed.

Especially are we surprised and astonished at the recent attitude of the church of Christ—on the increase of a desire to bow to racial prejudice, to narrow the bounds of human brotherhood, and to segregate black men in some outer sanctuary. This is wrong, unchristian and disgraceful to the twentieth century civilization.

Of the above grievances we do not hesitate to complain, and to complain loudly and insistently. To ignore, overlook, or apologize for these wrongs is to prove ourselves unworthy of freedom. Persistent manly agitation is the way of liberty, and toward this goal the Niagara Movement has started and asks the co-operation of all men of all races.

At the same time we want to acknowledge with deep thankfulness the help of our fellowmen from the abolitionist down to those who to-day still stand for equal opportunity and who have given and still give of their wealth and of their poverty for our advancement.

And while we are demanding, and ought to demand, and will continue to demand the rights enumerated above, God forbid that we should ever forget to urge corresponding duties upon our people:

The duty to vote.

The duty to respect the rights of others.

The duty to work.

The duty to obey the laws.

The duty to be clean and orderly.

The duty to send our children to school.

The duty to respect ourselves, even as we respect others.

This statement, complaint and prayer we submit to the American people, and Almighty God.

# The Crisis

## Statement of Principles

*The Crisis, W. E. B. Du Bois' journal founded in 1910, reflected the purposes of the National Association for the Advancement of Colored People.*

The object of this publication is to set forth those facts and arguments which show the danger of race prejudice, particularly as manifested today toward colored people. It takes its name from the fact that the editors believe that this is a critical time in the history of the advancement of men. Catholicity and tolerance, reason and forbearance can today make the world-old dream of human brotherhood approach realization; while bigotry and prejudice, emphasized race consciousness and force can repeat the awful history of the contact of nations and groups in the past. We strive for this higher and broader vision of Peace and Good Will.

The policy of THE CRISIS will be simple and well defined:

It will first and foremost be a newspaper: it will record important happenings and movements in the world which bear on the great problem of interracial relations, and especially those which affect the Negro American.

Secondly, it will be a review of opinion and literature, recording briefly books, articles, and important expressions of opinion in the white and colored press on the race problem.

Thirdly, it will publish a few short articles.

Finally, its editorial page will stand for the rights of men, irrespective of color or race, for the highest ideals of American democracy, and for reasonable but earnest and persistent attempt to gain these rights and realize these ideals. The magazine will be the organ of no clique or party and will avoid personal rancor of all sorts. In the absence of proof to the contrary it will assume honesty of purpose on the part of all men, North and South, white and black.

*Source: The Crisis* (November 1910).

# Marcus Garvey

## An Early Black Nationalist

*In this speech of November 25, 1922, Marcus Garvey explains a movement that made him one of the most visible black American leaders of the early twentieth century.*

Over five years ago the Universal Negro Improvement Association placed itself before the world as the movement through which the new and rising Negro would give expression of his feelings. This Association adopts an attitude not of hostility to other races and peoples of the world, but an attitude of self-respect, of manhood rights on behalf of 400,000,000 Negroes of the world.

We represent peace, harmony, love, human sympathy, human rights and human justice, and that is why we fight so much. Wheresoever human rights are denied to any group, wheresoever justice is denied to any group, there the U. N. I. A. finds a cause. And at this time among all the peoples of the world, the group that suffers most from injustice, the group that is denied most of those rights that belong to all humanity, is the black group of 400,000,000. Because of that injustice, because of that denial of our rights, we go forth under the leadership of the One who is always on the side of right to fight the common cause of humanity; to fight as we fought in the Revolutionary War, as we fought in the Civil War, as we fought in the Spanish-American War, and as we fought in the war between 1914–18 on the battle plains of France and of Flanders. As we fought on the heights of Mesopotamia; even so under the leadership of the U. N. I. A., we are marshaling the 400,000,000 Negroes of the world to fight for the emancipation of the race and of the redemption of the country of our fathers.

We represent a new line of thought among Negroes. Whether

*Source:* Speech delivered at Liberty Hall, New York City, November 25, 1922. Robert A. Hill, ed., *The Marcus Garvey and Universal Negro Improvement Association Papers, Vol. 5, September 1922–August 1924* (Berkeley: University of California Press, 1986).

you call it advanced thought or reactionary thought, I do not care. If it is reactionary for people to seek independence in government, then we are reactionary. If it is advanced thought for people to seek liberty and freedom, then we represent the advanced school of thought among the Negroes of this country. We of the U. N. I. A. believe that what is good for the other folks is good for us. If government is something that is worth while; if government is something that is appreciable and helpful and protective to others, then we also want to experiment in government. We do not mean a government that will make us citizens without rights or subjects without consideration. We mean a kind of government that will place our race in control, even as other races are in control of their own governments.

That does not suggest anything that is unreasonable. It was not unreasonable for George Washington, the great hero and father of the country, to have fought for the freedom of America giving to us this great republic and this great democracy; it was not unreasonable for the Liberals of France to have fought against the Monarchy to give to the world French Democracy and French Republicanism; it was no unrighteous cause that led Tolstoi to sound the call of liberty in Russia, which has ended in giving to the world the social democracy of Russia, an experiment that will probably prove to be a boon and a blessing to mankind. If it was not an unrighteous cause that led Washington to fight for the independence of this country, and led the Liberals of France to establish the Republic, it is therefore not an unrighteous cause for the U. N. I. A. to lead 400,000,000 Negroes all over the world to fight for the liberation of our country.

Therefore the U. N. I. A. is not advocating the cause of church building, because we have a sufficiently large number of churches among us to minister to the spiritual needs of the people, and we are not going to compete with those who are engaged in so splendid a work; we are not engaged in building any new social institutions, and Y. M. C. A. or Y. W. C. A.[,] because there are enough social workers engaged in those praise-worthy efforts. We are not engaged in politics because we have enough local politicians, Democrats, Socialists, Soviets, etc., and the political situation is well taken care of. We are not engaged in domestic politics, in church building or in social uplift work, but we are engaged in nation building. . . .

I desire to remove the misunderstanding that has been created in the minds of millions of peoples throughout the world in their relationship to the organization. The Universal Negro

Improvement Association stands for the Bigger Brotherhood; the Universal Negro Improvement Association stands for human rights, not only for Negroes, but for all races. The Universal Negro Improvement Association believes in the rights of not only the black race, but the white race, the yellow race and the brown race. The Universal Negro Improvement Association believes that the white man has as much right to be considered, the yellow man has as much right to be considered, the brown man has as much right to be considered as well as the black man of Africa. In view of the fact that the black man of Africa has contributed as much to the world as the white man of Europe, and the brown man and yellow man of Asia, we of the Universal Negro Improvement Association demand that the white, yellow and brown races give to the black man his place in the civilization of the world. We ask for nothing more than the rights of 400,000,000 Negroes. We are not seeking, as I said before, to destroy or disrupt the society or the government of other races, but we are determined that 400,000,000 of us shall unite ourselves to free our motherland from the grasp of the invader. We of the Universal Negro Improvement Association are determined to unite 400,000,000 Negroes for their own industrial, political, social and religious emancipation.

We of the Universal Negro Improvement Association are determined to unite the 400,000,000 Negroes of the world to give expression to their own feeling; we are determined to unite the 400,000,000 Negroes of the world for the purpose of building a civilization of their own. And in that effort we desire to bring together the 15,000,000 of the United States, the 180,000,000 in Asia, the West Indies and Central and South America, and the 200,000,000 in Africa. We are looking toward political freedom on the continent of Africa, the land of our fathers. . . .

The difference between the Universal Negro Improvement Association and the other movements of this country, and probably the world, is that the Universal Negro Improvement Association seeks independence of government, while the other organizations seek to make the Negro a secondary part of existing governments. We differ from the organizations in America because they seek to subordinate the Negro as a secondary consideration in a great civilization, knowing that in America the Negro will never reach his highest ambition, knowing that the Negro in America will never get his constitutional rights. All those organizations which are fostering the improvement of Negroes in the British Empire know that the Negro in the British Empire will never reach the height of his constitutional rights. What do I mean by constitutional rights in America? If the black man is to reach the height of his ambition in this country—if the black man is to get all of his constitutional rights in America—then the black man should have the same chance in the nation as any other man to become president of the nation, or a street cleaner in New York. If the black man in the British Empire is to have all his constitutional rights it means that the Negro in the British Empire should have at least the same right to become premier of Great Britain as he has to become street cleaner in the city of London. Are they prepared to give us such political equality? You and I can live in the United States of America for 100 more years, and our generations may live for 200 years or for 5000 more years, and so long as there is a black and white population, when the majority is on the side of the white race, you and I will never get political justice or get political equality in this country. Then why should a black man with rising ambition, after preparing himself in every possible way to give expression to that highest ambition, allow himself to be kept down by racial prejudice within a country? If I am as educated as the next man, if I am as prepared as the next man, if I have passed through the best schools and colleges and universities as the other fellow, why should I not have a fair chance to compete with the other fellow for the biggest position in the nation? I have feelings, I have blood, I have senses like the other fellow; I have ambition, I have hope. Why should he, because of some racial prejudice, keep me down and why should I concede to him the right to rise above me, and to establish himself as my permanent master? That is where the U. N. I. A. differs from other organizations. I refuse to stultify my ambition, and every true Negro refuses to stultify his ambition to suit any one, and therefore the U. N. I. A. decides if America is not big enough for two presidents, if England is not big enough for two kings, then we are not going to quarrel over the matter; we will leave one president in America, we will leave one king in England, we will leave one president in France and we will have one president in Africa. Hence, the Universal Negro Improvement Association does not seek to interfere with the social and political systems of France, but by the arrangement of things today the U. N. I. A. refuses to recognize any political or social system in Africa except that which we are about to establish for ourselves.

We are not preaching a propaganda of hate against anybody. We love the white man; we love all humanity, because we feel that we cannot live without the other. The white man is as necessary to the existence of the Negro as the Negro is necessary to his existence. There is a common relationship that we cannot escape. Africa has certain things that Europe wants, and Europe has certain things that Africa wants, and if a fair and square deal must bring white and black with each other, it is impossible for us to escape it. Africa has oil, diamonds, copper, gold and rubber and all the minerals that Europe wants, and there must be some kind of relationship between Africa and Europe for a fair exchange, so we cannot afford to hate anybody. . . .

The question often asked is what does it require to redeem a race and free a country? If it takes man power, if it takes scientific intelligence, if it takes education of any kind, or if it takes blood, then the 400,000,000 Negroes of the world have it. . . .

If we have been liberal minded enough to give our life's blood in France, in Mesopotamia and elsewhere, fighting for the white man, whom we have always assisted, surely we have not forgotten to fight for ourselves, and when the time comes that the world will again give Africa an opportunity for freedom, surely 400,000,000 black men will march out on the battle plains of Africa, under the colors of the red, the black and the green.

We shall march out, yes, as black American citizens, as black British subjects, as black French citizens, as black Italians or as black Spaniards, but we shall march out with a greater loyalty, the loyalty of race. We shall march out in answer to the cry of our fathers, who cry out to us for the redemption of our own country, our motherland, Africa.

We shall march out, not forgetting the blessings of America. We shall march out, not forgetting the blessings of civilization. We shall march out with a history of peace before and behind us, and surely that history shall be our breastplate, for how can man fight better than knowing that the cause for which he fights is righteous? How can man fight more gloriously than by knowing that behind him is a history of slavery, a history of bloody carnage and massacre inflicted upon a race because of its inability to protect itself and fight? Shall we not fight for the glorious opportunity of protecting and forever more establishing ourselves as a mighty race and nation, never more to be disrespected by men[?] Glorious shall be the battle when the time comes to fight for our people and our race.

We should say to the millions who are in Africa to hold the fort, for we are coming 400,000,000 strong.

# Langston Hughes

## The Harlem Renaissance

*The poet Langston Hughes was a participant in the period
of black artistic creativity during the 1920s known as the
Harlem Renaissance.*

On a bright September morning in 1921, I came up out of
the subway at 135th and Lenox into the beginnings of the Negro
Renaissance. I headed for the Harlem Y.M.C.A. down the block,
where so many new, young, dark, male arrivals in Harlem have
spent early days. The next place I headed to that afternoon was the
Harlem Branch Library just up the street. There, a warm and wonderful librarian, Miss Ernestine Rose, white, made newcomers feel
welcome, as did her assistant in charge of the Schomburg Collection, Catherine Latimer, a luscious café au lait. That night I went
to the Lincoln Theatre across Lenox Avenue where maybe one of
the Smiths—Bessie, Clara, Trixie, or Mamie—was singing the
blues. And as soon as I could, I made a beeline for *Shuffle Along*, the
all-colored hit musical playing on 63rd Street in which Florence
Mills came to fame.

I had come to New York to enter Columbia College as a fresh-
man, but *really* why I had come to New York was to see Harlem. I
found it hard a week or so later to tear myself away from Harlem
when it came time to move up the hill to the dormitory at Columbia. That winter I spent as little time as possible on the campus.
Instead, I spent as much time as I could in Harlem, and this I have
done ever since. I was in love with Harlem long before I got there,
and I still am in love with it. Everybody seemed to make me welcome. The sheer dark size of Harlem intrigued me. And the fact
that at that time poets and writers like James Weldon Johnson and
Jessie Fauset lived there, and Bert Williams, Duke Ellington, Ethel
Waters, and Walter White, too, fascinated me. Had I been a rich

*Source:* Langston Hughes, "My Early Days in Harlem," *Freedomways*, 3 (Summer
1963).

young man, I would have bought a house in Harlem and built musical steps up to the front door, and installed chimes that at the press of a button played Ellington tunes.

After a winter at Columbia, I moved back down to Harlem. Everywhere I roomed, I had the good fortune to have lovely land-ladies. If I did not like a landlady's looks, I would not move in with her, maybe that is why. But at finding work in New York, my fortune was less than good. Finally, I went to sea—Africa, Europe—then a year in Paris working in a night club where the band was from Harlem. I was a dishwasher, later bus boy, listening every night to the music of Harlem transplanted to Montmartre. And I was on hand to welcome Bricktop when she came to sing for the first time in Europe, bringing with her news of Harlem.

When I came back to New York in 1925 the Negro Renaissance was in full swing. Countee Cullen was publishing his early poems, Aaron Douglas was painting, Zora Neale Hurston, Rudolph Fisher, Jean Toomer and Wallace Thurman were writing, Louis Armstrong was playing, Cora La Redd was dancing, and the Savoy Ballroom was open with a specially built floor that rocked as the dancers swayed. Alain Locke was putting together *The New Negro*. Art took heart from Harlem creativity. Jazz filled the night air—but not everywhere—and people came from all around after dark to look upon our city within a city, Black Harlem. Had I not had to earn a living, I might have thought it even more wonderful than it was. But I could not eat the poems I wrote. Unlike the whites who came to spend their money in Harlem, only a few Harlemites seemed to live in even a modest degree of luxury. Most rode the subway downtown every morning to work or to look for work.

Downtown! I soon learned that it was seemingly impossible for black Harlem to live without white downtown. My youthful illusion that Harlem was a world unto itself did not last very long. It was not even an area that ran itself. The famous night clubs were owned by whites, as were the theatres. Almost all the stores were owned by whites, and many at that time did not even (in the very middle of Harlem) employ Negro clerks. The books of Harlem writers all had to be published downtown, if they were to be published at all. Downtown: *white*. Uptown: *black*. White downtown pulling all the strings in Harlem. Moe Gale, Moe Gale, Moe Gale, Lew Leslie, Lew Leslie, Lew Leslie, Harper's, Knopf, *The Survey Graphic*, the Harmon Foundation, the racketeers who kidnapped Casper Holstein and began to take over the numbers for whites. Negroes could not even play their own numbers with their *own* people. And almost all the policemen in Harlem were white. Negroes couldn't even get graft from *themselves* for themselves by themselves. Black

Harlem really was in white face, economically speaking. So I wrote this poem:

| | |
|---|---|
| Because my mouth | Because my mouth |
| Is wide with laughter | Is wide with laughter, |
| And my throat | You do not hear |
| Is deep with song, | My inner cry? |
| You do not think | Because my feet |
| I suffer after | Are gay with dancing, |
| I have held my pain | You do not know |
| So long? | I die? |

Harlem, like a Picasso painting in his cubistic period. Harlem—Southern Harlem—the Carolinas, Georgia, Florida—looking for the Promised Land—dressed in rhythmic words, painted in bright pictures, dancing to jazz—and ending up in the subway at morning rush time—*headed downtown*. West Indian Harlem—warm rambu[n]ctious sassy remembering Marcus Garvey. Haitian Harlem, Cuban Harlem, little pockets of tropical dreams in alien tongues. Magnet Harlem, pulling an Arthur Schomburg from Puerto Rico, pulling an Arna Bontemps all the way from California, a Nora Holt from way out West, an E. Simms Campbell from St. Louis, likewise a Josephine Baker, a Charles S. Johnson from Virginia, an A. Philip Randolph from Florida, a Roy Wilkins from Minnesota, an Alta Douglas from Kansas. Melting pot Harlem—Harlem of honey and chocolate and caramel and rum and vinegar and lemon and lime and gall. Dusky dream Harlem rumbling into a nightmare tunnel where the subway from the Bronx keeps right on downtown, where the money from the nightclubs goes right on back downtown, where the jazz is drained to Broadway, whence Josephine goes to Paris, Robeson to London, Jean Toomer to a Quaker Meeting House, Garvey to the Atlanta Federal Penitentiary, and Wallace Thurman to his grave; but Duke Ellington to fame and fortune, Lena Horne to Broadway, and Buck Clayton to China.

Before it was over—our New Negro Renaissance—poems became placards: DON'T BUY WHERE YOU CAN'T WORK! Adam Powell with a picket sign; me, too. BUY BLACK! Sufi long before the Black Muslims. FIRST TO BE FIRED, LAST TO BE HIRED! The Stock Market crash. The bank failures. Empty pockets. *God Bless The Child That's Got His Own*. Depression. Federal Theatre in Harlem, the making of Orson Welles. WPA, CCC, the Blue Eagle, Father Divine. In the midst of the Depression I got a cable from Russia inviting me to work on a motion picture there. I went to Moscow. That was the end of the early days of Langston Hughes in Harlem.

National Gardsmen, under federal command, escorted black students into Central High School in Little Rock, Arkansas, in 1957.

# Part 2

# INTEGRATION

*Integration is the term that has been most closely associated with the demands of the civil rights activists of the 1950s and the early sixties. It was over integration that many of the earlier rights battles took place; through the courts, as in the* Brown *decision, and through demonstrations and public campaigns in Montgomery, Greensboro, and scores of less visible localities throughout the South.*

*Much of what integrationists wanted may now appear symbolic rather than substantive: an end to segregation on buses, in public rest rooms, at counters serving quick lunches. Such places are incidental to the lives of people who make use of them: integrating them required running great risk for what can look to be small gain. Why, on a twenty-minute bus ride or in the length of time it takes to swallow a hastily snatched cup of coffee, would you care where you are sitting and who is sitting next to you; why would black and white demonstrators endure insult, arrest, or white violence to win a seat?*

*The simplest answer is that the symbol pointed beyond itself to the place of black Americans in white society. To be segregated denied dignity to the isolated race and reminded it of its subordinate status. White supremacists knew this, knew it enough to go to the trouble of imposing segregation and enough to be enraged and terrified when segregation came under attack; and black opponents of segregation knew it enough to know that their effort was worth the taunts, the arrests, the dangers.*

*In the case of the desegregation of public schools, of course, not only dignity was at stake but the quality of education. Then, too, the concept of integration refers to bringing African Americans into the wider economy. It represents its own version of what would later be called black power. But integrationists have aimed not to concentrate*

*power in separate black communities but rather to seek access to it
where it already exists, in the larger and mainly white society.*

*In its most profound significance, integration could have
meant—may still mean some day—the bringing together of two
largely separated societies and the forging of one cooperative people.*

The civil rights movement of the 1960s marched onward, seeking equality in
schooling, voting, employment, and housing. *(Courtesy, AP/Wide World Photos)*

# A. Philip Randolph

## First March on Washington Movement

*A. Philip Randolph, president of the Brotherhood of Sleeping Car Porters, organized the original March on Washington movement, which he describes here. He was also instrumental in the great March on Washington of 1963.*

Though I have found no Negroes who want to see the United Nations lose this war, I have found many who, before the war ends, want to see the stuffing knocked out of white supremacy and of empire over subject peoples. American Negroes, involved as we are in the general issues of the conflict, are confronted not with a choice but with the challenge both to win democracy for ourselves at home and to help win the war for democracy the world over.

There is no escape from the horns of this dilemma. There ought not to be escape. For if the war for democracy is not won abroad, the fight for democracy cannot be won at home. If this war cannot be won for the white peoples, it will not be won for the darker races.

Conversely, if freedom and equality are not vouchsafed the peoples of color, the war for democracy will not be won. Unless this double-barreled thesis is accepted and applied, the darker races will never wholeheartedly fight for the victory of the United Nations. . . .

When the defense program began and billions of the taxpayers' money were appropriated for guns, ships, tanks and bombs, Negroes presented themselves for work only to be given the cold shoulder. North as well as South, and despite their qualifications, Negroes were denied skilled employment. Not until their wrath and indignation took the form of a proposed protest march on Washington, scheduled for July 1, 1941, did things begin to move

*Source:* A. Philip Randolph, "Why Should We March?" *Survey Graphic*, 31 (November 1942).

in the form of defense jobs for Negroes. The march was postponed by the timely issuance (June 25, 1941) of the famous Executive Order No. 8802 by President Roosevelt. But this order and the President's Committee on Fair Employment Practice, established thereunder, have as yet only scratched the surface by way of eliminating discriminations on account of race or color in war industry. Both management and labor unions in too many places and in too many ways are still drawing the color line.

It is to meet this situation squarely with direct action that the March on Washington Movement launched its present program of protest mass meetings. Twenty thousand were in attendance at Madison Square Garden, June 16; sixteen thousand in the Coliseum in Chicago, June 26; nine thousand in the City Auditorium of St. Louis, August 14. Meetings of such magnitude were unprecedented among Negroes. The vast throngs were drawn from all walks and levels of Negro life—businessmen, teachers, laundry workers, Pullman porters, waiters, and red caps; preachers, crapshooters, and social workers; jitterbugs and Ph.D.'s. They came and sat in silence, thinking, applauding only when they considered the truth was told, when they felt strongly that something was going to be done about it.

The March on Washington Movement is essentially a movement of the people. It is all Negro and pro-Negro, but not for that reason anti-white or anti-Semitic, or anti-Catholic, or anti-foreign, or anti-labor. Its major weapon is the non-violent demonstration of Negro mass power. Negro leadership has united back of its drive for jobs and justice. "Whether Negroes should march on Washington, and if so, when?" will be the focus of a forthcoming national conference. For the plan of a protest march has not been abandoned. Its purpose would be to demonstrate that American Negroes are in deadly earnest, and all out for their full rights. No power on earth can cause them today to abandon their fight to wipe out every vestige of second class citizenship and the dual standards that plague them.

A community is democratic only when the humblest and weakest person can enjoy the highest civil, economic, and social rights that the biggest and most powerful possess. To trample on these rights of both Negroes and poor whites is such a commonplace in the South that it takes readily to anti-social, anti-labor, anti-Semitic and anti-Catholic propaganda. It was because of laxness in enforcing the Weimar constitution in republican Germany that Nazism made headway. Oppression of the Negroes in the

United States, like suppression of the Jews in Germany, may open the way for a fascist dictatorship.

By fighting for their rights now American Negroes are helping to make America a moral and spiritual arsenal of democracy. Their fight against the poll tax, against lynch law, segregation, and Jim Crow, their fight for economic, political, and social equality, thus becomes part of the global war for freedom.

The Supreme Court's decision in *Brown v. Board of Education* in 1954 was a triumph for civil rights and for the NAACP, which fought the legal battle for desegregation. Lawyers for the NAACP (chief attorney and future United States Supreme Court Justice Thurgood Marshall is in the center) express their feelings at the news of the Court's decision.

# Ralph J. Bunche

## "... I Like the American Way of Life"

*Ralph J. Bunche's distinguished career in education and in government service and diplomacy puts him among a small number of black Americans who even before midcentury seemed to have broken the barriers to black advancement in white society. This address was given at Fisk University on May 30, 1949.*

I am an American, and I like the American way of life. I like freedom and equality and respect for the dignity of the individual. I believe that these graduates like them too. They like them so well that they bitterly resent being denied them because of an accident of birth.

There is a certain irony in the situation with which we are faced here. These Negro graduates of Fisk University today are better Americans than they are Negroes. They are Negroes primarily in a negative sense—they reject that sort of treatment that deprives them of their birthright as Americans. Remove that treatment and their identification as Negroes in the American society would become meaningless—at least as meaningless as it is to be of English or French or German or Italian ancestry.

These graduates are 100 per cent Americans. Who, indeed, is a better American, a better protector of the American heritage, of the American way, than he who demands the fullest measure of respect for those cardinal principles which are the pillars of our society?

If we could probe deeply into the minds of these graduates we would discover, I am sure, that the basic longing, the aspiration of every one of them, is to be an American in full. Not a semi-American. Not a Negro-American. Not an Afro-American. Not a "Colored

*Source:* Glenn R. Capp, *The Great Society: A Sourcebook of Speeches* (Belmont, California: Dickenson Publishing Company, 1967).

Gentleman." Not "one of our Colored Brethren." Just an American—with no qualifications, no ifs or buts, no apologies, conde-
scension or patronization. Just Americans, with a fair and equal
opportunity as individuals to make or break their futures on the
basis of their individual abilities without the un-American handi-
cap of race.

Can it be doubted that these young men and women must
even now be calculating their chances to make their way into the
mainstream of American life? And can it be doubted that they
must be greatly tormented at the prospect that because of their
race they may be kept out of the mainstream and shunted onto the
bayous and creeks and backwashes of American life?

And what may be told to them? That as Americans and citizens of this great democracy they are as entitled as the next man
to negotiate the waters of the mainstream could be disputed only
by racial bigots. But to encourage them to believe that their course
is charted and the shoals of racialism no longer endanger them
would be criminally misleading.

This, it seems to me, is what they should know. The democratic framework of our society is their great hope. The American
Negro suffers cruel disabilities because of race which are in most
flagrant violation of the constitutional tenets and ideals of the
American democracy. But the saving grace for the Negro is the
democratic warp and woof of the society which permits the Negro
to carry on his incessant and heroic struggle to come into his own,
to win those rights, that dignity and respect for the Negro, individually and collectively, which are his birthright as an American.
And fortunately, the American, white and black alike, has a conscience. The Negro American daily wins increasing support for his
own struggle from all those other Americans who aspire toward
a democratic, not a semidemocratic, America; who wish a four-
fourths, not a three-fourths democracy. Moreover, the sympathy of
the world is with him. The Charter of the United Nations endorses
his aspirations. . . .

If I may be pardoned for a personal reference, I should like to
say that in my own struggle against the barriers of race, I have
from early age been strongly fortified by the philosophy taught me
by my maternal grandmother, and it may be of interest to you.

She was a tiny woman, but a personality of indomitable will
and invincible moral and spiritual strength. "Nana" we all called
her, and she was the ruler of our family "clan." She had come from
Texas, married in Indian territory, and on the premature death of
my grandfather, was left with five young children.

Nana had traveled the troubled road. But she has never flinched or complained. Her indoctrination of the youngsters of the "clan" began at an early age. The philosophy she handed down to us was as simple as it has proved invaluable. Your color, she counseled, has nothing to do with your worth. You are potentially as good as anyone. How good you may prove to be will have no relation to your color, but with what is in your heart and your head. That is something which each individual, by his own effort, can control. The right to be treated as an equal by all other men, she said, is man's birthright. Never permit anyone to treat you otherwise. For nothing is as important as maintaining your dignity and self-respect. She told us that there would be many and great obstacles in our paths and that this was the way of life. But only weaklings give up in the face of obstacles. Set a goal for yourself and determine to reach it despite all obstacles. Be honest and frank with yourself and the world at all times. Never compromise what you know to be the right. Never pick a fight, but never run from one if your principles are at stake. Never be content with any effort you make until you are certain you have given it the best you have in you. Go out into the world with your head high and keep it high at all times.

Nana's advice and philosophy is as good today for these graduates as it was when she gave it to me in my childhood. I certainly cannot improve upon it, nor would I try to do so. For me it has been a priceless heritage from a truly noble woman.

In conclusion, I may say only that I have great faith that the kind of world we all long for can and will be achieved. It is the kind of world the United Nations is working incessantly to bring about: a world at peace; a world in which people practice tolerance and live together in peace with one another as good neighbors; a world in which there is full respect for human rights and fundamental freedom for all without distinction as to race, sex, language, or religion; a world in which all men shall walk together as equals and with dignity.

I trust that among these graduates there are many who will consecrate their lives to the struggle to achieve that kind of a world.

# Supreme Court decision in *Brown v. Board of Education of Topeka* (1954)

*This excerpt from the most famous decision of the Court under Chief Justice of the United States Earl Warren over- turned the Court's ruling of 1896 in* Plessy v. Ferguson, *a case involving not schooling but transportation facilities. In* Plessy *the Court had held that facilities could be segre- gated just so long as the facilities provided for the separate races were equal in quality. That is the doctrine known as "separate but equal." The* Brown *decision took into account social and psychological factors that make segre- gation harmful to black students even if the physical provi- sions should happen to be adequate.*

Today, education is perhaps the most important function of state and local governments. Compulsory school attendance laws and the great expenditures for education both demonstrate our recognition of the importance of education to our democratic soci- ety. It is required in the performance of our most basic public responsibilities, even service in the armed forces. It is the very foundation of good citizenship. Today it is a principal instrument in awakening the child to cultural values, in preparing him for later professional training, and in helping him to adjust normally to his environment. In these days, it is doubtful that any child may reasonably be expected to succeed in life if he is denied the oppor- tunity of an education. Such an opportunity, where the state has undertaken to provide it, is a right which must be made available to all on equal terms.

We come to the question presented: Does segregation of chil- dren in public schools solely on the basis of race, even though the physical facilities and other "tangible" factors may be equal, de-

*Source: Brown v. Board of Education of Topeka,* 347 U.S. 483 (1954).

prive the children of the minority group of equal education opportunities? We believe that it does.

In *Sweatt v. Painter, supra,* in finding that a segregated law school for Negroes could not provide them equal educational opportunities, this Court relied in large part on "those qualities which are incapable of objective measurement but which make for greatness in a law school." In *McLaurin v. Oklahoma State Regents, supra,* the Court, in requiring that a Negro admitted to a white graduate school be treated like all other students, again resorted to intangible considerations: ". . . his ability to study, to engage in discussions and exchange views with other students, and, in general, to learn his profession." Such considerations apply with added force to children in grade and high schools. To separate them from others of similar age and qualifications solely because of their race generates a feeling of inferiority as to their status in the community that may affect their hearts and minds in a way unlikely to ever be undone. . . .

We conclude that in the field of public education the doctrine of "separate but equal" has no place. Therefore, we hold that the plaintiffs and others similarly situated for whom the actions have been brought are, by reason of the segregation complained of, deprived of equal protection of the laws guaranteed by the Fourteenth Amendment. This disposition makes unnecessary any discussion whether such segregation also violates the Due Process Clause of the Fourteenth Amendment.

Because these are class actions, because of the wide applicability of this decision, and because of the great variety of local conditions, the formulation of decrees in these cases presents problems of considerable complexity. On reargument, the consideration of appropriate relief was necessarily subordinated to the primary question—the constitutionality of segregation in public education. We have now announced that such segregation is a denial of the equal protection of the laws. . . .

*It is so ordered.*

# Mrs. Althea Simmons

## "We Sat There in Stunned Silence"

*At the time of the* Brown *decision, the commentator had been a legal counsel for the NAACP. Her remarks in this interview bear on one of the more noteworthy components of the argument presented against segregated schools: the contention that segregation is demonstrably harmful psychologically to the children of the minority race, and that the Court must take into account this effect of segregation. (Conservatives had argued that the Court could consider only tangible, measurable factors.)*

LUMUMBA: ... [S]ince you also attended Howard University, and were present at the school—the segregation case, I was concerned with the uniqueness of the approach used in that case in ... introducing a large scope of social scientist evidence in order to help resolve the case. Can you tell us something about whether or not it was the precedent in the courts and whether or not there has been any follow up in this type?

SIMMONS: I think this was very significant, Malaika, because you see, we had to overcome the Plessy v. Ferguson decision. Which really said in effect that the black man had no rights that a white man was bound to respect. Because we had certain rights accorded to all people under our United States Constitution, and the Constitution had not been interpreted in favor of the Negro. It was thought by the legal staff of NAACP that a new dimension would have to be brought to the attention of the court and that now we ought to deal with not just the legal aspects but how does this affect a young person, in his social adjustment. Dr. Kenneth Clark was one of the persons who were contacted to give his expert opinion with regard to how segregation affected young people.

*Source:* Transcript of Mrs. Althea Simmons, oral history interview, Moorland-Spingarn Research Center, Howard University. Interview on June 18, 1970; interviewer Malaika Lumumba.

This argument when it was presented to the court interested the court very much. And the court used the argument to boost up the opinion that segregation was harmful to the black child. Now we'll go a little further and we say segregation is harmful to the white children too, because if you have to live and work in a multi-racial society the sooner you get to know each other, in a multi-racial society the sooner you can get rid of misconceptions. And then you don't have one group of persons feeling they are superior to another group; and the next group feeling that it's inferior. This argument was one—it was a calculated risk....

... [E]very Monday is decision reading day. And of course, somebody would always go down to the Supreme Court then call back to say no, the decision would not be read today. And then that morning came May 17.... So we hopped into taxis and went down to the Supreme Court and sat there with bated breath and listened. Because we didn't know what Chief Justice Warren was going to say, and when he read that phrase it was a phrase that I would never forget: "that segregation in public education is unconstitutional" we sat there in stunned silence. We knew it should have been that way, but nobody really dared to believe it would happen.

Rosa Parks, whose action sparked the Montgomery boycott, is fingerprinted after her indictment for violating a seldom-invoked antiboycott law.
*Photo: Wide World Photos, Inc.*

# Rosa Parks

## "... I Tried Not to Think About What Might Happen"

*Rosa Parks' defiance of bus policy was the immediate
cause of the Montgomery bus boycott.*

I knew [the opponents of the bus rules] needed a plaintiff who
was beyond reproach, because I was in on the discussions about
the possible court cases. But that is not why I refused to give up my
bus seat to a white man on Thursday, December 1, 1955. I did not
intend to get arrested. If I had been paying attention, I wouldn't
even have gotten on that bus.

I was very busy at that particular time. I was getting an
NAACP workshop together for the 3rd or 4th of December, and I
was trying to get the consent of Mr. H. Council Trenholm at Alabama State to have the Saturday meeting at the college. He did
give permission, but I had a hard time getting to him to get permission to use the building. I was also getting notices in the mail
for the election of officers of the Senior Branch of the NAACP,
which would be the next week.

When I got off from work that evening of December 1, I went
to Court Square as usual to catch the Cleveland Avenue bus home.
I didn't look to see who was driving when I got on, and by the time
I recognized him, I had already paid my fare. It was the same
driver who had put me off the bus back in 1943, twelve years earlier. He was still tall and heavy, with red, rough-looking skin. And
he was still mean-looking. I didn't know if he had been on that
route before—they switched the drivers around sometimes. I do
know that most of the time if I saw him on a bus, I wouldn't get
on it.

I saw a vacant seat in the middle section of the bus and took
it. I didn't even question why there was a vacant seat even though
there were quite a few people standing in the back. If I had thought

*Source:* Rosa Parks with Jim Haskins, *Rosa Parks: My Story* (New York: Dial Books,
1992).

about it at all, I would probably have figured maybe someone saw me get on and did not take the seat but left it vacant for me. There was a man sitting next to the window and two women across the aisle.

The next stop was the Empire Theater, and some whites got on. They filled up the white seats, and one man was left standing. The driver looked back and noticed the man standing. Then he looked back at us. He said, "Let me have those front seats," because they were the front seats of the black section. Didn't anybody move. We just sat right where we were, the four of us. Then he spoke a second time: "Y'all better make it light on yourselves and let me have those seats."

The man in the window seat next to me stood up, and I moved to let him pass me, and then I looked across the aisle and saw the two women were also standing. I moved over to the window seat. I could not see how standing up was going to "make it light" for me. The more we gave in and complied, the worse they treated us. . . .

The driver of the bus saw me still sitting there, and he asked was I going to stand up. I said, "No." He said, "Well, I'm going to have you arrested." Then I said, "You may do that." These were the only words we said to each other. . . .

As I sat there, I tried not to think about what might happen. I knew anything was possible. I could be manhandled or beaten. I could be arrested. People have asked me if it occurred to me then that I could be the test case the NAACP had been looking for. I did not think that at all. In fact if I had let myself think too deeply about what might happen to me, I might have gotten off the bus. But I chose to remain.

**Montgomery, Alabama,** 1956. Evidence of the effectiveness of the year-long bus boycott.

# Joseph Francis Rummel

## Segregation as Sin

*This pastoral letter denouncing segregation, which Joseph Francis Rummel issued as Archbishop of New Orleans, invokes Roman Catholic moral teaching. On February 19, 1956, the letter was read in all the Catholic churches of the archdiocese of New Orleans. Rummel went further: he held the threat of excommunication against Catholics, including legislators, who resisted integration of private schools.*

Difficult indeed is the approach to a propitious solution, according to Christian principles of justice and charity, of the problem of racial integration in our schools, especially in the Deep South where for more than a century and a half segregation has been accepted without serious question or challenge.

For months we have prayed, studied and consulted about the problem with a sense of our responsibility for the welfare of all souls that constitute the spiritual family for which, in virtue of our office as Archbishop, we are responsible before God. With an appeal to the Holy Spirit we now submit for careful consideration the following results, especially regarding the moral difficulties which segregation presents.

Racial segregation as such is morally wrong and sinful because it is a denial of the unity and solidarity of the human race as conceived by God in the creation of man in Adam and Eve. . . .

Racial segregation is morally wrong and sinful because it is a denial of the unity and universality of the Redemption. . . .

Racial segregation is morally wrong and sinful because it is basically a violation of the dictates of justice and the mandate of love, which in obedience to God's will must regulate the relations between all men. To deny to members of a certain race, just because they are members of that race, certain rights and opportu-

*Source: The Catholic Mind,* 54 (May 1956).

nities, civic or economic, educational or religious, recreational or social, imposes upon them definite hardships and humiliations, frustrations and impediments to progress which condemn them to perpetual degradation which is only a step removed from slavery. Such indignities are grievous violations of Christian justice and charity, which cannot be justified in this modern age of enlightenment and loudly proclaimed democracy. Of violations of charity St. Thomas Aquinas says in his work about the two precepts of charity, that men having the same nature are morally bound to love one another. It is Thomas' teaching that "... 'every animal loves its like' (Eccles. 13:19), wherefore since all men are alike in nature, they ought to love one another. Therefore to hate one's neighbor is contrary to, not only the divine law, but also the law of nature."

Because the emancipation during the War between the States involved certain physical and economic hardships, racial segregation was regarded with toleration but never justifiable as a permanent racial adjustment. Even the Catholic Church considered it wise and necessary to give separate church and school facilities to Negroes to afford them the opportunity to practice their faith more freely and educate their children more fully than was often possible in mixed congregations, but this arrangement was never intended to be permanent. . . .

We come now to the reasons for segregation at least in the school. These reasons are for the most part unwarranted generalizations in which it is aimed to give the impression that all members of the Negro race and especially all Negro children are tainted with virtually all the alleged defects. The amazing fact is that "as a race" they are not still more generally lacking in mental ability, culture, moral self-control, immunity from social diseases, criminal propensities, etc., when you consider the neglect and barriers to which they have been exposed in education, general culture, economic opportunities, respectable housing facilities, contact with stable social institutions and the more dignified ways of life. Although living and moving in the maelstrom of city or rural life, the laws and customs built up around the mystic term "segregation" have practically relegated Negroes to an island-like existence. They emerge to work, toil and serve even in the intimacy of the white home and family, but "segregation" cuts off the free avenues to progress in the better things of life that are synonymous with Christian civilization. This condition in itself is an indictment against continuing segregation "indefinitely" as its advocates envision.

# The Southern Manifesto

*This pronouncement, signed by most Senators and Representatives from eleven southern states and reflecting a widespread determination to resist the Supreme Court's* Brown *decision of 1954, was introduced into the Congressional Record on March 12, 1956. The Manifesto carries ninety-six signatures, nineteen from the Senate and seventy-seven from the House of Representatives. Five more Representatives signed later.*

## Declaration of Constitutional Principles

The unwarranted decision of the Supreme Court in the public school cases is now bearing the fruit always produced when men substitute naked power for established law.

The Founding Fathers gave us a Constitution of checks and balances because they realized the inescapable lesson of history that no man or group of men can be safely entrusted with unlimited power. They framed this Constitution with its provisions for change by amendment in order to secure the fundamentals of government against the dangers of temporary popular passion or the personal predilections of public officeholders.

We regard the decision of the Supreme Court in the school cases as a clear abuse of judicial power. It climaxes a trend in the Federal Judiciary undertaking to legislate, in derogation of the authority of Congress, and to encroach upon the reserved rights of the States and the people.

The original Constitution does not mention education. Neither does the 14th amendment nor any other amendment. The debates preceding the submission of the 14th amendment clearly show that there was no intent that it should affect the system of education maintained by the States.

*Source: Congressional Record*, 84th Cong., 2nd Sess. (March 12, 1956).

The very Congress which proposed the amendment subsequently provided for segregated schools in the District of Columbia.

When the amendment was adopted in 1868, there were 37 States of the Union. Every one of the 26 States that had any substantial racial differences among its people, either approved the operation of segregated schools already in existence or subsequently established such schools by action of the same law-making body which considered the 14th amendment.

As admitted by the Supreme Court in the public school case *(Brown v. Board of Education)*, the doctrine of separate but equal schools "apparently originated in *Roberts v. City of Boston* (1849), upholding school segregation against attack as being violative of a State constitutional guarantee of equality." This constitutional doctrine began in the North, not in the South, and it was followed not only in Massachusetts, but in Connecticut, New York, Illinois, Indiana, Michigan, Minnesota, New Jersey, Ohio, Pennsylvania and other northern States until they, exercising their rights as States through the constitutional processes of local self-government, changed their school systems.

In the case of *Plessy v. Ferguson* in 1896 the Supreme Court expressly declared that under the 14th amendment no person was denied any of his rights if the States provided separate but equal public facilities. This decision has been followed in many other cases. It is notable that the Supreme Court, speaking through Chief Justice Taft, a former President of the United States, unanimously declared in 1927 in *Lum v. Rice* that the "separate but equal" principle is "within the discretion of the State in regulating its public schools and does not conflict with the 14th amendment."

This interpretation, restated time and again, became a part of the life of the people of many of the States and confirmed their habits, customs, traditions, and way of life. It is founded on elemental humanity and commonsense, for parents should not be deprived by Government of the right to direct the lives and education of their own children.

Though there has been no constitutional amendment or act of Congress changing this established legal principle almost a century old, the Supreme Court of the United States, with no legal basis for such action, undertook to exercise their naked judicial power and substituted their personal political and social ideas for the established law of the land.

This unwarranted exercise of power by the Court, contrary to the Constitution, is creating chaos and confusion in the States principally affected. It is destroying the amicable relations between the white and Negro races that have been created through 90 years of patient effort by the good people of both races. It has planted hatred and suspicion where there has been heretofore friendship and understanding.

Without regard to the consent of the governed, outside agitators are threatening immediate and revolutionary changes in our public-school systems. If done, this is certain to destroy the system of public education in some of the States.

With the gravest concern for the explosive and dangerous condition created by this decision and inflamed by outside meddlers:

We reaffirm our reliance on the Constitution as the fundamental law of the land.

We decry the Supreme Court's encroachments on rights reserved to the States and to the people, contrary to established law, and to the Constitution.

We commend the motives of those States which have declared the intention to resist forced integration by any lawful means.

We appeal to the States and people who are not directly affected by those decisions to consider the constitutional principles involved against the time when they too, on issues vital to them, may be the victims of judicial encroachment.

Even though we constitute a minority in the present Congress, we have full faith that a majority of the American people believe in the dual system of government which has enabled us to achieve our greatness and will in time demand that the reserved rights of the States and of the people be made secure against judicial usurpation.

We pledge ourselves to use all lawful means to bring about a reversal of this decision which is contrary to the Constitution and to prevent the use of force in its implementation.

In this trying period, as we all seek to right this wrong, we appeal to our people not to be provoked by the agitators and troublemakers invading our States and to scrupulously refrain from disorder and lawless acts.

# Elizabeth Eckford

## "Don't Let Them See You Cry"

*Elizabeth Eckford was one of the nine black students required to confront the racist mobs that awaited the arrival of integrated schooling at Little Rock in 1957.*

That night I was so excited I couldn't sleep. The next morning I was about the first one up. While I was pressing my black-and-white dress—I had made it to wear on the first day of school—my little brother turned on the TV set. They started telling about a large crowd gathered at the school. The man on TV said he wondered if we were going to show up that morning. Mother called from the kitchen, where she was fixing breakfast, "Turn that TV off!" She was so upset and worried. I wanted to comfort her, so I said, "Mother, don't worry."

Dad was walking back and forth, from room to room, with a sad expression. He was chewing on his pipe and he had a cigar in his hand, but he didn't light either one. It would have been funny, only he was so nervous.

Before I left home Mother called us into the living room. She said we should have a word of prayer. Then I caught the bus and got off a block from the school. I saw a large crowd of people standing across the street from the soldiers guarding Central. As I walked on, the crowd suddenly got very quiet. Superintendent Blossom had told us to enter by the front door. I looked at all the people and thought, "Maybe I will be safer if I walk down the block to the front entrance behind the guards."

At the corner I tried to pass through the long line of guards around the school so as to enter the grounds behind them. One of the guards pointed across the street. So I pointed in the same direction and asked whether he meant for me to cross the street and

*Source:* Elizabeth Eckford with Daisy Bates, "The First Day: Little Rock, 1957," in *Growing Up Southern: Southern Exposure Looks at Childhood, Then and Now,* edited by Chris Mayfield (New York: Pantheon Books, 1981).

walk down. He nodded "yes." So, I walked across the street conscious of the crowd that stood there, but they moved away from me.

For a moment all I could hear was the shuffling of their feet. Then someone shouted, "Here she comes, get ready!" I moved away from the crowd on the sidewalk and into the street. If the mob came at me I could then cross back over so the guards could protect me.

The crowd moved in closer and then began to follow me, calling me names. I still wasn't afraid. Just a little bit nervous. Then my knees started to shake all of a sudden and I wondered whether I could make it to the center entrance a block away. It was the longest block I ever walked in my whole life.

Even so, I still wasn't too scared because all the time I kept thinking that the guards would protect me.

When I got in front of the school, I went up to a guard again. But this time he just looked straight ahead and didn't move to let me pass him. I didn't know what to do. Then I looked and saw that the path leading to the front entrance was a little further ahead. So I walked until I was right in front of the path to the front door.

I stood looking at the school—it looked so big! Just then the guards let some white students through.

The crowd was quiet. I guess they were waiting to see what was going to happen. When I was able to steady my knees, I walked up to the guard who had let the white students in. He too didn't move. When I tried to squeeze past him, he raised his bayonet and then the other guards moved in and raised their bayonets.

They glared at me with a mean look and I was very frightened and didn't know what to do. I turned around and the crowd came toward me.

They moved closer and closer. Somebody started yelling, "Lynch her! Lynch her!"

I tried to see a friendly face somewhere in the mob—someone who maybe would help. I looked into the face of an old woman and it seemed a kind face, but when I looked at her again, she spat on me.

They came closer, shouting, "No nigger bitch is going to get in our school. Get out of here!"

I turned back to the guards but their faces told me I wouldn't get any help from them. Then I looked down the block and saw a bench at the bus stop. I thought, "If I can only get there I will be safe." I don't know why the bench seemed a safe place to me, but I started walking toward it. I tried to close my mind to what they were shouting, and kept saying to myself, "If I can only make it to the bench I will be safe."

When I finally got there, I don't think I could have gone another step. I sat down and the mob crowded up and began shouting all over again. Someone hollered, "Drag her over to this tree! Let's take care of that nigger." Just then a white man sat down beside me, put his arm around me and patted my shoulder. He raised my chin and said, "Don't let them see you cry."

White students and adults jeer Elizabeth Eckford, one of the nine black students admitted to Little Rock High School. *Photo: Wide World Photos, Inc*

# Lawrence C. Dum

## Discovering History in the Making

*Lawrence C. Dum, later a journalist, was a white student at Central High School in Little Rock. His memories of the year of integration are an honest confession of how difficult it is for people to understand or react adequately to the events in which they are placed.*

MARTIN: ... When does this whole situation break to the point that you become aware of what is happening, that you begin to become sensitive to these developments?

DUM: Well, I think, of course, the first day of school or the second day. The troops were out, the National Guard.

MARTIN: Yes.

DUM: And again, I began to hear more and more about it as the start of school approached and I was a little bit appalled that it took this many troops to handle this kind of situation. I just personally couldn't see how all these people felt so threatened by nine children, no matter what color they were or what size they were or anything else....

MARTIN: I guess you began to see newspapermen, cameramen for the first time really?

DUM: Well, this was the first contact I had had, I remember really one reporter, I think he was from Chicago. After football practice one day, we were sitting, a group of football players were sitting in the stands resting after practice and there were some reporters sitting there and I remember this one reporter vividly saying, this is the biggest thing since the Civil War....

MARTIN: And it took a newspaper reporter from a distant city to indicate to you the importance of it? This had not seemed to you to be so terribly important?

*Source:* Transcript of Lawrence C. Dum, oral history interview, Moorland-Spingarn Research Center, Howard University. Interview on July 29, 1969; interviewer Robert E. Martin.

DUM: I say it seemed a matter of concern and a matter of importance because it involved me and my school and my friends and the community around me.

MARTIN: Yes.

DUM: Yes, but I think that this was a point that I realized something bigger [was happening] than just Little Rock Central High School or even the town of Little Rock or one side of the city as opposed to another part of the city and I think this—it was the first time I tried to grasp something that big that wasn't in the history book.

MARTIN: Yes, yes. Do you recall any comments from any of your classmates as they began to see this drama unfold? Any comments that would indicate what impressions this was having on them?

DUM: Well, . . . I would say a majority, perhaps not as large a majority as some would think . . . [were] against integration or desegregation, . . . and I would say there is another group perhaps that I was mostly in that . . . were in favor of [integration] but our main concern, I regret to say at this point, was that we just didn't want to get involved. . . .

. . . On the other hand there were some students and some of the student leaders who made an effort to sit with some of the black students and of course were highly criticized and I remember one, Ralph Brody, who I think was the student body president and Ralph was a very religious man and a student who I admired very much and [I] now wish I had been more like him at that particular point. He attempted . . . in small ways [to] try to make things a little easier.

# Jimmy McDonald

## A Freedom Rider Reflects

*Jimmy McDonald reveals the determination beneath the peaceful antisegregation tactic of the freedom rides.*

Now, I have been asked on many occasions, "Do you hate these people?" And, as pathetic as it sounds, I do not. In order for me to hate them, they must do something to me which harms me—and this they cannot do. But what I do hate is the society that produces such people, a society in which the white man has set himself up as the undisputed spokesman for the Negro. After all, if only the white can speak for the colored, how can the Negro object to this arrangement? All this, of course, disregards the obvious biological fact that the Negro has a mind and a mouth of his own and is as capable of using them as anyone else. Not to mention what also should be evident: only the Negro knows what the Negro wants and, at last, although he still cannot say it at the polls, he is letting the world know what it is: to be treated like a human being.

In spite of this, we find responsible people demanding "cooling-off" periods and moderation. This is not a new request, and we often have complied with it. I would be happy if they would moderately respect me as a human being and afford me the same dignities that are the right of every one of us to expect and receive—which include the right to life, liberty, and the pursuit of happiness. But according to these so-called moderates, I already am going too fast. They would rather I did nothing to secure the civil rights that have been denied me and my people since the first Negro slave was brought here in the seventeenth century. For 300 years we have been cooling off. More recently, we were cooling off when they lynched our mothers and fathers. And did we not cool off when they raped and jailed Mrs. Rose Lee Ingram? Perhaps she, too, was disturbing the peace and refusing to obey an officer. We

*Source:* Jimmy McDonald, "A Freedom Rider Speaks His Mind," *Freedomways,* 1 (Summer 1961).

also were prepared to cool off when they told the Jim Crow school boards to let us get a decent education "with all deliberate speed," and Miss Autherine Lucy discovered which word they valued most. But after a while, a cooling-off becomes a deep freeze. Now we are trying to take a bus ride, on an interstate carrier, through several Southern states, and the Ku Klux Klan, white Citizens Councils, and their brethren bomb our buses, board them, and beat us; all with the semiofficial blessing of the governor of the state of Alabama and the chief of police of the city of Birmingham. It is not the Negro people who should cool off—they are cool enough already. Those who should cool off are the bomb throwers and their legalistic counterparts, the constabulary and judiciary of Anniston, Alabama, Birmingham and Jackson, Mississippi.

I am tempted to say, so far, so good. But, although we have made appreciable gains while remaining cooled-off, several rights remain for us to reclaim. Things are not so good. We intend to remain cooled-off—we can count on the Klan and the Council for all the heat we shall need; but we will not become docile. We will keep sending Freedom Riders down South—and these are not "so-called" Freedom Riders; they are exposing themselves to all sorts of danger to insure the freedom not just of the Negro, but of every American. Segregation is a dangerous precedent, and if we accept it—shall we say, "sitting down"—not one American is free. Least of all those who segregate. We will continue to ride for freedom, in the bus terminals and in the rest of the country!

Women of the Klan bow their heads in prayer at a rally near Salisbury, North Carolina. The Klan tried to portray itself as a family organization steeped in godliness.

# Charlayne Hunter-Gault

## A University Integrated

*Today a nationally known newswoman, Charlayne Hunter-Gault (then Charlayne Hunter) along with Hamilton Holman—"Hamp" in the first passage—in January 1961 entered the University of Georgia: the first black students at the institution. Their first days there involved legal maneuverings by the state, which was trying to keep them out. After a riot, described in the article in* The Urbanite *partially reproduced here, the two were temporarily suspended. Thereupon a court order required the university to admit them.*

It was with a heady sense of history that we started out for Athens early Monday, just as the sun was rising on a cold Georgia morning. My mother, Vernon Jordan, and I were in one car, and Hamp and his father in another. We had no security, and no plan for what we would do in the event that we were attacked on the way or after we got there, despite the history of white violence on this route. No, this was the morning when I thought about how I was going to take my first steps onto the campus as if I knew my place, only this time, for the first time, it would be I who would be defining my place on *my* terms, on territory that was their pride but was now mine, too. . . .

I captured the rest of the events of [an evening of violence] in an article I wrote soon after for *The Urbanite*. The new Black entry into the magazine world was published by Byron Lewis, the former private in my father's glee club in Alaska, who was now out of the army and living in New York. I wrote:

> The lobby of the dormitory was almost empty, but after I had gone to my room many of the girls came down as they had

*Source:* Charlayne Hunter-Gault, *In My Place* (New York: Farrar, Straus, Giroux, 1992). Reprinted by permission.

the day before—to welcome, observe, inspect. Mrs. Porter, the housemother, came down and told the girls not to stay too long because I was tired. She had advised me earlier that it would be best to have my dinner in my room that night. This, again, seemed only a normal precaution, considering the circumstances.

It began getting dark around six o'clock. After the last of the girls had gone, everything became amazingly quiet inside the dorm. I picked up a book and tried to study, but then firecrackers began popping outside, as they had the night before. I decided there was nothing to do but go to bed, despite the racket outside. Mrs. Porter came in again to see if I had eaten and to ask how I was feeling. She suggested that I keep the blinds closed and stay away from the windows. "We expect some trouble," she said.

Later, as I went into the hall for a drink of water, I caught a glimpse of the faculty members the students had nicknamed "The Baby-Sitting Crew," because they had volunteered to patrol the building. It seemed to me the group was larger than it had been the night before. I returned to my room. After a while, the noise outside gradually grew larger and uglier. Though I did not know it at the time, a hotly disputed last-minute defeat of the basketball team at the hands of Georgia Tech had helped create anything but a mood of sweet reasonableness in the crowd that had marched from the gym to the dormitory. Reading or sleeping was out of the question. I was in the first room of the duplex apartment. Suddenly there was a loud crash in the bedroom. Not stopping to think, I rushed in, only to be stopped in my tracks by another crash, as a Coca-Cola bottle followed the brick that had ripped through the window a moment before. Jagged splinters of window glass and fragments of the bottle had spattered across my dress, slippers, and the skirts and blouses that I had not yet had time to unpack.

Strangely, I was not at all afraid at this moment. Instead, I found myself thinking, as I stood there in the midst of the wreckage, So this is how it is.

At this time, I did not know that all the students had been told by the riot planners to turn off the lights in their rooms when it got dark. With the rest of the building in darkness, the three brightly lit windows of my apartment must have made an inviting target for the mob out on the lawn. . . .

I realized that it was nearing time for the eleven o'clock news and that my mother in Atlanta would be waiting up for it. I called her and told her that I was all right. Though I knew she could hear the noise in the background, she seemed relatively calm. But I could not get her to promise that she would go to bed at once, without waiting to look at the television news program.

After I hung up, [Paula Leiter], one of the most genuine persons it has been my good luck to meet, came down and began talking to me. Though it was clear that she herself was nervous, she did all she could under the circumstances to take my mind off what was going on. This was anything but easy, since by now the hostility from outside was being echoed by some of the girls inside the dorm. Perhaps it was partially out of hysteria, or partially because the girl upstairs had been hurt. At any rate, a group of girls began tramping in a continuous circle, yelling insults first at me and then at the schoolmate who had come in to befriend me.

It was hard to sit there and listen to some of the things that were said about me without being able to answer. I was told I was about to become "a Black martyr, getting fifty dollars a day for this from the NAACP"—a piece of news that would have considerably surprised my family.

The city police outside, after having waited in vain for the state patrol, finally resorted to tear gas. The gas fumes began seeping into the dorm, and the girls were told to change the linen on their beds. This prompted deliberately loud offers of a dime or a quarter to Charlayne for changing the sheets of these same residents who professed to believe that I was already being paid at a rate of over six dollars an hour, if figured on the basis of an eight-hour day.

My new friend was beginning to get drowsy, though she tried not to show it, and I suggested that she go to bed, assuring her that I would be all right. After she had left, I wondered how many people, myself included, would have had the courage to do what she had done. . . .

Sit-in at the Woolworth's Lunch Counter in Greensboro, North Carolina, February 2, 1960.

# Joanne Grant

## Youth in the Civil Rights Movement

*These reflections are a reminder that at least from the time of the Greensboro sit-ins the young were noted for their participation.*

Who knows the name Dion Diamond? Who has heard of Chuck McDew? Are there many in this land—above the Mason-Dixon Line—who know of Brenda Travis, of Bob Zellner?

These are faceless names to most. But they are not just names; they are people. Diamond, McDew, Brenda Travis and Zellner are behind bars.

Brenda Travis is a 16-year-old Negro girl who is now in a reformatory because she took part in a sit-in demonstration and then was arrested during a prayer meeting on the steps of City Hall in a Southern Town (that was in violation of her parole). She is not in high school any more; she was suspended. She is in a Colored Girls Industrial School for one year. Where? In Raymond, Mississippi.

Dion Diamond, Charles McDew and Bob Zellner are in a jail in Baton Rouge, Louisiana. Diamond was arrested as he alighted from a taxi on the campus of a Negro University, Louisiana Southern University, whose student body had protested by the hundreds segregation in Baton Rouge. Diamond is field secretary for the Student Nonviolent Coordinating Committee, a loosely-knit group of courageous Southern Negro students. He had visited the University in support of those hundreds who had marched in the streets of Baton Rouge and whose march had caused the University's President to at first close the school, and then refuse to readmit student leaders when school reopened.

McDew, chairman of SNCC, and Zellner, another field secretary (white Alabaman), went to the jail to visit Diamond. They

---

*Source:* Joanne Grant, "The Time Is Always Now," *Freedomways*, 2 (Spring 1962).

were told that they could not see him, but that they could bring him some books and fruit. When they returned to the jail with books and fruit for their friend they were arrested and charged with vagrancy. Later their charge was changed to "criminal anarchy," with a maximum sentence of ten years. Bail for the three was $25,000. . . .

What has continued to amaze me about the civil rights movement which dramatically shook America and the world with a lunch counter sit-in two years ago in February, 1960 is the attitude of the students, of students like Zellner and McDew and Diamond and so many others. Their confidence that they would eventually be supported; their determination that they would not fail has wrought such changes as no one would have dared dream of until the placid waters were roiled by a handful of young people. They created a ripple and then ever-enlarging waves which moved ever outward, until the whole South had felt the spray.

When they began the students heard few words of encouragement from their elders, but many words of caution. But the young people had had enough. They said: "Freedom NOW!" And they would continue to fight with little but that goal to sustain them for a long time to come. There have been small victories. In the words of one of the young leaders, Rev. James Lawson: "I do not wish to minimize the gains we have made thus far. But it would be well to recognize that we have been receiving concessions, not real changes." Rev. Lawson has called for a nonviolent army of thousands to bring the young people from the threshold of revolution to "real revolution." He has said that the time has come, not for wringing concessions from the system, but for transforming it.

Already that revolution is under way. Something has happened to thousands of people in the South as a result of the small victories. A mayor of a Deep South city has expressed in 1962 what at last the white South has come to recognize: "Even Robert E. Lee finally had to surrender, didn't he?" This realization is revolutionary.

So too, is the knowledge, solidly held by the Southern Negro community, that what is needed before the Negro can be free is a dismantling of the power structure of the South and a rebuilding in a new pattern. The adult Southern Negro has learned painfully by watching his children walk through howling mobs to school, or march before a "white" department store or theater or church and be spat upon. He has learned by sitting with his children trapped inside an airless church in Montgomery, Alabama all night while mobs raged outside. He has learned by hearing his children answer his pleas from behind a prison's bars: "No, Daddy, I will not stop."

The children have said: No, we will not stop, in many places. They have said it as the mobs armed with sticks and bricks and guns piled out of cars on the University of Georgia campus to "get" two young Negro students; they have said it as they were herded into a stockade at Orangeburg, South Carolina; they have said it as they lay in hospital beds swathed in bandages in Huntsville, Alabama, where they had been burned by mustard gas and in Birmingham where they had been beaten so near to death that the police finally came.

They have said, no, we will not stop, to the government. Justice Department men asked so many new Freedom Riders after the first group had been nearly pulverized in Alabama: Don't go. Cool off. But the young Riders kept on riding. They said, no. They said it to the judges, too. Judges, who, upholding the Southern Way of Life, increased the sentences of each new wave of Freedom Riders, each new wave of sit-ins. They have said, No, we will not stop, to members of Congress like Mississippi's James Whitten, who told his constituents (the fifty percent to whom he speaks and who are allowed to vote): "The first consideration in Mississippi should be that of retaining control in stable and conservative people . . . if we are to prevent our government from being dominated by irresponsible people. Destruction of our nation from within remains a much greater threat than danger of destruction from abroad."

We do not know they have suffered. We can appreciate only in too small measure what they have sacrificed, for what we have gained.

In Clarksdale, Mississippi a 19-year-old Negro woman was forced by police to lie on a concrete floor, expose her body and submit to a belt whipping. They told her not to tell anyone what they had done. She sent a signed affidavit to the U.S. Department of Justice.

Such brutality is sometimes simply part of the Southern Way of Life, the last spasms of a dead beast. More often it is a means to an end—intimidation of those who sit in the front seats of buses, return doggedly day after day to the voting registrar's office, sit at the lunch counters until they close or desegregate and intimidation of those who help by giving food and shelter, comfort and love. The homes of ministers who house the students are bombed; the churches are invaded by the police—the agents of the enemy; many lose their jobs.

For those who carry on the struggle there is nothing else.

They live the Movement each day. It is a round-the-clock, seven-day reality. They sleep little, they are ready to move into any trouble spot where help is needed. They give to each other whatever each has to give. The South of those in the Movement is a network of way stations on the Underground Railway.

Though all of us cannot be so intimately involved as they, we must at least know and understand what it is they suffer. We must not ever forget their faces. We must not forget that they live in a land of terror, a land with an overlay of warmth, of calm and of humor which hides—sometimes—fear, violence and death.

**Birmingham, 1963.** Photographs of white brutality against African-American protesters, such as this view of blacks enduring the cannonlike force of water shot from high-pressure fire hoses, galvanized the nation's conscience and forced President Kennedy to submit a comprehensive civil rights bill to Congress.

# F. L. Shuttlesworth and N. H. Smith

## The Birmingham Manifesto

*The manifesto was issued to the public on April 3, 1963, at the beginning of a rights campaign under the leadership of the Rev. Fred Shuttlesworth. It would turn out to be a massive campaign, closely followed by the national media. Especially remembered are the fire hoses and attack dogs used by the police, and a bomb planted in a church that in September 1963 left four black children dead. The second passage here is from a later interview with Shuttlesworth.*

The patience of an oppressed people cannot endure forever. The Negro citizens of Birmingham for the last several years have hoped in vain for some evidence of good faith resolution of our just grievances.

Birmingham is part of the United States and we are *bona fide* citizens. Yet the history of Birmingham reveals that very little of the democratic process touches the life of the Negro in Birmingham. We have been segregated racially, exploited economically, and dominated politically. Under the leadership of the Alabama Christian Movement for Human Rights, we sought relief by petition for the repeal of city ordinances requiring segregation and the institution of a merit hiring policy in city employment. We were rebuffed. We then turned to the system of the courts. We weathered set-back after set-back, with all of its costliness, finally winning the terminal, bus, parks and airport cases. The bus decision has been implemented begrudgingly and the parks decision prompted the closing of all municipally-owned recreational facilities with the exception of the zoo and Legion Field. The airport case has been a slightly better experience with the exception of hotel accommodations and the subtle discrimination that continues in the limousine service.

*Source: Freedomways,* 4 (Winter 1964).

We have always been a peaceful people, bearing our oppression with super-human effort. Yet we have been the victims of repeated violence, not only that inflicted by the hoodlum element but also that inflicted by the blatant misuse of police power. Our memories are seared with painful mob experience of Mother's Day 1961 during the Freedom Rides. For years, while our homes and churches were being bombed, we heard nothing but the rantings and ravings of racist city officials.

The Negro protest for equality and justice has been a voice crying in the wilderness. Most of Birmingham has remained silent, probably out of fear. In the meanwhile, our city has acquired the dubious reputation of being the worst big city in race relations in the United States. Last fall, for a flickering moment, it appeared that sincere community leaders from religion, business and industry discerned the inevitable confrontation in race relations approaching. Their concern for the city's image and commonweal of all its citizens did not run deep enough. Solemn promises were made, pending a postponement of direct action, that we would be joined in a suit seeking the relief of segregation ordinances. Some merchants agreed to desegregate their rest-rooms as a good-faith start, some actually complying, only to retreat shortly thereafter. We hold in our hands now, broken faith and broken promises.

We believe in the American Dream of democracy, in the Jeffersonian doctrine that "all men are created equal and are endowed by their Creator with certain inalienable rights, among these being life, liberty and the pursuit of happiness."

Twice since September we have deferred our direct action thrust in order that a change in city government would not be made in the hysteria of community crisis. We act today in full concert with our Herbraic-Christian tradition, the law of morality and the Constitution of our nation. The absence of justice and progress in Birmingham demands that we make a moral witness to give our community a chance to survive. We demonstrate our faith that we believe that The Beloved Community can come to Birmingham.

We appeal to the citizenry of Birmingham, Negro and white, to join us in this witness for decency, morality, self-respect and human dignity. Your individual and corporate support can hasten the day of "liberty and justice for all." This is Birmingham's moment of truth in which every citizen can play his part in her larger destiny. The Alabama Christian Movement for Human Rights, in behalf of the Negro community of Birmingham.

F. L. SHUTTLESWORTH, President
N. H. SMITH, Secretary

*    *    *

MOSBY: I'd like to talk about something now, Reverend Shuttlesworth, that we hit on through our entire interview. That is non violence. What does it mean? What does non violence mean to you?

SHUTTLESWORTH: Well non violence to me—and I don't know as much about Gandhi as King did. King made it a study. This was a part of his studies. But non violence to me means, too, a way of life. It means try not to think evil of people. Jesus said . . . resist not evil; man can pay you to go one mile; go two. And I best experienced this in my own life, here, when I had a right-wing attack upon my church down there, eleven hundred members. It just went on so bad, and I told the few people who were praying with me not to resist, not to fight, not to attack them and I'll get up and preach and do my job. So, finally, . . . we're doing better than ever before. So that non violence does work.

MOSBY: But it's not a tactic. It's a way of life?

SHUTTLESWORTH: Well it's a tactic. It's a way of life, because I'm a preacher; because I can't believe in violence . . . and be a preacher. Do violence to no man, John the Baptist said that out on the wilderness.

MOSBY: This means that when struck you would not retaliate under any circumstances?

SHUTTLESWORTH: I don't know whether it means under any circumstances, and I'm not too sure that you would not retaliate under certain circumstances, that is, if somebody came in to kill my family or something. But, I mean, if I'm out there marching for a cause and I'm struck in that cause I take that blow for that cause, because I'm trying to disprove the evil that's being [done].

Source: Transcript of the Rev. Fred L. Shuttlesworth, oral history interview, Moorland-Spingarn Research Center, Howard University. Interview in September 1968; interviewer James M. Mosby, Jr.

# Whitney M. Young, Jr.

## Passion and Professionalism

*The Urban League, for which Whitney Young spoke, has been characterized by a concern for practical social and economic programs. Taken together, Young's comments in this work published in 1964 catch differing components of the thought of the civil rights movement. He affirms both the virtues of hard-headed professional skill and the need for spiritual regeneration; and unlike both white racists and black separatists, he insists that a mixed and integrated society is the richer in culture.*

Race relations is no longer a hobby for the well-intentioned, the idle, or the status-seeking. We can no longer play by ear in intergroup relations. We have advanced far enough in social science research so that intelligent, scientific planning can and must replace hit-or-miss action. . . .

Back in 1910 several small agencies banded together in New York to form the National League on Urban Conditions Among Negroes to improve social and economic conditions of Negro citizens through interracial teamwork. Initially, the League sought jobs for Negroes. It was at a time when jobs of any kind were needed, and the League did its work effectively, though hampered then as at all times during its history by lack of money and staff. The League worked for housing, health and welfare services, and education—then as well as now. Because of the halfhearted approaches to Negro needs by existing agencies, the League was forced to be the direct service organization to which Negroes came, whatever their problems. In return for taking over this catch-all responsibility, guilt-compensating token financial support was given the League and its affiliates.

An increasing number of Americans know now what the

*Source:* Whitney M. Young, Jr., *To Be Equal* (New York: McGraw-Hill, 1964).

League knew and has tried to tell the nation's citizens for fifty-four years: that segregation is not only inherently bad, but produces even greater problems. Segregated jobs may reserve better jobs for non-Negro citizens, but they deny to society excellent talents and skills; they destroy incentives for Negroes. Segregated housing may make some realtors wealthy through the carefully nurtured myth of exclusive neighborhoods, but it breeds slums, crime, *de facto* segregation in schools; it multiplies health and welfare costs. For too long, custom had referred all Negro problems to a single agency—the League—bypassing the numerous specialized, all-white services. This practice was not only unfair, but made it humanly impossible for the League to handle Negro problems adequately, to say nothing of executing its far more important job of social engineering. It was, as Lester Granger, past executive director of the League put it, "like bailing out a sinking ship with a teaspoon."

Nevertheless, the basic soundness of the League's efforts, the intense need for its services, and the solid record of achievement in more than sixty urban centers have won respect, recognition, and, at last, moderate financial support. With five hundred professional staff members and more than six thousand board members, both white and Negro, the League has proved that understanding and teamwork *do* make for community progress. The incredible element in the League story has been the dedication of its staff, who, as recently as 1950 were existing on average salaries of $3,500 and operating League programs in crucial urban areas on an average of $21,000 per year—scarcely enough to run a second-rate cigar store.

Wherein responsibility here?

The League as an organization has proposed a special effort, domestic Marshall Plan deliberately, to recall America's action in rehabilitating war-torn Europe. Our nation also has helped to rehabilitate and given asylum to Cuban and Hungarian refugees. If America is serious and honest about closing the discrimination gap that exists in our society between white and Negro citizens, we must do something equally special.

Neither the Negro nor the Urban League is asking for three hundred years of preferential treatment such as white citizens have had. We are asking for only a decade of dedicated special effort.

Who can call this irresponsibility? ...

Integration is an opportunity for white citizens to show to the whole world their maturity and their security. It is time for them consciously to proclaim the creative possibilities in that diversity from which they have unconsciously benefitted. People do not grow through similarity to one another. One grows from the stimulus of people who are different, people whose cultural backgrounds are heterogeneous. One contributes to the other. In my own case, I moved into a neighborhood where there are no other Negroes. Until then, my children had never had an opportunity to light Hannukah candles and until then many of my neighbors' children had never had a chance to decorate a Christmas tree. These children grew and learned simply by knowing each other.

When you surround yourself with people who drive the same cars and have the same skin color and go to the same churches, clubs and parties and read the same books all you do is perpetuate a type of homogenized mediocrity. Probably no nation owes so much to diversity as does ours. We have benefitted in myriad ways from the vast variety of contributions to our way of life by people of all manner of backgrounds. Think of the foods, stemming from different cultures, that we enjoy every day; look at the art, dance, clothing, toys and games, music, even the words in our American language that derive from other countries—all of these make life in this nation zestful. In centuries past, the county fair was the annual occasion that introduced to an area the exotic and stimulating features of faraway places. In the United States, with our mobility and our communications media, ours is a 24-hour-a-day, 365-days-a-year interchange with the rest of the world. And how much more we enjoy and absorb from life when we open our senses to the manifold varieties of "otherness" available to us. Men grow to the extent that they are the beneficiaries of diverse ideas, not through the process of having their ideas reflected and reinforced by people whose backgrounds and cultures are identical.

We are, through integration, seeking to help all our citizens realize their true, creative potentials and to move toward a new type of society that is not a replica of any past culture or any single group, but is a culture that has absorbed the best from each.

# Slater King

## The Albany Movement

*Slater King's commentary on the wide-ranging civil rights movement in Albany, Georgia, of which he was a leader, presents integration as a means to economic and political power.*

In all of the small and rural communities that surround Albany, the Negroes have been so "cowed" down and intimidated by hangings, being burned alive and all sorts of mayhem and torture, physical as well as psychological, until they will not even attempt to use the integrated facilities presumably made available to them through the recently enacted Civil Rights Bill. In one neighboring community where a few young Negroes have attempted to use the local previously "all white" theatre, police have stood in front of the theatre allowing whites to come and go but blocking the paths of Negroes attempting to enter. Their excuse is that they are keeping order. It is a definite axiom to say that in the majority, the police force and the machinery of the Southern local and state enforcement agencies will be used not for the Negroes' protection but as a repressive instrument against them. The city of Albany hired six Negro policemen. There is a tremendous rapport between them and the Negroes of Albany. They have been very humane men who have restrained themselves greatly in the exercise of their police powers. . . .

We in Albany, Georgia feel a great sense of reward in the enactment of the Civil Rights Bill despite its many limitations. There were college students who were "sitting in" and conducting other demonstrations to protest segregation but we were the first

---

*Source:* Slater King, "Our Main Battle in Albany," *Freedomways*, 5 (Summer 1965).

community where there was the involvement of the total community protesting segregation. This caused thousands of blacks to be jailed (in 1961–62). After other communities such as Birmingham and others followed our example, it was clear that this country would have to enact the Civil Rights Bill to stop the developments of embarrassing spectacles such as Albany and Birmingham, which were being viewed by an international audience.

It is pathetic that most of the Negroes who were arrested here for marching and sitting in and for the whole spectrum of Civil Rights activities will not enjoy the fruits of their labors because many aren't employed and many who are employed don't make enough to eat out or travel to enjoy these facilities that are now open to them. The people who will enjoy these new freedoms are the small group composing the "Black Bourgeoisie." Not only have most of them not helped financially nor physically in the Civil Rights struggles, but many of them ridiculed those Negroes who did.

The Civil Rights Bill has helped in many ways in desegregating the restaurants, gas stations' rest rooms and many other places. It will also help in opening a few jobs, but for the majority of these jobs the Negroes do not have the technical training necessary.

There are still thousands of Negroes here who are part of what is called the sub-strata of American society. The Civil Rights Bill will not help them. These black families have grown up generation after generation bordering on illiteracy. But most regrettable, they have lost all hope that America will help them. Today for these Negroes who form the sub-strata of American life, it looks more bleak and hopeless than ever. With the Civil Rights Bill passed, the lines in the battle are not as clearly demarcated as in the past. It is harder to get issues around which people will rally and yet the average Negro family finds that economically if anything it is *recessing* instead of *progressing.* . . .

There were many white gas stations in the Negro community that had segregated rest rooms and Negroes working only in menial positions. The movement caused a re-evaluation. The Gulf Oil Company sold a franchise to a Negro to operate a first class Gulf Station. Negroes rallied to his support so, until he won the "Award" repeatedly for the greatest volume in gallons pumped of any Gulf Station in Albany.

The other large stations such as Shell, Texaco and others were so impressed by what they saw of the Negroes' urgent desire to patronize other Negroes until all of them located in Negro neighborhoods have built large new modern stations and have sold the franchises to Negroes, all of whom are doing very well.

One of the largest employers of Negro women in the city of Albany, Bobs Candy Company, had a vote supervised by the National Labor Relations Board and they voted overwhelmingly for the union. There are also other factories where Negroes are heavily employed where they are working to bring the unions and they will do so!

In my opinion the most important thing that the Movement has done is that it has touched the blighted lives of youngsters where not a ray of hope shone through before. Our Movement has given them hope because for the first time they feel that there is a possibility of changing the order through a belief in themselves and hard work.

I have looked at the black and white workers of SNCC and felt that if there is any such thing as God working through people, I know that he works through them. For I have seen the hope, the faith and belief which they have instilled into other youngsters' lives. I have seen the new vistas of the heart and mind that have been opened; and I have seen the conservatives, black and white, almost go into a state of apoplexy whenever a discussion of SNCC comes up. And for the first time, I can imagine what type of persons the Pharisees must have been and I can imagine what type of persons the Disciples must have been—intense, devoted, earthy, erring, but still moving forwards.

As we looked harder and more objectively at the Negro community and saw the many scars and the signs of the internal wounds that affect us we felt that rehabilitative surgery would have to be performed. We also felt that the Negro community would have to begin practicing an "In-group" type of socialism. Such as the establishment of a "National Association for the Economic Advancement of Negroes," that wealthy Negroes and more "advanced" whites would make heavy contributions to help educate the Negro in proper business methods. We have for so many generations been intentionally kept out of the mainstream of American life until proper managerial methods are very hard for us to come by. The little wealth that Negroes have accomplished prior to this time has been through the white man's paternalism towards a Negro, or by the lone Negro through hard work singularly and painfully being able to accumulate. I say *painfully* because he had to discover the proper method through trial and error and most often does not see fit to pass his skills and "know how" on to other Negroes but jealously and selfishly guards the secrets with the attitude "I caught hell getting mine, now you get yours." No longer do we have the time for trial and error. It does not work in our highly competitive society, especially with communications as highly developed as they presently are. Further there are very few paternalistic feelings left with most whites and it is not white paternalism that we seek anyway.

Many celebrities joined the march to Montgomery and entertained the marchers on Wednesday evening. From left: writer James Baldwin; Mary Travers of the trio Peter, Paul, and Mary.

# John L. Perry

## A Lesson at Selma

*John L. Perry witnessed the great demonstrations of 1965 at Selma, Alabama.*

Two days of light rain on Selma, Alabama, made all it touched seem unreal.

Yellow slickers on state troopers clad in blue, clear plastic sheeting under which huddled SNCC kids and priests and nuns and students from tony private schools and Negro field-hands and grand white ladies from old New England families, greasy rope across a muddy street in front of the Negro church, network TV cameras—all reflected the unreal glare of white headlights and flashing red beacons from half a hundred highway patrol cars.

The light focused on the "compound," two city blocks of Selma's blacktown in which scores of "freedom marchers" from across the nation had come together, in a half-voluntary, half-coerced concentration camp, to beseech and demand Freedom Now in the blackest section of whitest Alabama. Pointing at them from around the compass were leveled rifles and blinding lights of Alabama law.

"What's going on in there?" I had asked one Selma cop the night I arrived, indicating the black-and-white mass praying and singing freedom songs.

"Aw, they still just a-hucklebuckin.' "

"What are you all doing out here in the circle?"

He removed a toothpick from his upper teeth and grinned: "Protectin' 'em."

The unreality reflected in the floodlit mud and rain of that minor town of a minor state was the only unreal thing there.

Nothing was more real than Selma, 1965. No dateline in the

*Source:* John L. Perry, "Farewell, Hell!" *The Center Magazine*, 1 (1968).

world was better known then. For that brief period Selma *was* America—America on trial before the world, and before itself, perhaps more than at any time since 1865. . . .

. . . I stood within the compound, talking with a handful of "freedom marchers." An occasional "thap" of an air-rifle pellet being fired from behind the circle of cops could be heard amid freedom songs and prayers.

As I turned away from the circle, to go back into the church which had been converted into a combination field headquarters-field kitchen-field hospital, my place was taken by a young Negro woman dressed in the chicken-feed-sack cotton print so familiar to those of us who grew up in the rural South.

I do not recall hearing the "thap" that time but did hear the cry as the young woman sank to one knee in the mud, blood pouring between her fingers from her mouth.

We brought her through the rain and mud into the parsonage and managed finally to awaken an aging Negro doctor, who was slumped, exhausted, on a battered sofa in a dark corner of the parlor. He had seen more than his share of the results of white violence that week. It had begun with near-slaughter, when Alabama troopers smashed heads of "freedom marchers" trying to cross the river bridge. There followed a succession of isolated incidents of violence—a Negro shot in the leg, another beaten, and, a few hours before, a white minister slain downtown. The girl in the feed-sack dress was merely the latest injured, and by no means the most seriously.

Like all mouth wounds hers bled profusely, and partially on me as I cradled her head. I was trying to say something comforting, and cannot forget what she said through the red bubbles: "Thass awright. It mought jess as leave be you."

Despite the pain from the air pellet which had drilled a hole the size and shape of a pencil eraser through her lower lip and gone on to knock out a tooth and then unhinge the tender tissue under her tongue, her face was happy and peaceful.

I do not know why she had come in from the Alabama cotton fields or poultry pens or nigger-town home laundries to join that unlikely mixture of "freedom marchers" and their allies who had wound up in the squalor of the Selma compound. I had no idea whether she had in mind brotherhood or desegregation or integration or black power or racial separatism.

But there was no doubt that in her moment of agony she had found something of whatever it was she was seeking and that something had to do with whites and Negroes sharing—in this instance, a common danger. "It mought jess as leave be" a young white man as a young black woman.

When whites issue statements on what is best for Negroes or what Negroes are going to have to accept or what whites are going to have to accept about Negroes, I wonder if they have bothered to consult a young woman in Alabama with a hole in her lip the size and shape of a pencil eraser. . . .

This Greyhound bus carrying the first Freedom Riders into Alabama was set afire by a mob outside the town of Anniston. *(Courtesy, AP/Wide World Photos)*

# Roy Wilkins

## Standing Fast

*Roy Wilkins, a leader of the NAACP and one of the older figures in the civil rights movement, was an unbending champion of longstanding integrationist principles. In the late 1960s he argued with black separatists.*

At the risk of belaboring the obvious, I want to point out that the school cases were a legal victory, a fitting reward for the N.A.A.C.P.'s faith in the basic institutions of the country and for its patient strategy of correcting injustices by taking them to the courts. Within ten years, many impatient folks would find it easy to criticize the N.A.A.C.P. for that very faith. I can still hear their epithets—from "babe in the woods" to "Uncle Tom"—ringing in my ears. No matter what was said later, the real point is that without the N.A.A.C.P. there would have been no fight against lynching, no victory over the white primary, no defeat for restrictive covenants, no triumph over Jim Crow in the military, no liberating action for the schools. The N.A.A.C.P. had been fighting the good fight for a very long time. It cleared the underbrush and opened the way for the civil rights movement in the fifties and sixties. Nat Turner and Mahatma Gandhi may have provided some new models as the years went on, but the N.A.A.C.P. was the grand-daddy of us all. . . .

I was working at the office when word of Dr. King's assassination came from Memphis. A rattlesnake had struck the civil rights movement, slipping into its hole before anyone could grab a shovel and crush it. Those bodyguards I had seen with Dr. King on the road several weeks before had not been able to save him. Dr. King, our Great Exhorter, was gone.

*Source:* Roy Wilkins with Tom Mathews, *Standing Fast: The Autobiography of Roy Wilkins* (New York: The Viking Press, 1982).

That night in Washington, D.C., there were flames and black smudges of smoke only a few blocks away from the White House. The TV news reports the next day caught youngsters hauling their loot to park benches, handling it, picking and choosing whatever caught their eye. There was almost a carnival mood. All that was missing was the calliope. The rioters were not up in arms at the death of Dr. King; his murder had only provided the spark for the riot. It was impossible that his belief in brotherhood and human dignity could lead to such mayhem. The rioters were dragging his dream through the mud.

Even as the carnage was going on, the ABC television station in Manhattan invited me to its studio to talk things over. When I arrived I found Sammy Davis, Jr., on the set. He looked anguished. "I don't see sad faces, people in mourning," he said. "I see laughing and giggling . . . less than forty-eight hours after our leader died: those are not really brothers." . . .

I still believe that the way S.N.C.C. and C.O.R.E. took over the Meredith march was a tragedy for the civil rights movement. Scores of organizations might otherwise have been encouraged to rally around the Civil Rights Bill. Instead, Stokely set off down the road for Jackson, with Dr. King in tow, to draw crowds and reporters. In Greenwood, Mississippi, Stokely got up and yelled, "The only way we gonna stop them white men from whuppin' us is to take over. We been sayin' freedom for six years and we got nothin'. What we gonna start saying now is 'Black Power.' "

Those two words—and what havoc they caused. If Stokely had not joined S.N.C.C. he would have made a wonderful Madison Avenue sloganeer. He had an absolute genius for the provocative phrase. Black power was just a slogan, loaded words, not a real program, but it crystallized resentments that had been building for years, the frustrations of black folks on one hand—and all the animosity of the white backlash on the other. The phrase couldn't have been more destructive if Senator Eastland had contrived it. I imagine he sat there saying to himself, "Now, why didn't I think of that?"

No sooner were the words out than Stokely and everyone else had to scramble to define them. Over the next few weeks and months they were defined, redefined, and defined all over again. No one ever seemed able to agree on just what black power really meant.

The issue was not new. There have been Negro banks and savings-and-loans for nearly seventy-five years. Obviously black people had been thinking of economic power for a long time. For sixty years the N.A.A.C.P. had asserted the right of Negroes to self-defense against the violence of white oppression. During the Parker affair in the thirties and the elections of 1948 and 1960, Negroes had amply shown how aware they were of their own political power. None of these things was new. The younger people were either ignorant of the long record or they chose to ignore it.

Martin Luther King, Jr. at a rally on the steps of the state Capitol in Montgomery, Alabama.

# Martin Luther King, Jr.

## The Dream

*These are two of the best known addresses of Martin Luther King, Jr. Spoken by the symbolic leader of the civil rights movement in its fight against segregation, they make an appropriate summary to this section of the readings. The first selection is the famous address recognized as "I Have a Dream," remembered for King's delivery of it at the 1963 March on Washington. The passages in the second selection are from a sermon he gave at Mason Temple in Memphis, Tennessee, on April 3, 1968. He was in Memphis to support a strike by garbage collectors. Its ending reads like an anticipation of Dr. King's murder, which came shortly afterwards.*

I am happy to join with you today in what will go down in history as the greatest demonstration for freedom in the history of our nation.

Fivescore years ago, a great American, in whose symbolic shadow we stand today, signed the Emancipation Proclamation. This momentous decree came as a great beacon light of hope to millions of Negro slaves who had been seared in the flames of withering injustice. It came as a joyous daybreak to end the long night of their captivity.

But one hundred years later, the Negro still is not free; one hundred years later, the life of the Negro is still sadly crippled by the manacles of segregation and the chains of discrimination; one hundred years later, the Negro lives on a lonely island of poverty in the midst of a vast ocean of material prosperity; one hundred years later, the Negro is still languished in the corners of American society and finds himself in exile in his own land.

So we've come here today to dramatize a shameful condition.

*Source: Negro History Bulletin,* 21 (May 1968).

In a sense we've come to our nation's capital to cash a check. When the architects of our republic wrote the magnificent words of the Constitution and the Declaration of Independence, they were signing a promissory note to which every American was to fall heir. This note was the promise that all men, yes, black men as well as white men, would be guaranteed the unalienable rights of life, liberty and the pursuit of happiness.

It is obvious today that America has defaulted on this promissory note in so far as her citizens of color are concerned. Instead of honoring this sacred obligation, America has given the Negro people a bad check; a check which has come back marked "insufficient funds." We refuse to believe that there are insufficient funds in the great vaults of opportunity of this nation. And so we've come to cash this check, a check that will give us upon demand the riches of freedom and the security of justice.

We have also come to this hallowed spot to remind America of the fierce urgency of now. This is no time to engage in the luxury of cooling off or to take the tranquilizing drug of gradualism. Now is the time to make real the promises of democracy; now is the time to rise from the dark and desolate valley of segregation to the sunlit path of racial justice; now is the time to lift our nation from the quicksands of racial injustice to the solid rock of brotherhood; now is the time to make justice a reality for all God's children. It would be fatal for the nation to overlook the urgency of the moment. This sweltering summer of the Negro's legitimate discontent will not pass until there is an invigorating autumn of freedom and equality.

Nineteen sixty-three is not an end, but a beginning. And those who hope that the Negro needed to blow off steam and will now be content, will have a rude awakening if the nation returns to business as usual.

There will be neither rest nor tranquility in America until the Negro is granted his citizenship rights. The whirlwinds of revolt will continue to shake the foundations of our nation until the bright day of justice emerges.

But there is something that I must say to my people who stand on the warm threshold which leads into the palace of justice. In the process of gaining our rightful place we must not be guilty of wrongful deeds.

Let us not seek to satisfy our thirst for freedom by drinking from the cup of bitterness and hatred. We must forever conduct our struggle on the high plane of dignity and discipline. We must not allow our creative protest to degenerate into physical violence.

Again and again we must rise to the majestic heights of meeting physical force with soul force.

The marvelous new militancy which has engulfed the Negro community must not lead us to a distrust of all white people, for many of our white brothers, as evidenced by their presence here today, have come to realize that their destiny is tied up with our destiny and they have come to realize that their freedom is inextricably bound to our freedom. This offense we share mounted to storm the battlements of injustice must be carried forth by a bi-racial army. We cannot walk alone.

And as we walk, we must make the pledge that we shall always march ahead. We cannot turn back. There are those who are asking the devotees of civil rights, "When will you be satisfied?" We can never be satisfied as long as the Negro is the victim of the unspeakable horrors of police brutality.

We can never be satisfied as long as our bodies, heavy with fatigue of travel, cannot gain lodging in the motels of the highways and the hotels of the cities. We cannot be satisfied as long as the Negro's basic mobility is from a smaller ghetto to a larger one.

We can never be satisfied as long as our children are stripped of their selfhood and robbed of their dignity by signs stating "for whites only." We cannot be satisfied as long as a Negro in Mississippi cannot vote and a Negro in New York believes he has nothing for which to vote. No, we are not satisfied, and we will not be satisfied until justice rolls down like waters and righteousness like a mighty stream.

I am not unmindful that some of you have come here out of excessive trials and tribulation. Some of you have come fresh from narrow jail cells. Some of you have come from areas where your quest for freedom left you battered by the storms of persecution and staggered by the winds of police brutality. You have been the veterans of creative suffering. Continue to work with the faith that unearned suffering is redemptive.

Go back to Mississippi; go back to Alabama; go back to South Carolina; go back to Georgia; go back to Louisiana; go back to the slums and ghettos of the northern cities, knowing that somehow this situation can and will be changed. Let us not wallow in the valley of despair.

So I say to you, my friends, that even though we must face the difficulties of today and tomorrow, I still have a dream. It is a dream deeply rooted in the American dream that one day this nation will rise up and live out the true meaning of its creed—we hold these truths to be self-evident, that all men are created equal.

I have a dream that one day on the red hills of Georgia, sons of former slaves and sons of former slave-owners will be able to sit down together at the table of brotherhood.

I have a dream that one day, even the state of Mississippi, a state sweltering with the heat of injustice, sweltering with the heat of oppression, will be transformed into an oasis of freedom and justice.

I have a dream my four little children will one day live in a nation where they will not be judged by the color of their skin but by the content of their character. I have a dream today!

I have a dream that one day, down in Alabama, with its vicious racists, with its governor having his lips dripping with the words of interposition and nullification, that one day, right there in Alabama, little black boys and black girls will be able to join hands with little white boys and white girls as sisters and brothers. I have a dream today!

I have a dream that one day every valley shall be exalted, every hill and mountain shall be made low, the rough places shall be made plain, and the crooked places shall be made straight and the glory of the Lord will be revealed and all flesh shall see it together.

This is our hope. This is the faith that I go back to the South with.

With this faith we will be able to bear out of the mountain of despair a stone of hope. With this faith we will be able to transform the jangling discords of our nation into a beautiful symphony of brotherhood.

With this faith we will be able to work together, to pray together, to struggle together, to go to jail together, to stand up for freedom together, knowing that we will be free one day. This will be the day when all of God's children will be able to sing with new meaning—"my country 'tis of thee; sweet land of liberty; of thee I sing; land where my fathers died, land of the pilgrim's pride; from every mountain side, let freedom ring"—and if America is to be a great nation, this must become true.

So let freedom ring from the prodigious hilltops of New Hampshire.

Let freedom ring from the mighty mountains of New York.

Let freedom ring from the heightening Alleghenies of Pennsylvania.

Let freedom ring from the snow-capped Rockies of Colorado.

Let freedom ring from the curvaceous slopes of California.

But not only that.

Let freedom ring from Stone Mountain of Georgia.

Let freedom ring from Lookout Mountain of Tennessee.

Let freedom ring from every hill and molehill of Mississippi, from every mountainside, let freedom ring.

And when we allow freedom to ring, when we let it ring from every village and hamlet, from every state and city, we will be able to speed up that day when all of God's children—black men and white men, Jews and Gentiles, Catholics and Protestants—will be able to join hands and to sing in the words of the old Negro spiritual, "Free at last, free at last; thank God Almighty, we are free at last."

*    *    *

I'm delighted to see each of you here tonight in spite of a storm warning. You reveal that you are determined to go on anyhow. Something is happening in Memphis, something is happening in our world.

As you know, if I were standing at the beginning of time, with the possibility of general and panoramic view of the whole human history up to now, and the Almighty said to me, "Martin Luther King, which age would you like to live in?"—I would take my mental flight by Egypt through, or rather across the Red Sea, through the wilderness on toward the promised land. And in spite of its magnificence, I wouldn't stop there. I would move on by Greece, and take my mind to Mount Olympus. And I would see Plato, Aristotle, Socrates, Euripides and Aristophanes assembled around the Parthenon as they discussed the great and eternal issues of reality.

But I wouldn't stop there. I would go on, even to the great heyday of the Roman Empire. And I would see developments around there, through various emperors and leaders. But I wouldn't stop there. I would even come up to the day of the Renaissance, and get a quick picture of all that the Renaissance did for the cultural and esthetic life of man. But I wouldn't stop there. I would even go by the way that the man for whom I'm named had his habitat. And I would watch Martin Luther as he tacked his ninety-five theses on the door at the church in Wittenberg.

But I wouldn't stop there. I would come on up even to 1863, and watch a vacillating president by the name of Abraham Lincoln finally come to the conclusion that he had to sign the Emancipa-

*Source: Martin Luther King, Jr.: A Documentary, Montgomery to Memphis,* edited by Flip Schulke (New York and London: Norton, 1976).

tion Proclamation. But I wouldn't stop there. I would even come up to the early thirties, and see a man grappling with the problems of the bankruptcy of his nation. And come with an eloquent cry that we have nothing to fear but fear itself.

But I wouldn't stop there. Strangely enough, I would turn to the Almighty, and say, "If you allow me to live just a few years in the second half of the twentieth century, I will be happy." Now that's a strange statement to make, because the world is all messed up. The nation is sick. Trouble is in the land. Confusion all around. That's a strange statement. But I know, somehow, that only when it is dark enough, can you see the stars. And I see God working in this period of the twentieth century in a way that men, in some strange way, are responding—something is happening in our world. The masses of people are rising up. And wherever they are assembled today, whether they are in Johannesburg, South Africa; Nairobi, Kenya; Accra, Ghana; New York City; Atlanta, Georgia; Jackson, Mississippi; or Memphis, Tennessee—the cry is always the same—"We want to be free."

And another reason that I'm happy to live in this period is that we have been forced to a point where we're going to have to grapple with the problems that men have been trying to grapple with through history, but the demands didn't force them to do it. Survival demands that we grapple with them. Men, for years now, have been talking about war and peace. But now, no longer can they just talk about it. It is no longer a choice between violence and nonviolence in this world; it's nonviolence or nonexistence.

That is where we are today. And also in the human rights revolution, if something isn't done, and in a hurry, to bring the colored peoples of the world out of their long years of poverty, their long years of hurt and neglect, the whole world is doomed. Now, I'm just happy that God has allowed me to live in this period, to see what is unfolding. And I'm happy that he's allowed me to be in Memphis....

Always anchor our external direct action with the power of economic withdrawal. Now, we are poor people, individually, we are poor when you compare us with white society in America. We are poor. Never stop and forget that collectively, that means all of us together, collectively we are richer than all the nations in the world, with the exception of nine. Did you ever think about that? After you leave the United States, Soviet Russia, Great Britain, West Germany, France, and I could name the others, the Negro collectively is richer than most nations of the world. We have an annual income of more than thirty billion dollars a year, which is more than all of the exports of the United States, and more than the national budget of Canada. Did you know that? That's power right there, if we know how to pool it.

We don't have to argue with anybody. We don't have to curse and go around acting bad with our words. We don't need any bricks and bottles, we don't need any Molotov cocktails, we just need to go around to these stores, and to these massive industries in our country, and say, "God sent us by here, to say to you that you're not treating his children right. And we've come by here to ask you to make the first item on your agenda—fair treatment, where God's children are concerned. Now, if you are not prepared to do that, we do have an agenda that we must follow. And our agenda calls for withdrawing economic support from you." . . .

Well, I don't know what will happen now. We've got some difficult days ahead. But it doesn't matter with me now. Because I've been to the mountaintop. And I don't mind. Like anybody, I would like to live a long life. Longevity has its place. But I'm not concerned about that now. I just want to do God's will. And He's allowed me to go up to the mountain. And I've looked over. And I've seen the promised land. I may not get there with you. But I want you to know tonight, that we, as a people will get to the promised land. And I'm happy, tonight. I'm not worried about anything. I'm not fearing any man. Mine eyes have seen the glory of the coming of the Lord.

# Part 3

# NONVIOLENCE

*The term can be mistaken to imply a mere absence, a nonactivity. It refers, to the contrary, to an active resistance to an unjust law or custom. In an act of defiance—sitting in, for example, at a segregated lunch counter—practitioners of nonviolence resist the outward forces of society: its ordinances and customs, its police, the threats and insults of its bigots. Simultaneously, the demonstrators resist forces within themselves: the urge to flee, and the urge to react with violence to the violent police officer or mob. Nonviolence, then, is an effort to overcome or at least to hold at bay primitive impulses that exist in society and in the individual.*

*The civil rights practitioners of nonviolence, the most prominent of whom was Martin Luther King, Jr., took as a model Mahatma Gandhi, the leader of the campaign that had forced the British to relinquish their control of India. Gandhi's concept of nonviolence, drawing on diverse elements of the religions and the spirituality of India, embraced a complex perception of truth, soul, and life that were not readily transferable from Indian to American culture. It was more Gandhi's example than the detail of his teaching that was useful to the activists in Montgomery and later campaigns against white supremacy. Much of their vocabulary was Christian. They also stressed the virtue of self-control: a practice session might enact scenes of racial insult, so that the attendants could learn to internalize composure in the face of abuse. In all this, nonviolence requires its adherents in some sense to remake themselves, to make its demands a condition of character. That is so whether nonviolence is employed only as a tactic or embraced as a principle of living.*

*A closely related concept is that of civil disobedience. That could mean disobedience to a law, or simply disobedience to the commands of police or other local officials (who might in fact be breaking the law themselves), followed by acceptance of arrest. Rosa Parks committed such an act when on that December Montgomery day she stayed in her bus seat against an order to move; so do demonstrators who block an entrance to a public building. Not all nonviolence involves civil disobedience; peaceful defiance of a mob qualifies as much as does peaceful defiance of a statute.*

*The most strongly symbolic employment of nonviolence is against an instance of social violence. The practice therefore passed quite easily from the civil rights movement to some opponents of the Vietnam war. In recent years protesters against nuclear weapons, nuclear power itself, or abortion clinics have used nonviolent action in resistance to an activity that, by their definition, is violent.*

*Not all of the selections in this section specifically discuss the idea of nonviolence. We include a range of materials on arrests and jailing, for the conduct of civil rights activists who made themselves subject to arrest and then endured imprisonment was an enactment, not always conscious or philosophical, of the practice of nonviolence.*

Particularly in the South, racial discrimination was evident in the segregation of schools, neighborhoods, bathroom facilities, and even drinking fountains.

# Wilma Dykeman and James Stokely

## Greensboro and Beyond

*These passages, which define the practice of nonviolence as
it grew out of the Greensboro sit-ins of early 1960, make it
clear that nonviolence was radical not only in its attack on
segregation but in its demands on the practitioner and its
defiance of normal ways of conduct.*

" 'There is one thing stronger than all the armies in the world
and that is an idea whose time has come.' An idea whose time has
come is sweeping the South today. It is the lunch counter protests.
From Greensboro to Chattanooga, to Florida, a new young Negro
leadership is asserting itself.

"It will do the South no good to bury its head in the sand and
hope the trouble will go away. It will do no good to blame the newspapers for telling what happens. It will do no good to assert that
'local custom' sufficient for fifty years ago or even twenty-five years
ago must prevail forever. It may not suffice even to fill up the jails.

"The idea's moral force—that colored men no longer will tol-
erate being served at nine counters and rejected at the tenth—cannot be denied . . ."

So spoke the influential and moderate Greensboro *Daily News*
in the North Carolina city where the initial impetus for the present
Negro student movement in the South began February 1. . . .

At 4:30 Monday afternoon, February 1, four freshmen attend-
ing the Negro Agricultural and Technical College at Greensboro,
North Carolina, took seats at the lunch counter at the downtown
Woolworth store. Ezell Blair and David Richmond had lived in
Greensboro all their lives and experienced the lunch counter segre-
gation "all along, with intentions of doing something about it
eventually." Franklin [McCain] was from Washington, D.C., and
Joseph McNeil from Wilmington, N.C. Before they sat down to eat,

*Source:* Wilma Dykeman and James Stokely, "Sit Down Chillun, Sit Down!" *The
Progressive*, 24 (June 1960). Reprinted by permission.

the students had purchased one or two small articles at a nearby counter. Later, Blair gave this account of his conversation with the waitress:

BLAIR: "I'd like a cup of coffee, please."

WAITRESS: "I'm sorry. We don't serve colored here."

BLAIR: "I beg to disagree with you. You just finished serving me at a counter only two feet from here."

WAITRESS: "Negroes eat at the other end."

BLAIR: "What do you mean? This is a public place, isn't it? If it isn't, then why don't you sell membership cards? If you do that, then I'll understand that this is a private concern."

WAITRESS: "Well, you won't get any service here!"

Blair said the waitress left then and went to the other end of the counter. A Negro girl, a helper on the counter, confronted the four students: "You are stupid, ignorant! You're dumb! That's why we can't get anywhere today. You know you are supposed to eat at the other end."

The manager of the lunch counter did not talk with them then, and neither did the police who came and watched them until they left at 5:30, when the store closed.

Before two and a half months had passed, every Southern state was caught up in a wave of passive resistance to segregation, a wave of such scope and force, extending from Charleston to Houston, from Louisville to Miami, embracing imprisonment and intimidation without faltering, that many observers have come to believe it is a movement of impressive passive persistence, as well. . . .

Approximately 1,500 arrests, most of them Negro students, have been made since that February day. One example is the town of Orangeburg, South Carolina. On March 15, 388 students were arrested there during a peaceful march from two Negro colleges—one state-supported, the other a Methodist institution—to the downtown area, about eight blocks away, where they intended to sing *America* and offer a public prayer for equal rights. About two blocks from the campuses they were met by the police chief and the fire department. The heaviest ammunition the Negroes were carrying were their Bibles and hymn books. The firemen held their hoses ready to blast forth a stream of water.

"The police chief asked who the leader was," one of the Negro boys related, "and twelve hundred students shouted, 'I am the leader.'

" 'Well,' the police chief said, 'I am going to arrest the leader. Step forward,' and twelve hundred students stepped forward.

"One or two of those in front were arrested then and the

police chief said, 'Get those niggers.' The fire hoses were turned on. Many of the boys and girls were knocked down, the force of the water was so strong. Some of their dresses and shirts were torn. Hats and coats were ruined. One fellow's ear began to bleed, but he stood there and took it."

Then the students began to sing *The Battle Hymn of the Republic* and still moved forward. Tear gas was thrown into their midst. Still they came. Then the arrests began, so many that only a parking lot converted into a temporary stockade could hold all the prisoners. It was ten o'clock that night before the Negro community could raise sufficient bail to get the students back to their campuses, where at least forty were treated for injuries and exposure in the near-freezing drizzle of rain.

"We're being tried in groups of fifty," one of them reported a few weeks later, "and one of the state lawyers told us, 'We'll give you boys a fair trial before we find you guilty.' " . . .

Orangeburg was the site of the most massive arrests, but numerous other Southern cities have followed the same reaction: Nashville, with some 150 arrests in lunch counter and picketing conflicts where Negroes were spat upon, hit, and had cigarette butts stuffed down the backs of their shirt collars; Atlanta, eighty arrests; some forty-five in Tallahassee; about sixty-five in Memphis; more than seventy in Marshall, Texas. But there is no evidence that arrests have discouraged any prospective demonstrators, and there is much evidence that they have encouraged a strong unity among Negroes. After arrests of students in Portsmouth, Virginia, a minister said that the adult Negroes had paid little heed to sit-downs until some of the young people were arrested by the police; then adults rallied behind them in solid support.

So the demonstrations have spread and varied according to localities, but they are indicating, in the words of the Southern Regional Council, that "the South is in a time of change, the terms of which cannot be dictated by white Southerners. To react to these events with the old conditioned reflexes—indignation, reprisal, new laws, and prosecutions—is absurd. The deeper meaning of the 'sit-in' demonstrations is to show that segregation cannot be maintained in the South short of continuous coercion and the intolerable social order which would result." . . .

In Virginia a more recent lyric has combined both the old qualities of the spiritual and the new message of non-violence. Its first verse:

> "Sit down Chillun—sit down!
> In every Jim Crow state and town.

*Bear your cross and wear your crown,*
*Sit down Chillun, sit down!"* ...

The method of non-violence is difficult and calls for a rugged discipline. (It will be ironic indeed if the region which has the highest rate and reputation for violence—due partly to the frustrations and aggressions of an unequally treated minority—should develop a significant non-violent approach to its major problem.) There are many friends, both black and white, who wonder if the complex understanding and stern self-control required by non-violence can be maintained by the students who have thus far met the challenge stoutly.

College students in Nashville drew up a code of conduct to govern their sit-ins:

*"Don't strike back or curse if abused.*
*Don't laugh out.*
*Don't hold conversations with floor workers.*
*Don't block entrances to the stores and aisles.*
*Show yourself courteous and friendly at all times.*
*Sit straight and always face the counter.*
*Remember love and non-violence.*
*May God bless each of you."*

Even more impressive than this code has been the system of workshops conducted for some of the students who plan sit-in demonstrations. In a strange but effective training, young Negro men and women unlearn all the manners customary in civilized society. They budge and shove, humiliate and intimidate each other, testing the strength of their endurance for future ordeals. They call each other "coon" and "nigger" with a harshness and frequency that belies how deeply such terms have wounded them in the past. They spit in each other's face.

"I couldn't stand it for a white man to strike me," one student confesses, and the workshop leader advises him to stay home and participate in the cause in some other way.

"If you can't take it," an Alabama student says, "if you're so weak you've got to fight, find another movement. This is not for you."

The theme of several of these workshops has been "the redemptive power of unmerited suffering." Against the dignity and determination of people who can confront suffering without flinching, the paucity of imagination and courage in the methods of some of their white opposition stands stripped and barren.

# James Farmer

## Origins and Development of CORE

*James Farmer was instrumental in the formation in 1942 of the Congress of Racial Equality (CORE), an offshoot of the antiwar Fellowship of Reconciliation (FOR). Under Farmer's directorship, CORE would send freedom riders south in the early 1960s testing segregation in southern interstate bus facilities.*

CORE came into being in 1942. Like most war babies, I suppose, it was born into a time of violence, but out of a hope for peace. Its founders were young men and women deeply concerned with social justice, most of whom were also pacifists. To the profound and terrible violence of the war, we and many others of similar convictions had experienced correspondingly deep and troubled reactions. Total war was being waged in the name of freedom and democracy. We were all mobilized to fight for the American Way of Life. Yet in the glare of the conflagration overseas we could see clearly how much unfreedom and inequality went into that way of life. Many victims of the Depression were still hungry and terrified; labor all over the country was bound to long hours and low wages. And always there was the Negro, a full-fledged soldier on the battlefields of France, but at home still the son of Ham, a servant of servants unto his brethren.

We wanted desperately to render him equal and free. In our search for a method, we were drawn inevitably to Gandhi. I had presented a long memorandum, "Provisional Plans for Brotherhood Mobilization," to the pacifist Fellowship of Reconciliation (FOR), for which I was then working as race relations secretary. It proposed the establishment of an interracial organization which would apply Gandhian techniques of non-violent direct action to attack segregation in this country: "... not to make housing in

*Source:* James Farmer, *Freedom—When?* with an introduction by Jacob Cohen (New York: Random House, 1965). Reprinted by permission.

ghettos more tolerable, but to destroy residential segregation; not to make racial discrimination more bearable, but to wipe it out; ... effectively to repudiate every form of racism ... [and to] forge the instrumentalities through which that nation-wide repudiation can be effected!" The small interracial group of Chicago students who were to form the nucleus of CORE had independently evolved a similar idea. While I was drafting a memo, they had already begun formulating action projects. So that when I was authorized by the FOR to set up a pilot project in Chicago, we had only to stretch out our hands to one another, and a movement was created.

There was something extremely audacious in our attempt to apply Gandhi's theories to the American race problem. The Hindu mind, radically different from the American, is much more inclined to perceive battles as spiritual. The Hindu religion conditions its adherents both to the self-discipline and to the setting-the-self-at-naught so necessary to the success of direct action. Furthermore, although the Indians had little political power, they were a vast numerical majority in their country and were working toward the single goal of independence from England, a goal which, however difficult to achieve, was quite simple to define and recognize and which could, indeed, be consummated by a stroke of the pen. Above all, their movement had as its soul the kind of divinely inspired leader who comes perhaps once in a millennium. Gandhi was a man who possessed strategic brilliance and great political shrewdness combined with the charisma of a saint.

Yet it is also true that an American classic, Thoreau's *Civil Disobedience*, exercised a great influence on Gandhi. The belief that each man's actions should have a direct bearing upon his own destiny is quite in accord with the American tradition. And Americans generally prefer to act rather than to withdraw; for that reason, Gandhian militance was much more likely to appeal to Americans than was the passive resistance generally being advocated by our native pacifists. Gandhi's disciple Krishnalal Shridharani, whose *War Without Violence* became our rule book and Bible, remarked that "most American pacifists were less interested than militant liberals in my work. This was as it should have been, as Gandhi's *satyagraha* has more in common with war than with pacifism."

In point of fact, most of us were American pacifists, accustomed to understanding non-violence largely in Tolstoyan terms of non-resistance: the Christian injunction to love thine enemy and turn the other cheek; and non-co-operation: the peaceful refusal to obey unjust laws. But we were also militant pacifists, anxious to change the world, or at least our corner of it. Gandhi, whose assumptions about the power of love and righteousness resembled those of Jesus in the Sermon on the Mount, had nevertheless superimposed upon them a specific and viable program of action. This was what appealed to us, and we adopted it, at least in the beginning, to the letter. . . .

Gandhi coined the word *satyagraha* to describe his movement, partly to shake off the misleading connotations of "passive resistance," and partly to give his All-India movement an all-Indian name. Ironically, there is no English phrase which can adequately translate *satyagraha*. It means something like "soul force" or "the firmness engendered by truth, or love." Westernized Indians have offered the word *Kristograha* to express an equivalent meaning in Christian terms. However it is translated, several different English expressions would be required to cover all its implications. It is *satyagraha* as "the truth which cannot be denied" that stands behind Gandhi's insistence on negotiation and public education. We too, in the early years of CORE, believed that truth alone, the transparent justice of our demands, would convert the segregationists, once they agreed to listen. That was why *satyagraha* as "the firmness engendered by love" was so essential to our discipline. Our own unshakable good will, which left no room in us for violence and helped us endure the violence of others, was the key with which we intended to unlock their hearts.

We were very young and idealistic. We had not yet discovered that Southern sheriffs could respond to non-violent protest with police dogs and cattle prods. We revered Gandhi for his saintliness, but we remembered less vividly that at various times his Congress Party had resorted to hunger strikes, jail-ins, a boycott of foreign cloth, a nation-wide general strike, and even the illegal distillation of salt from the sea in order to circumvent and render unenforceable a compulsory salt tax. That kind of heavy artillery lay beyond the range of our expectations. What could we know about mass desperation, working as we did in small groups, in Northern cities, desegregating one restaurant or one movie house at a time?

The infinite number of tactics that can be improvised in non-violent warfare had not yet excited our attention. We were attracted by other possibilities, somewhat more utopian in nature. Gandhi's program to revitalize rural handicraft in order to make Indian villages economically self-sufficient suggested to us an analogous program for America. Rural Negroes carve quite amazing objects out of gourds and wood, and the women sew and knit beautifully. These skills, which have been passed down from generation to generation, are among the few possessions of some of the poorest people in the country. Why not turn them to profit? Why not, in fact, form an economic base for our movement by establishing a network of co-operatives—housing co-operatives, producers' and farmers' co-operatives—extending throughout the country, North and South? So we asked ourselves, ready to remake the country before we had really begun to find out what it was made of.

Actually, in the very beginning, we did set up a co-operative house, although in this case economy was only a secondary motive. Our first project as a group, plunging eagerly into action before we had formulated a proper organization or even decided upon a name for ourselves, was to test discrimination in housing. Chicago at that time had a blanket of restrictive covenants which kept the ever-growing Negro population out of 80 per cent of the city. In defiance of the covenant we established a men's interracial co-operative house in a residential area restricted to whites. When the real estate company discovered that Negroes were living in the house, they began legal proceedings to get us evicted. Evidently not daring to test the legality of the covenant, they claimed instead that the neighbors objected to our presence. We went to call on the neighbors. They were not enthusiastic about having Negroes in the building, but they had no complaints about our behavior and they saw the justice of our position. They refused to testify for the prosecution. We won by their default a victory for decency, and the co-operative house flourished for many years. For all I know, it is there still. . . .

The sit-ins taught us much about the nature of the revolution. The mass movement of which we had hardly dared to dream in our days of youthful idealism was now becoming a reality. If CORE was to continue in a position of significance and authority, we would have to learn to embrace these masses of willing revolutionaries. No longer could we indulge in the luxury of the perfectly designed, perfectly executed action project, in which each individual had a voice in every step of the planning and all the demonstrators were steeped in the philosophy and tactics and discipline of non-violence. Nor would the local chapters be able to retain quite the same autonomy. With the movement achieving national dimensions, CORE too would have to operate on a national scale, formulating policies and organizing projects far beyond the scope of individual chapters, making on-the-spot decisions that would allow no time for referendums. The challenging task confronting

CORE and all the other civil rights organizations was that of giving a certain amount of direction to the movement and imposing upon it the control of non-violence, without inhibiting the spontaneity or self-expression of thousands of newly aroused Negroes. . . .

What happened to the movement and to CORE after Montgomery was a kind of wedding of two forces, both bred by the war: the means-oriented idealists of pacifistic turn of mind, for whom non-violence was a total philosophy, a way of life—we had founded CORE; and the ends-oriented militants, the New Jacobins, disillusioned with America's rhetoric of equality, who saw in direct action a useful weapon and viewed non-violence only as a tactic.

Without such a fusion, no revolutionary mass movement could have emerged. Without the Young Turks the movement could never have grown to mass proportions, and without the idealists it could not have developed revolutionary dimensions. The anger of one without the disciplined idealism of the other could have produced only nihilism. Without the indigenous anger of the Negro masses, the idealists for all their zeal would have remained largely irrelevant and would have gone on talking to themselves and whispering through an occasional keyhole to another human heart.

As in any working marriage, each party speaks much truth to the other. The idealists warn that the ends do not justify the means, and the militants assert with equal validity that means are worthless which do not achieve substantial reform. Each tempers the other, and out of the creative tension between the two has come a third position which I believe more accurately reflects the movement. Today, non-violence is neither a mere tactic which may be dropped on any occasion nor an inviolable spiritual commitment. It is somewhere between the two—not a philosophy, not a tactic, but a strategy involving both philosophical and tactical elements, in a massive and widening direct-action campaign to redeem the American promise of full freedom for the Negro.

# Statement of Purpose at the Origins of the Student Nonviolent Coordinating Committee, 1960

*At a conference in mid-April 1960 at Shaw University initiated by Ella Baker, then an official of the Southern Christian Leadership Conference (SCLC), and attended by students involved in sit-ins, plans shaped up for the formation of what was to become the Student Nonviolent Coordinating Committee. The adoption of this statement came at the insistence of James Lawson, one of the leaders of the Nashville representatives to the conference and a former theology student, who was determined to have SNCC stress the religious foundation of nonviolence.*

We affirm the philosophical or religious ideal of nonviolence as the foundation of our purpose, the presupposition of our faith, and the manner of our action. Nonviolence as it grows from Judaic-Christian tradition seeks a social order of justice permeated by love. Integration of human endeavor represents the crucial first step toward such a society.

Through nonviolence, courage displaces fear; love transforms hate. Acceptance dissipates prejudice; hope ends despair. Peace dominates war; faith reconciles doubt. Mutual regard cancels enmity. Justice for all overthrows injustice. The redemptive community supercedes systems of gross social immorality.

Love is the central motif of nonviolence. Love is the force by which God binds man to Himself and man to man. Such love goes to the extreme; it remains loving and forgiving even in the midst of hostility. It matches the capacity of evil to inflict suffering with an even more enduring capacity to absorb evil, all the while persisting in love.

By appealing to conscience and standing on the moral nature of human existence, nonviolence nurtures the atmosphere in which reconciliation and justice become actual possibilities.

*Source:* Clayborne Carson, *In Struggle: SNCC and the Black Awakening of the 1960s* (Cambridge, Massachusetts: Harvard University Press, 1981).

# Howell Raines

## Freedom Riders

*These interviews, conducted by Howell Raines, indicate the discipline that the freedom riders had to practice in the face of racist attacks during their bus trips to the South in the early 1960s.*

### Interview with James Farmer

JF: I was impressed by the fact that most of the activity thus far had been of local people working on their local problems—Greensborans sitting-in in Greensboro and Atlantans sitting-in in Atlanta—and the pressure of the opposition against having outsiders come was very, very great. If any outsider came in . . . , "Get that outside agitator." . . . I thought that this was going to limit the growth of the Movement. . . . We somehow had to cut across state lines and establish the position that we were entitled to act any place in the country, no matter where we hung our hat and called home, because it was our country.

We also felt that one of the weaknesses of the student sit-in movement of the South had been that as soon as arrested, the kids bailed out. . . . This was not quite Gandhian and not the best tactic. A better tactic would be to remain in jail and to make the maintenance of segregation so expensive for the state and the city that they would hopefully come to the conclusion that they could no longer afford it. Fill up the jails, as Gandhi did in India, fill them to bursting if we had to. In other words, stay in without bail.

So those were the two things: cutting across state lines, putting the movement on wheels, so to speak, and remaining in jail, not only for its publicity value but for the financial pressure it would put upon the segregators. We decided that a good approach

*Source:* "Freedom Riders" by Howell Raines. Reprinted with permission of G. P. Putnam's Sons from *My Soul Is Rested: Movement Days in the Deep South Remembered,* by Howell Raines. Copyright © 1977 by Howell Raines.

here would be to move away from restaurant lunch counters. That had been the Southern student sit-in movement, and anything we would do on that would be anticlimactic now. We would have to move into another area and so we decided to move into the transportation, interstate transportation. . . .

So we, following the Gandhian technique, wrote to Washington. We wrote to the Justice Department, to the FBI, and to the President, and wrote to Greyhound Bus Company and Trailways Bus Company and told them that on May first or May fourth— whatever the date was, I forget now—we were going to have a Freedom Ride. Blacks and whites were going to leave Washington, D.C., on Greyhound and Trailways, deliberately violating the segregated seating requirements and at each rest stop would violate the segregated use of facilities. And we would be nonviolent, absolutely nonviolent, throughout the campaign, and we would accept the consequences of our actions. This was a deliberate act of civil disobedience. . . .

*Did Justice try to head you off?*

JF: No, we got no reply. We got no reply from Justice. Bobby Kennedy, no reply. We got no reply from the FBI. We got no reply from the White House, from President Kennedy. We got no reply from Greyhound or Trailways. *We got no replies.* [Laughs]

*He recruited an interracial group of thirteen and brought them to Washington for a week's training.*

JF: We had some of the group of thirteen sit at a simulated counter asking for coffee. Somebody else refused them service, and then we'd have others come in as white hoodlums to beat 'em up and knock them off the counter and club 'em around and kick 'em in the ribs and stomp 'em, and they were quite realistic, I must say. I thought they bent over backwards to be realistic. I was aching all over. [Laughs] And then we'd go into a discussion as to how the roles were played, whether there was something that the Freedom Riders did that they shouldn't have done, said that they shouldn't have said, something that they didn't say or do that they should have, and so on. Then we'd reverse roles and play it over and over again and have lengthy discussions of it.

I felt, by the way, that by the time that group left Washington, they were prepared for anything, even death, and this was a possibility, and we knew it, when we got to the Deep South.

Through Virginia we had no problem. In fact they had heard we were coming, Greyhound and Trailways, and they had taken down the For Colored and For Whites signs, and we rode right through. Yep. The same was true in North Carolina. Signs had come down just the previous day, blacks told us. And so the letters in advance did something.

In South Carolina it was a different story.... John Lewis started into a white waiting room in some town in South Carolina ... and there were several young white hoodlums, leather jackets, ducktail haircuts, standing there smoking, and they blocked the door and said, "Nigger, you can't come in here." He said, "I have every right to enter this waiting room according to the Supreme Court of the United States in the Boynton case."

They said, "Shit on that." He tried to walk past, and they clubbed him, beat him, and knocked him down. One of the white Freedom Riders ... Albert Bigelow, who had been a Navy captain during World War II, big, tall, strapping fellow, very impressive, from Connecticut—then stepped right between the hoodlums and John Lewis. Lewis had been absorbing more of the punishment. They then clubbed Bigelow and finally knocked him down, and that took some knocking because he was a pretty strapping fellow, and he didn't hit back at all. [They] knocked him down, and at this point police arrived and intervened. They didn't make any arrests. Intervened....

## Interview with Hank Thomas

HT: The Freedom Ride didn't really get rough until we got down in the Deep South. Needless to say, Anniston, Alabama, I'm never gonna forget that, when I was on the bus that they threw some kind of incendiary device on....

I got real scared then. You know, I was thinking—I'm looking out the window there, and people are out there yelling and screaming. They just about broke every window out of the bus.... I really thought that that was going to be the end of me.

*How did the bus get stopped?*

HT: They shot the tires out, and the bus driver was forced to stop.... He got off, and man, he took off like a rabbit, and might well have. I couldn't very well blame him there. And we were trapped on the bus. They tried to board. Well, we did have two FBI men aboard the bus. All they were there to do were to observe and gather facts, but the crowd apparently recognized them as FBI men, and they did not try to hurt them.

It wasn't until the thing was shot on the bus and the bus caught afire that everything got out of control, and . . . when the bus was burning, I figured . . . [pauses] . . . panic did get ahold of me. Needless to say, I couldn't survive that burning bus. There was a possibility I could have survived the mob, but I was just so afraid of the mob that I was gonna stay on that bus. I mean, I just got that much afraid. And when we got off the bus . . . first they closed the doors and wouldn't let us off. But then I'm pretty sure they realized, that somebody said, "Hey, the bus is gonna explode," because it had just gassed up, and so they started scattering then, and I guess that's the way we got off the bus. Otherwise, we probably all would have been succumbed by the smoke, and not being able to get off, probably would have been burned alive or burned on there anyway. That's the only time I was really, really afraid. I got whacked over the head with a rock or I think some kind of a stick as I was coming off the bus.

*What happened in Anniston after the bus was attacked?*

HT: We were taken to the hospital. The bus started exploding, and a lot of people were cut by flying glass. We were taken to the hospital, most of us, for smoke inhalation.

*By whom?*

HT: I don't remember. I think I was half out of it, half dazed, as a result of the smoke, and, gosh, I can still smell that stuff down in me now. You got to the point where you started having the dry heaves. Took us to the hospital, and it was incredible. The people at the hospital would not do anything for us. They would not. And I was saying, "You're *doctors*, you're medical personnel." They wouldn't. Governor Patterson got on statewide radio and said, "Any rioters in this state will not receive police protection." And then the crowd started forming outside the hospital, and the hospital told us to leave. And we said, "No, we're not going out there," and there we were. A caravan from Birmingham, about a fifteen-car caravan led by the Reverend Fred Shuttlesworth, came up from Birmingham to get us out.

*Without police escort, I take it?*

HT: Without police escort, but every one of those cars had a shotgun in it. And Fred Shuttlesworth had got on the radio and said—you know Fred, he's very dramatic—"I'm going to get my people." [Laughs] He said, "I'm a nonviolent man, but I'm going to get my people." And apparently a hell of a lot of people believed in him. Man, they came there and they were a welcome sight. And each one of 'em got out with their guns and everything and the state police were there, but I think they all realized that this was not a time to say anything because, I'm pretty sure, there would have been a lot of people killed.

*The black drivers were openly carrying guns?*

HT: Oh, yeah. They had rifles and shotguns. And that's how we got back to Birmingham. . . . I think I was flown to New Orleans for medical treatment, because still they were afraid to let any of us go to the hospitals in Birmingham, and by that time—it was what, two days later—I was fairly all right. I had gotten most of the smoke out of my system.

*No one received any attention in the hospital in Anniston?*

HT: No, no. Oh, we did have one girl, Genevieve Hughes, a white girl, who had a busted lip. I remember a nurse applying something to that, but other than that, nothing. Now that I look back on it, man, we had some vicious people down there, wouldn't even so much as *treat* you. But that's the way it was. But strangely enough, even those bad things then don't stick in my mind that much. Not that I'm full of love and goodwill for everybody in my heart, but I chalk it off to part of the things that I'm going to be able to sit on my front porch in my rocking chair and tell my young'uns about, my grandchildren about.

*Postscript: That same day, Mother's Day, May 14, 1961, the second bus escaped the mob in Anniston and made it to Birmingham. At the Trailways station there, white men armed with baseball bats and chains beat the Freedom Riders at will for about fifteen minutes before the first police arrived. In 1975 a former Birmingham Klansman, who was a paid informant of the FBI at the time, told the Senate Select Committee on Intelligence that members of the Birmingham police force had promised the Klansmen that no policemen would show up to interfere with the beatings for at least fifteen minutes. In 1976 a Birmingham detective who refused to be interviewed on tape told me that account was correct—as far as it went. The detective said that word was passed in the police department that Public Safety Commissioner Eugene "Bull" Connor had watched from the window of his office in City Hall as the crowd of Klansmen, some brandishing weapons, gathered to await the Freedom Riders. Asked later about the absence of his policemen, Connor said most of them were visiting their mothers. . . .*

## Interview with John Lewis

[John Lewis] It was a nice ride between Birmingham and Montgomery. A few miles outside of Montgomery you just didn't see anything. You didn't see the plane, didn't see the state patrol car. It seemed like everything sort of disappeared, and the moment that we arrived in that station, it was the strangest feeling to me. It was something strange, that you knew something. It was really weird. It was an eerie feeling. There was a funny peace there, a quietness. You didn't see anything happening. Apparently, when you really look back, the mob there must have been so planned and was so out of sight. . . . it just sorta appeared, just appeared on the scene.

*You didn't see any sign of it as you went into the bus station?*

JL: None. Just didn't see anything. When we drove up, we didn't see anything. . . . We got most of the young ladies in a cab. So they got in a cab and the black cab driver didn't want to drive, because at that time there was two white students, young ladies from Peabody or Scarritt, and in Alabama there was a law that you couldn't have an integrated cab. So the two young ladies got out, and at that very time, this mob started all over the place. So everybody, all the young ladies, got away, and the two young white girls were running down the street trying to get away. That's when John Siegenthaler got hit. And at that time, the rest of us, mostly fellas, just literally standing there because we couldn't run—no place to go really.

*This was out in the lot?*

JL: Just out in the lot. And if you've been at the bus station, there's a rail there. . . . Down below is the entrance to the courthouse, the Post Office building. So when the mob kept coming, several of the people, several of the fellas jumped over and were able to get in the basement of the Post Office, and the postmaster there opened it and made it possible for people to come in and escape the mob. And I said—I remember saying that we shouldn't run, we should just stand there, 'cause the mob was beating people. And the last thing that I recall, I was hit with a crate, a wooden crate what you have soda in, and was left lying in the street. And I remember the Attorney General of Alabama, MacDonald Gallion, serving this injunction that Judge Walter B. Jones had issued saying that it was unlawful for interracial groups to travel. While I was lying there on the ground, he brought this injunction.

# James Farmer

## In a Mississippi Jail

*Confined in Jackson City, Mississippi, and then briefly in the dreaded Hinds County Prison Farm, Farmer and other freedom riders had to maintain the self-possession required by the practice of nonviolence.*

The jailer came to the cell block. We thought, of course, that he had come with the official word. But, no, he just wanted to talk.

His usual salutation summoned me to the bars. "How y'all feeling?"

I told him not bad, but we'd feel a lot better if they'd just let us all out, drop the charges, and serve us in the bus terminal restaurant without any commotion. Then I told him that I could stop the Freedom Rides, at least on buses in Mississippi.

"Mr. Farmer, you know good'n well they ain't gonna do that," he said, a bit sadly, I thought. He quietly continued: "Maybe when my grandchildren grow up, they'll do something like that. Lot 'a the young people down here don't feel like the old folks do; these things ain't goin' to go on forever. They cain't.

"Them boys with you is good boys," he continued. "They ain't criminals. They hadn't oughta be in jail here. They ain't done nothing—they ain't killed nobody, or robbed, or raped. They just wanta be treated like everybody else." He lowered his eyes and his chin quivered. He knew of the imminent transfer, no doubt, but was not aware that I shared that knowledge.

He went on: "If I was a ni—If I was colored, I'd be doin' the same thing as them boys is. I understan' these boys. But I cain't understan' them white boys up there. They can go anywhere they wanna go, they're white. What they come down here for?"

I ventured an answer: "Well, they believe, as Jesus said, that all men are brothers."

*Source:* James Farmer, *Lay Bare the Heart: An Autobiography of the Civil Rights Movement* (New York: Arbor House, 1986). Reprinted by permission.

His glance was still averted and his shoulders shook. Reaching my arm through the bars, I patted his shoulder. The *jailed* comforting the *jailer!*

Our jailer shook his head slowly and walked out without looking back. . . .

A caravan of police vans moved swiftly through the night with an escort of state and county police. Arriving at the county prison farm, we filed into the prison on order. Surrounded by guards, armed and ominous, we were herded together while the superintendent spoke to us.

Like an army sergeant spitting out orders, he told us that we were going to be put in our cells and the lights turned out for the night and there wasn't going to be any singing or any other noise. None at all! At six in the morning, we'd get breakfast. Then, one at a time, we'd be processed, and when asked questions we were going to answer "yes, sir" and "no, sir." There wasn't going to be any "yeah" or "naw." If anybody disobeyed this order, the guards standing by would correct his manners immediately. That was all.

As the cell gates slammed shut, I fervently hoped that attorney Jack Young remembered my request that he bail someone out quickly. Surreptitiously, we held a strategy conference, with each person's comments relayed from cell to cell. We readily agreed to forgo singing for a day, and to reassess on the morrow. Then we tackled the issue at hand.

"I'd die before I'd say sir to these crackers," declared Six-Two. "I ain't gonna kiss *no* red-neck's ass."

"What's the big deal about saying sir?" asked Little Gandhi. "We say sir and ma'am to our professors and our parents and to a lot of people we don't even know, don't we?"

"Yeah," said someone else, "but these ain't our professors or our parents. These creeps want to see us dead."

"Right, but why you wanna take the bait and give them an excuse to kill us?"

"Man, they ain't going to kill nobody. They're just trying to scare us. If they killed any of us, Bobby Kennedy'd be down here the next day."

"Man, you know Bobby Kennedy ain't go'n bring his skinny ass down here. Or his brother, neither. They'd whip their butts, too."

"How they gonna whip their asses when they got the whole United States Army, Navy, and Marines to back 'em up?"

"They ain't never goin' to use all that to help *us*."

"They might use it to help themselves, though."

"Well, if they don't come, I bet they'd send somebody. And that'd be the same thing."

Someone asked what I thought. Clearly, this was no time to pontificate; the pros and cons were both compelling, and the best response unclear to me. And broken heads were at stake.

I did not know what to do, but my gut reaction was to comply rather than be savaged over an issue of protocol instead of principle. But was this mere protocol when the method of addressing one another was the very essence of southern caste: the enforcement code of a racist society? Could we yield to this command and at the same time maintain dignity? Or would the next compromise, whatever it was, then come easier? Protocol could force one to bend the knee. Would there be a step-by-step process, eroding dignity and dragging us over the brink into the chasm of bowing and scraping, shuffling and scratching like many of the blacks down there? Who was strong enough or wise enough to draw the line where it could be moved no farther?

The fundamental issue was dignity. With that in mind, I tried, without confidence, to formulate an acceptable compromise.

"Let us keep our dignity at all costs. Why not say yes or no loudly. Then, after a brief pause, even more firmly, say sir. We will have complied with the letter of the command. But not its spirit. The *spirit* is the important thing."

Several riders said "Uh-huh." But Six-Two demurred: "Naw, I don't wanna compromise with no nigger-killin' racist bastards. Let's die like men insteada livin' like dogs."

Silence followed. No one else felt like venturing an opinion.

Clearly, there was no consensus. A unified policy was not available to us. Each was left to the counsel of his conscience and his God. I did ask, though, that each man processed reply loudly enough for us to hear, so we could prepare our response. . . .

Two beefy guards lumbered down the corridor, stopped at one cell, and called out the name of one of its occupants. The Rider summoned walked out of the cell and disappeared down the corridor between the two guards.

None of us spoke a word, but all ears strained. We did not hear the question, but the answer came clear. "No," and then a louder "sir." The latter word was spat out with a vengeance. A long pause followed. Then the questioning continued.

After the interrogation, the Freedom Rider walked down the corridor accompanied by the guards, blackjacks in hand. "I did it, man," he whispered as he passed my cell. His meaning eluded the guards.

Next came the Reverend C. T. Vivian. This time, we heard the question: "Do you live in this state?" The answer was in a firm voice. And "sir" did not follow "no."

Almost instantly, came the sound of weapons against flesh. The thud of a slight body falling to the floor. Rapid voices, and the beating stopped. There was panic in the interrogation room. Moments later, male nurses were seen running through the corridor.

When C. T. was led back down the corridor, there were bandages over his right eye and his T-shirt was covered with blood. The huge guards, half carrying him, appeared frightened. There was a smile on C. T.'s face.

Those blackjacks—flat leather thongs stuffed with lead—were designed to beat into unconsciousness without leaving any telltale signs. But C. T.'s assailants had been overeager, striking with the edge of the weapon instead of its flush side. Blood had been shed.

After that, the processing was halted.

An hour later, Jack Young came with $500 bail-bond money for one Rider who had previously indicated a desire for release. The timing was exquisite! The Freedom Rider bailed out had his press conference and called the FBI.

Two hours after the bail-out, the FBI arrived, and the lions of the county farm became mice, scurrying about. There was a hang-dog look about them as they kowtowed to their superiors.

That night, we were transported back to the Hinds County Jail in Jackson without incident.

# Martin Luther King, Jr.

## Nonviolence and Civil Disobedience

*These two selections, a speech delivered on November 16, 1961, to the Presbyterian Fellowship of the Concerned and the famous 1963 "Letter from Birmingham Jail," are statements of the concept of nonviolence that King was instrumental in making a component of the civil rights movement.*

Now there are three ways that oppressed people have generally dealt with their oppression. One way is the method of acquiescence, the method of surrender; that is, the individuals will somehow adjust themselves to oppression, they adjust themselves to discrimination or to segregation or colonialism or what have you. The other method that has been used in history is that of rising up against the oppressor with corroding hatred and physical violence. Now of course we know about this method in western civilization, because in a sense it has been the hallmark of its grandeur, and the inseparable twin of western materialism. But there is a weakness in this method because it ends up creating many more social problems than it solves. And I am convinced that if the Negro succumbs to the temptation of using violence in his struggle for freedom and justice, unborn generations will be the recipients of a long and desolate night of bitterness. And our chief legacy to the future will be an endless reign of meaningless chaos.

But there is another way, namely the way of non-violent resistance. This method was popularized in our generation by a little man from India, whose name was Mohandas K. Gandhi. He used this method in a magnificent way to free his people from the economic exploitation and the political domination inflicted upon them by a foreign power.

*Source:* Reprinted by permission from *Rhetoric of Racial Revolt*, edited by Roy L. Hill (Denver: Golden Bell Press, 1964).

This has been the method used by the student movement in the South and all over the United States. And naturally whenever I talk about the student movement I cannot be totally objective. I have to be somewhat subjective because of my great admiration for what the students have done. For in a real sense they have taken our deep groans and passionate yearnings for freedom, and filtered them in their own tender souls, and fashioned them into a creative protest which is an epic known all over our nation. As a result of their disciplined, non-violent, yet courageous struggle, they have been able to do wonders in the South, and in our nation. But this movement does have an underlying philosophy, it has certain ideas that are attached to it, it has certain philosophical precepts. These are the things that I would like to discuss for the few moments left.

I would say that the first point or the first principle in the movement is the idea that means must be as pure as the end. This movement is based on the philosophy that ends and means must cohere. Now this has been one of the long struggles in history, the whole idea of means and ends. Great philosophers have grappled with it, and sometimes they have emerged with the idea, from Machiavelli on down, that the end justifies the means. There is a great system of thought in our world today, known as Communism. And I think that with all of the weakness and tragedies of Communism, we find its greatest tragedy right here, that it goes under the philosophy that the end justifies the means that are used in the process. So we can read or we can hear the Lenins say that lying, deceit, or violence, that many of these things justify the ends of the classless society.

This is where the student movement and the non-violent movement that is taking place in our nation would break with Communism and any other system that would argue that the end justifies the means. For in the long run, we must see that the end represents the means in process and the ideal in the making. In other words, we cannot believe, or we cannot go with the idea that the end justifies the means because the end is pre-existent in the means. So the idea of non-violent resistance, the philosophy of non-violent resistance, is the philosophy which says that the means must be as pure as the end, that in the long run of history, immoral destructive means cannot bring about moral and constructive ends.

There is another thing about this philosophy, this method of non-violence which is followed by the student movement. It says that those who adhere to or follow this philosophy must follow a consistent principle of non-injury. They must consistently refuse to inflict injury upon another. Sometimes you will read the literature of the student movement and see that, as they are getting ready for the sit-in or stand-in, they will read something like this, "if you are hit do not hit back, if you are cursed do not curse back." This is the whole idea, that the individual who is engaged in a non-violent struggle must never inflict injury upon another. Now this has an external aspect and it has an internal one. From the external point of view it means that the individuals involved must avoid external physical violence. So they don't have guns, they don't retaliate with physical violence. If they are hit in the process, they avoid external physical violence at every point. But it also means that they avoid internal violence of spirit. This is why the love ethic stands so high in the student movement. We have a great deal of talk about love and non-violence in this whole thrust. . . .

There is something else: that one seeks to defeat the unjust system, rather than individuals who are caught in that system. And that one goes on believing that somehow this is the important thing, to get rid of the evil system and not the individual who happens to be misguided, who happens to be misled, who was taught wrong. The thing to do is to get rid of the system and thereby create a moral balance within society.

Another thing that stands at the center of this movement is another idea: that suffering can be a most creative and powerful social force. Suffering has certain moral attributes involved, but it can be a powerful and creative social force. Now, it is very interesting at this point to notice that both violence and non-violence agree that suffering can be a very powerful social force. But there is this difference: violence says that suffering can be a powerful social force by inflicting the suffering on somebody else; so this is what we do in war, this is what we do in the whole violent thrust of the violent movement. It believes that you achieve some end by inflicting suffering on another. The non-violent say that suffering becomes a powerful social force when you willingly accept that violence on yourself, so that self-suffering stands at the center of the non-violent movement and the individuals involved are able to suffer in a creative manner, feeling that unearned suffering is redemptive, and that suffering may serve to transform the social situation.

Another thing in this movement is the idea that there is within human nature an amazing potential for goodness. There is within human nature something that can respond to goodness. I know somebody's liable to say that this is an unrealistic movement if it goes on believing that all people are good. Well, I didn't say that. I think the students are realistic enough to believe that there is a strange dichotomy of disturbing dualism within human nature. Many of the great philosophers and thinkers through the ages have seen this. It caused Ovid the Latin poet to say, "I see and approve the better things of life, but the evil things I do." It caused even St. Augustine to say, "Lord, make me pure, but not yet." So that that is in human nature. Plato, centuries ago said that the human personality is like a charioteer with two headstrong horses, each wanting to go in different directions, so that within our own individual lives we see this conflict and certainly when we come to the collective life of man, we see a strange badness. But in spite of this there is something in human nature that can respond to goodness. So that man is neither innately good nor is he innately bad; he has potentialities for both. So in this sense, Carlyle was right when he said that "there are depths in man which go down to the lowest hell, and heights which reach the highest heaven, for are not both heaven and hell made out of him, ever-lasting miracle and mystery that he is?" Man has the capacity to be good, man has the capacity to be evil.

And so the non-violent resister never lets this idea go, that there is something within human nature that can respond to goodness. So that a Jesus of Nazareth or a Mohandas Gandhi can appeal to human beings and appeal to that element of goodness within them, and a Hitler can appeal to the element of evil within them. But we must never forget that there is something within human nature that can respond to goodness, that man is not totally depraved, to put it in theological terms, the image of God is never totally gone. And so the individuals who believe in this movement and who believe in non-violence and our struggle in the South somehow believe that even the worst segregationist can become an integrationist. Now sometimes it is hard to believe that this is what this movement says, and it believes it firmly, that there is something within human nature that can be changed, and this stands at the top of the whole philosophy of the student movement and the philosophy of non-violence.

It says something else. It says that it is as much a moral obligation to refuse to cooperate with evil as it is to cooperate with good. Non-cooperation with evil is as much a moral obligation as the cooperation with good. So that the student movement is willing to stand up courageously on the idea of civil disobedience. Now

I think this is the part of the student movement that is probably misunderstood more than anything else. And it is a difficult aspect, because on the one hand the students would say, and I would say, and all the people who believe in civil rights would say, obey the Supreme Court's decision of 1954 and at the same time, we would disobey certain laws that exist on the statutes of the South today....

Now there are one or two other things that I want to say about this student movement, moving out of the philosophy of non-violence, something about what it is a revolt against. On the one hand it is a revolt against the negative peace that had encompassed the South for many years. I remember when I was in Montgomery, Ala., one of the white citizens came to me one day and said—and I think he was very sincere about this—that in Montgomery for all of these years we have been such a peaceful community, we have had so much harmony in race relations and then you people have started this movement and boycott, and it has done so much to disturb race relations, and we just don't love the Negro like we used to love them, because you have destroyed the harmony and the peace that we once had in race relations. And I said to him, in the best way I could say and I tried to say it in non-violent terms, we have never had peace in Montgomery, Ala., we have never had peace in the South. We have had a negative peace, which is merely the absence of tension; we've had a negative peace in which the Negro patiently accepted his situation and his plight, but we've never had true peace, we've never had positive peace, and what we're seeking now is to develop this positive peace. For we must come to see that peace is not merely the absence of some negative force, it is the presence of a positive force. True peace is not merely the absence of tension, but it is the presence of justice and brotherhood. I think this is what Jesus meant when he said, I come not to bring peace but a sword. Now Jesus didn't mean he came to start war, to bring a physical sword, and he didn't mean, I come not to bring positive peace. But I think what Jesus was saying in substance was this, that I come not to bring an old negative peace, which makes for stagnant passivity and deadening complacency, I come to bring something different, and whenever I come, a conflict is precipitated, between the old and the new, whenever I come a struggle takes place between justice and injustice, between the forces of light and the forces of darkness. I come not to bring a negative peace, but a positive peace, which is brotherhood, which is justice, which is the Kingdom of God.

\*     \*     \*

My Dear Fellow Clergymen:

While confined here in the Birmingham city jail, I came across your recent statement calling my present activities "unwise and untimely." Seldom do I pause to answer criticism of my work and ideas. If I sought to answer all the criticisms that cross my desk, my secretaries would have little time for anything other than such correspondence in the course of the day, and I would have no time for constructive work. But since I feel that you are men of genuine good will and that your criticisms are sincerely set forth, I want to try to answer your statement in what I hope will be patient and reasonable terms.

I think I should indicate why I am here in Birmingham, since you have been influenced by the view which argues against "outsiders coming in." I have the honor of serving as president of the Southern Christian Leadership Conference, an organization operating in every southern state, with headquarters in Atlanta, Georgia. We have some eighty-five affiliated organizations across the South, and one of them is the Alabama Christian Movement for Human Rights. Frequently we share staff, educational and financial resources with our affiliates. Several months ago the affiliate here in Birmingham asked us to be on call to engage in a nonviolent direct-action program if such were deemed necessary. We readily consented, and when the hour came we lived up to our promise. So I, along with several members of my staff, am here because I was invited here, I am here because I have organizational ties here.

But more basically, I am in Birmingham because injustice is here. Just as the prophets of the eighth century B.C. left their villages and carried their "thus saith the Lord" far beyond the boundaries of their home towns, and just as the Apostle Paul left his village of Tarsus and carried the gospel of Jesus Christ to the far corners of the Greco-Roman world, so am I compelled to carry the gospel of freedom beyond my own home town. Like Paul, I must constantly respond to the Macedonian call for aid.

Moreover, I am cognizant of the interrelatedness of all communities and states. I cannot sit idly by in Atlanta and not be concerned about what happens in Birmingham. Injustice anywhere is a threat to justice everywhere. We are caught in an inescapable

*Source:* From *Why We Can't Wait* by Martin Luther King, Jr. Copyright © 1963, 1964 by Martin Luther King, Jr. Reprinted by permission of Harper & Row Publishers Inc.

network of mutuality, tied in a single garment of destiny. What-ever affects one directly, affects all indirectly. Never again can we afford to live with the narrow, provincial "outside agitator" idea. Anyone who lives inside the United States can never be considered an outsider anywhere within its bounds.

You deplore the demonstrations taking place in Birmingham. But your statement, I am sorry to say, fails to express a similar concern for the conditions that brought about the demonstrations. I am sure that none of you would want to rest content with the superficial kind of social analysis that deals merely with effects and does not grapple with underlying causes. It is unfortunate that demonstrations are taking place in Birmingham, but it is even more unfortunate that the city's white power structure left the Negro community with no alternative.

In any nonviolent campaign there are four basic steps: collec-tion of the facts to determine whether injustices exist; negotiation; self-purification; and direct action. We have gone through all these steps in Birmingham. There can be no gainsaying the fact that racial injustice engulfs this community. Birmingham is probably the most thoroughly segregated city in the United States. Its ugly record of brutality is widely known. Negroes have experienced grossly unjust treatment in the courts. There have been more unsolved bombings of Negro homes and churches in Birmingham than in any other city in the nation. These are the hard, brutal facts of the case. On the basis of these conditions, Negro leaders sought to negotiate with the city fathers. But the latter consistently re-fused to engage in good-faith negotiation.

Then, last September, came the opportunity to talk with lead-ers of Birmingham's economic community. In the course of the negotiations, certain promises were made by the merchants—for example, to remove the stores' humiliating racial signs. On the basis of these promises, the Reverend Fred Shuttlesworth and the leaders of the Alabama Christian Movement for Human Rights agreed to a moratorium on all demonstrations. As the weeks and months went by, we realized that we were the victims of a bro-ken promise. A few signs, briefly removed, returned; the others remained.

As in so many past experiences, our hopes had been blasted, and the shadow of deep disappointment settled upon us. We had no alternative except to prepare for direct action, whereby we would present our very bodies as a means of laying our case before the conscience of the local and the national community. Mindful of the difficulties involved, we decided to undertake a process of self-purification. We began a series of workshops on nonviolence, and we repeatedly asked ourselves: "Are you able to accept blows without retaliating?" "Are you able to endure the ordeal of jail?" We decided to schedule our direct-action program for the Easter season, realizing that except for Christmas, this is the main shopping period of the year. Knowing that a strong economic-withdrawal program would be the by-product of direct action, we felt that this would be the best time to bring pressure to bear on the merchants for the needed change.

Then it occurred to us that Birmingham's mayoralty election was coming up in March, and we speedily decided to postpone action until after election day. When we discovered that the Commissioner of Public Safety, Eugene "Bull" Connor, had piled up enough votes to be in the run-off, we decided again to postpone action until the day after the run-off so that the demonstrations could not be used to cloud the issues. Like many others, we waited to see Mr. Connor defeated, and to this end we endured postponement after postponement. Having aided in this community need, we felt that our direct-action program could be delayed no longer.

You may well ask: "Why direct action? Why sit-ins, marches and so forth? Isn't negotiation a better path?" You are quite right in calling for negotiation. Indeed, this is the very purpose of direct action. Nonviolent direct action seeks to create such a crisis and foster such a tension that a community which has constantly refused to negotiate is forced to confront the issue. It seeks so to dramatize the issue that it can no longer be ignored. My citing the creation of tension as part of the work of the nonviolent-resister may sound rather shocking. But I must confess that I am not afraid of the word "tension." I have earnestly opposed violent tension, but there is a type of constructive, nonviolent tension which is necessary for growth. Just as Socrates felt that it was necessary to create a tension in the mind so that individuals could rise from the bondage of myths and half-truths to the unfettered realm of creative analysis and objective appraisal, so must we see the need for nonviolent gadflies to create the kind of tension in society that will help men rise from the dark depths of prejudice and racism to the majestic heights of understanding and brotherhood.

The purpose of our direct-action program is to create a situation so crisis-packed that it will inevitably open the door to negotiation. I therefore concur with you in your call for negotiation. Too long has our beloved Southland been bogged down in a tragic effort to live in monologue rather than dialogue.

One of the basic points in your statement is that the action that I and my associates have taken in Birmingham is untimely. Some have asked: "Why didn't you give the new city administration time to act?" The only answer that I can give to this query is that the new Birmingham administration must be prodded about as much as the outgoing one, before it will act. We are sadly mistaken if we feel that the election of Albert Boutwell as mayor will bring the millennium to Birmingham. While Mr. Boutwell is a much more gentle person than Mr. Connor, they are both segregationists, dedicated to maintenance of the status quo. I have hope that Mr. Boutwell will be reasonable enough to see the futility of massive resistance to desegregation. But he will not see this without pressure from devotees of civil rights. My friends, I must say to you that we have not made a single gain in civil rights without determined legal and nonviolent pressure. Lamentably, it is an historical fact that privileged groups seldom give up their privileges voluntarily. Individuals may see the moral light and voluntarily give up their unjust posture; but, as Reinhold Niebuhr has reminded us, groups tend to be more immoral than individuals.

We know through painful experience that freedom is never voluntarily given by the oppressor; it must be demanded by the oppressed. Frankly, I have yet to engage in a direct-action campaign that was "well timed" in the view of those who have not suffered unduly from the disease of segregation. For years now I have heard the word "Wait!" It rings in the ear of every Negro with piercing familiarity. This "Wait" has almost always meant "Never." We must come to see, with one of our distinguished jurists, that "justice too long delayed is justice denied."

We have waited for more than 340 years for our constitutional and God-given rights. The nations of Asia and Africa are moving with jet-like speed toward gaining political independence, but we still creep at horse-and-buggy pace toward gaining a cup of coffee at a lunch counter. Perhaps it is easy for those who have never felt the stinging darts of segregation to say, "Wait." But when you have seen vicious mobs lynch your mothers and fathers at will and drown your sisters and brothers at whim; when you have seen hate-filled policemen curse, kick and even kill your black brothers and sisters; when you see the vast majority of your twenty million Negro brothers smothering in an airtight cage of poverty in the midst of an affluent society; when you suddenly find your tongue twisted and your speech stammering as you seek to explain to your six-year-old daughter why she can't go to the public amusement park that has just been advertised on television, and see tears welling up in her eyes when she is told that Funtown is closed to colored children, and see ominous clouds of inferiority beginning to form in her little mental sky, and see her beginning to distort her personality by developing an unconscious bitterness toward white people; when you have to concoct an answer for a five-year-old son who is asking: "Daddy, why do white people treat colored people so mean?"; when you take a cross-country drive and find it necessary to sleep night after night in the uncomfortable corners of your automobile because no motel will accept you; when you are humiliated day in and day out by nagging signs reading "white" and "colored"; when your first name becomes "nigger," your middle name becomes "boy" (however old you are) and your last name becomes "John," and your wife and mother are never given the respected title "Mrs."; when you are harried by day and haunted by night by the fact that you are a Negro, living constantly at tiptoe stance, never quite knowing what to expect next, and are plagued with inner fears and outer resentments; when you are forever fighting a degenerating sense of "nobodiness"—then you will understand why we find it difficult to wait. There comes a time when the cup of endurance runs over, and men are no longer willing to be plunged into the abyss of despair. I hope, sirs, you can understand our legitimate and unavoidable impatience.

You express a great deal of anxiety over our willingness to break laws. This is certainly a legitimate concern. Since we so diligently urge people to obey the Supreme Court's decision of 1954 outlawing segregation in the public schools, at first glance it may seem rather paradoxical for us consciously to break laws. One may well ask: "How can you advocate breaking some laws and obeying others?" The answer lies in the fact that there are two types of laws: just and unjust. I would be the first to advocate obeying just laws. One has not only a legal but a moral responsibility to obey just laws. Conversely, one has a moral responsibility to disobey unjust laws. I would agree with St. Augustine that "an unjust law is no law at all."

Now, what is the difference between the two? How does one determine whether a law is just or unjust? A just law is a manmade code that squares with the moral law or the law of God. An unjust law is a code that is out of harmony with the moral law. To put it in the terms of St. Thomas Aquinas: An unjust law is a human law that is not rooted in eternal law and natural law. Any law that uplifts human personality is just. Any law that degrades human personality is unjust. All segregation statutes are unjust because segregation distorts the soul and damages the personality. It gives the segregator a false sense of superiority and the segregated a false sense of inferiority. Segregation, to use the terminology of the Jewish philosopher Martin Buber, substitutes an "I-it" relationship for an "I-thou" relationship and ends up relegating persons to the status of things. Hence segregation is not only politically, economically and sociologically unsound, it is morally wrong and sinful. Paul Tillich has said that sin is separation. Is not segregation an existential expression of man's tragic separation, his awful estrangement, his terrible sinfulness? Thus it is that I can urge men to obey the 1954 decision of the Supreme Court, for it is morally right; and I can urge them to disobey segregation ordinances, for they are morally wrong.

Let us consider a more concrete example of just and unjust laws. An unjust law is a code that a numerical or power majority group compels a minority group to obey but does not make binding on itself. This is *difference* made legal. By the same token, a just law is a code that a majority compels a minority to follow and that it is willing to follow itself. This is *sameness* made legal.

Let me give another explanation. A law is unjust if it is inflicted on a minority that, as a result of being denied the right to vote, had no part in enacting or devising the law. Who can say that the legislature of Alabama which set up that state's segregation laws was democratically elected? Throughout Alabama all sorts of devious methods are used to prevent Negroes from becoming registered voters, and there are some counties in which, even though Negroes constitute a majority of the population, not a single Negro is registered. Can any law enacted under such circumstances be considered democratically structured?

Sometimes a law is just on its face and unjust in its application. For instance, I have been arrested on a charge of parading without a permit. Now, there is nothing wrong in having an ordinance which requires a permit for a parade. But such an ordinance becomes unjust when it is used to maintain segregation and to deny citizens the First-Amendment privilege of peaceful assembly and protest.

I hope you are able to see the distinction I am trying to point out. In no sense do I advocate evading or defying the law, as would the rabid segregationist. That would lead to anarchy. One who breaks an unjust law must do so openly, lovingly, and with a willingness to accept the penalty. I submit that an individual who breaks a law that conscience tells him is unjust, and who willingly accepts the penalty of imprisonment in order to arouse the conscience of the community over its injustice, is in reality expressing the highest respect for law.

Of course, there is nothing new about this kind of civil disobedience. It was evidenced sublimely in the refusal of Shadrach, Meshach and Abednego to obey the laws of Nebuchadnezzar, on the ground that a higher moral law was at stake. It was practiced superbly by the early Christians, who were willing to face hungry lions and the excruciating pain of chopping blocks rather than submit to certain unjust laws of the Roman Empire. To a degree, academic freedom is a reality today because Socrates practiced civil disobedience. In our own nation, the Boston Tea Party represented a massive act of civil disobedience.

We should never forget that everything Adolf Hitler did in Germany was "legal" and everything the Hungarian freedom fighters did in Hungary was "illegal." It was "illegal" to aid and comfort a Jew in Hitler's Germany. Even so, I am sure that, had I lived in Germany at the time, I would have aided and comforted my Jewish brothers. If today I lived in a Communist country where certain principles dear to the Christian faith are suppressed, I would openly advocate disobeying that country's antireligious laws.

I must make two honest confessions to you, my Christian and Jewish brothers. First, I must confess that over the past few years I have been gravely disappointed with the white moderate. I have almost reached the regrettable conclusion that the Negro's great stumbling block in his stride toward freedom is not the White Citizen's Counciler or the Ku Klux Klanner, but the white moderate, who is more devoted to "order" than to justice; who prefers a negative peace which is the absence of tension to a positive peace which is the presence of justice; who constantly says: "I agree with you in the goal you seek, but I cannot agree with your methods of direct action"; who paternalistically believes he can set the timetable for another man's freedom; who lives by a mythical concept of time and who constantly advises the Negro to wait for a "more convenient season." Shallow understanding from people of good will is more frustrating than absolute misunderstanding from people of ill will. Lukewarm acceptance is much more bewildering than outright rejection.

I had hoped that the white moderate would understand that law and order exist for the purpose of establishing justice and that when they fail in this purpose they become the dangerously structured dams that block the flow of social progress. I had hoped that the white moderate would understand that the present tension in the South is a necessary phase of the transition from an obnoxious negative peace, in which the Negro passively accepted his unjust plight, to a substantive and positive peace, in which all men will respect the dignity and worth of human personality. Actually, we who engage in nonviolent direct action are not the creators of tension. We merely bring to the surface the hidden tension that is already alive. We bring it out in the open, where it can be seen and dealt with. Like a boil that can never be cured so long as it is covered up but must be opened with all its ugliness to the natural medicines of air and light, injustice must be exposed, with all the tension its exposure creates, to the light of human conscience and the air of national opinion before it can be cured.

In your statement you assert that our actions, even though peaceful, must be condemned because they precipitate violence. But is this a logical assertion? Isn't this like condemning a robbed man because his possession of money precipitated the evil act of robbery? Isn't this like condemning Socrates because his unswerving commitment to truth and his philosophical inquiries precipitated the act by the misguided populace in which they made him drink hemlock? Isn't this like condemning Jesus because his unique God-consciousness and never-ceasing devotion to God's will precipitated the evil act of crucifixion? We must come to see that, as the federal courts have consistently affirmed, it is wrong to urge an individual to cease his efforts to gain his basic constitutional rights because the quest may precipitate violence. Society must protect the robbed and punish the robber.

I had also hoped that the white moderate would reject the myth concerning time in relation to the struggle for freedom. I have just received a letter from a white brother in Texas. He writes: "All Christians know that the colored people will receive equal rights eventually, but it is possible that you are in too great a religious hurry. It has taken Christianity almost two thousand years to accomplish what it has. The teachings of Christ take time to come to earth." Such an attitude stems from a tragic misconception of time, from the stangely irrational notion that there is something in the very flow of time that will inevitably cure all ills. Actually, time itself is neutral; it can be used either destructively or constructively. More and more I feel that the people of ill will have used time much more effectively than have the people of good will. We will have to repent in this generation not merely for the hateful words and actions of the bad people but for the appalling silence of the good people. Human progress never rolls in on wheels of inevitability; it comes through the tireless efforts of men willing to be co-workers with God, and without this hard work, time itself becomes an ally of the forces of social stagnation. We must use time creatively, in the knowledge that the time is always ripe to do right. Now is the time to make real the promise of democracy and transform our pending national elegy into a creative psalm of brotherhood. Now is the time to lift our national policy from the quicksand of racial injustice to the solid rock of human dignity.

You speak of our activity in Birmingham as extreme. At first I was rather disappointed that fellow clergymen would see my non-violent efforts as those of an extremist. I began thinking about the fact that I stand in the middle of two opposing forces in the Negro Community. One is a force of complacency, made up in part of Negroes who, as a result of long years of oppression, are so drained of self-respect and a sense of "somebodiness" that they have adjusted to segregation; and in part of a few middle-class Negroes who, because of a degree of academic and economic security and because in some ways they profit by segregation, have become insensitive to the problems of the masses. The other force is one of bitterness and hatred, and it comes perilously close to advocating violence. It is expressed in the various black nationalist groups that are springing up across the nation, the largest and best known being Elijah Muhammad's Muslim movement. Nourished by the Negro's frustration over the continued existence of racial discrimination, this movement is made up of people who have lost faith in America, who have absolutely repudiated Christianity, and who have concluded that the white man is an incorrigible "devil."

I have tried to stand between these two forces, saying that we need emulate neither the "do-nothingism" of the complacent nor the hatred and the despair of the black nationalist. For there is the more excellent way of love and nonviolent protest. I am grateful to God that, through the influence of the Negro church, the way of nonviolence became an integral part of our struggle.

If this philosophy had not emerged, by now many streets of the South would, I am convinced, be flowing with blood. And I am further convinced that if our white brothers dismiss as "rabble-rousers" and "outside agitators" those of us who employ nonviolent direct action, and if they refuse to support our nonviolent efforts, millions of Negroes will, out of frustration and despair, seek solace and security in black-nationalist ideologies—a development that would inevitably lead to a frightening racial nightmare.

Oppressed people cannot remain oppressed forever. The

yearning for freedom eventually manifests itself, and that is what has happened to the American Negro. Something within has reminded him of his birthright of freedom, and something without has reminded him that it can be gained. Consciously or unconsciously, he has been caught up by the *Zeitgeist,* and with his black brothers of Africa and his brown and yellow brothers of Asia, South America and the Caribbean, the United States Negro is moving with a sense of great urgency toward the promised land of racial justice. If one recognizes this vital urge that has engulfed the Negro community, one should readily understand why public demonstrations are taking place. The Negro has many pent-up resentments and latent frustrations, and he must release them. So let him march; let him make prayer pilgrimages to the city hall; let him go on freedom rides—and try to understand why he must do so. If his repressed emotions are not released in nonviolent ways, they will seek expression through violence; this is not a threat but a fact of history. So I have not said to my people: "Get rid of your discontent." Rather, I have tried to say that this normal and healthy discontent can be channeled into the creative outlet of nonviolent direct action. And now this approach is being termed extremist.

But though I was initially disappointed at being categorized as an extremist, as I continued to think about the matter I gradually gained a measure of satisfaction from the label. Was not Jesus an extremist for love: "Love your enemies, bless them that curse you, do good to them that hate you, and pray for them which despitefully use you, and persecute you." Was not Amos an extremist for justice: "Let justice roll down like waters and righteousness like an ever-flowing stream." Was not Paul an extremist for the Christian gospel: "I bear in my body the marks of the Lord Jesus." Was not Martin Luther an extremist: "Here I stand; I cannot do otherwise, so help me God." And John Bunyan: "I will stay in jail to the end of my days before I make a butchery of my conscience." And Abraham Lincoln: "This nation cannot survive half slave and half free." And Thomas Jefferson: "We hold these truths to be self-evident, that all men are created equal . . ." So the question is not whether we will be extremists, but what kind of extremists we will be. Will we be extremists for hate or for love? Will we be extremists for the preservation of injustice or for the extension of justice? In that dramatic scene on Calvary's hill three men were crucified. We must never forget that all three were crucified for the same crime—the crime of extremism. Two were extremists for immorality, and thus fell below their environment. The other, Jesus Christ, was an extremist for love, truth and goodness, and thereby rose above his environment. Perhaps the South, the nation and the world are in dire need of creative extremists. . . .

If I have said anything in this letter that overstates the truth and indicates an unreasonable impatience, I beg you to forgive me. If I have said anything that understates the truth and indicates my having a patience that allows me to settle for anything less than brotherhood, I beg God to forgive me.

I hope this letter finds you strong in the faith. I also hope that circumstances will soon make it possible for me to meet each of you, not as an integrationist or a civil-rights leader but as a fellow clergyman and a Christian brother. Let us all hope that the dark clouds of racial prejudice will soon pass away and the deep fog of misunderstanding will be lifted from our fear-drenched communities, and in some not too distant tomorrow the radiant stars of love and brotherhood will shine over our great nation with all their scintillating beauty.

Yours for the cause of Peace and Brotherhood,
Martin Luther King, Jr.

Dressed alike in workingman's clothes, King and Abernathy lead a line of demonstrators to a confrontation with the police that they knew would result in their arrest. From solitary confinement King wrote the inspiring "Letter From Birmingham City Jail."

# John Salter

## A Mississippi Demonstration

*"Medgar" in this passage refers to Medgar Evers, leader of the civil rights movement in Jackson, Mississippi. His murder in 1963 would bring further national attention to the struggle in the Deep South.*

A number of students from Brinkley High came into the church. They told us that other Brinkley students, walking the long trek from their school to Farish Street, had been followed by police and many had been arrested and, presumably, taken to the State Fairgrounds. Students from Lanier and Jim Hill arrived. A number of college youth were also present. Before long, there were almost 600 students gathered at Farish Street Baptist. Everyone was talking at once, everyone was excited, everyone was enthusiastic.

Outside, hundreds of police were assembled all around the church.

The strategy upon which we decided was that the students, two and three abreast, would walk from the church, down the sidewalk, toward Capitol Street—which was many blocks away. They would carry American flags and would sing songs. Willie Ludden would lead the march. When arrested, as many as possible would remain in jail.

The Rev. S. Leon Whitney, pastor of Farish Street Baptist, collected from the students anything that the police might, when they searched the demonstrators, construe as being "deadly weapons," such as pocket knives. The collection plates used during the church services were soon filled. Then we mounted the platform and addressed the students—Gloster Current, I, Medgar, and others—but the best talks were given by the student leaders themselves. These young people had supported the Youth Council

*Source:* John R. Salter, Jr., *Jackson, Mississippi: An American Chronicle of Struggle and Schism*, with a foreword by the Rev. R. Edwin King, Jr. (Malabar, Florida: Robert E. Krieger Publishing Company, 1987).

movement for many long, lean months. This was their day, and their talks were short and to the point: "Let's march!"

So, two and three abreast, carrying American flags and singing freedom songs, they marched out of the church, turned right on the sidewalk toward Capitol Street, and slowly walked toward what awaited them. And a great deal was waiting.

The whole area was surrounded by police in riot helmets, but down a block in the direction of Capitol Street were hundreds and hundreds of law officers. They stretched from the buildings on one side of the street straight across to the buildings on the other side, rank after rank after rank of them. Their blue helmets, their clubs, their guns glinted in the hot sunlight. Behind this solid wall were large numbers of state highway patrolmen, recognizable in their brown helmets, and behind them were sheriff's deputies. And behind all of this were city garbage trucks.

Newsmen were being kept back by the police.

Straight into all of this marched the students, singing and with their flags held high. When they reached the first rank of police, the officers yelled, "Run! Run!"

Some students in panic broke ranks and ran, chased by lawmen who fired shots above their heads. But the others marched straight into the wall of police, had their flags torn from their hands and thrown into the dirt of Farish Street. Some were clubbed, such as Willie Ludden, who was surrounded by police and knocked to the ground.

The students were hustled and shoved through the ranks of police, back into the groups of highway patrolmen, then to the sheriff's deputies, and finally were thrown into the garbage trucks.

Many Jackson black people had withdrawn into houses and buildings when the police arrived in the area and began setting up their human barricade, but some were standing and watching. Several were also clubbed.

With cold-blooded, mechanical efficiency, the demonstration was "handled"—each step obviously well planned and each step executed with ruthless precision made all the more vicious by the utter calm with which it was carried out. Medgar and I watched it together, on the sidewalk, and saw almost everything that happened.

The grim lines in his face seemed more deeply cut than ever. "Just like Nazi Germany," he said.

Several representatives from the U.S. Department of Justice quietly observed the proceedings.

The whole affair was over in a matter of minutes. The fleet of garbage trucks moved off to the State Fairgrounds, and we heard freedom singing coming from the back of every one. Almost 500 had been arrested in Jackson that afternoon.

A woman standing on the sidewalk picked up one of the fallen American flags. She was crying softly.

Another group of demonstrators is hauled off to jail in the demonstrations in Birmingham, 1963.

# Anne Moody

## Detention Center and Church

*Anne Moody, twenty-one years old at the time of these incidents, was a black student at Tougaloo College and a leader in the civil rights movement in Jackson, Mississippi. The arrest and confinement described here occurred just after the death of the civil rights leader Medgar Evers.*

[On the occasion of Medgar Ever's funeral] I was called to the front of the church to help lead the marchers in a few freedom songs. We sang "Woke Up This Morning With My Mind on Freedom" and "Ain't Gonna Let Nobody Turn Me 'Round." After singing the last song we headed for the streets in a double line, carrying small American flags in our hands. The cops had heard that there were going to be Negroes in the streets all day protesting Medgar's death. They were ready for us.

On Rose Street we ran into a blockade of about two hundred policemen. We were called to a halt by Captain Ray, and asked to disperse. "Everybody ain't got a permit get out of this here parade," Captain Ray said into his bull horn. No one moved. He beckoned to the cops to advance on us.

The cops had rifles and wore steel helmets. They walked right up to us very fast and then sort of engulfed us. They started snatching the small American flags, throwing them to the ground, stepping on them, or stamping them. Students who refused to let go of the flags were jabbed with rifle butts. There was only one paddy wagon on the scene. The first twenty of us were thrown into it, although a paddy wagon is only large enough to seat about ten people. We were sitting and lying all over each other inside the wagon when garbage trucks arrived. We saw the cops stuff about fifty demonstrators in one truck as we looked out through the back

*Source:* Anne Moody, *Coming of Age in Mississippi* (New York: Dell Publishing Company, 1968).

glass. Then the driver of the paddy wagon sped away as fast as he could, often making sudden stops in the middle of the street so we would be thrown around.

We thought that they were going to take us to the city jail again because we were college students. We discovered we were headed for the fairgrounds. When we got there, the driver rolled up the windows, turned the heater on, got out, closed the door and left us. It was over a hundred degrees outside that day. There was no air coming in. Sweat began dripping off us. An hour went by. Our clothes were now soaked and sticking to us. Some of the girls looked as though they were about to faint. A policeman looked in to see how we were taking it. Some of the boys begged him to let us out. He only smiled and walked away.

Looking out of the back window again, we noticed they were now booking all the other demonstrators. We realized they had planned to do this to our group. A number of us in the paddy wagon were known to the cops. After the Woolworth sit-in, I had been known to every white in Jackson. I can remember walking down the street and being pointed out by whites as they drove or walked past me.

Suddenly one of the girls screamed. Scrambling to the window, we saw John Salter with blood gushing out of a large hole in the back of his head. He was just standing there dazed and no one was helping him. And we were in no position to help either.

After they let everyone else out of the garbage trucks, they decided to let us out of the paddy wagon. We had now been in there well over two hours. As we were getting out, one of the girls almost fell. A guy started to help her.

"Get ya hands off that gal. Whatta ya think, ya goin' to a prom or somethin'?" one of the cops said.

Water was running down my legs. My skin was soft and spongy. I had hidden a small transistor radio in my bra and some of the other girls had cards and other things in theirs. We had learned to sneak them in after we discovered they didn't search the women but now everything was showing through our wet clothes.

When we got into the compound, there were still some high school students there, since the NAACP bail money had been exhausted. There were altogether well over a hundred and fifty in the girls' section. The boys had been put into a compound directly opposite and parallel to us. Some of the girls who had been arrested after us shared their clothes with us until ours dried. They told us what had happened after we were taken off in the paddy wagon. They said the cops had stuffed so many into the garbage trucks that some were just hanging on. As one of the trucks pulled off, thirteen-year-old John Young fell out. When the driver stopped, the truck rolled back over the boy. He was rushed off to a hospital and they didn't know how badly he had been hurt. They said the cops had gone wild with their billy sticks. They had even arrested Negroes looking on from their porches. John Salter had been forced off some Negro's porch and hit on the head.

The fairgrounds were everything I had heard they were. The compounds they put us in were two large buildings used to auction off cattle during the annual state fair. They were about a block long, with large openings about twenty feet wide on both ends where the cattle were driven in. The openings had been closed up with wire. It reminded me of a concentration camp. It was hot and sticky and girls were walking around half dressed all the time. We were guarded by four policemen. They had rifles and kept an eye on us through the wired sides of the building. As I looked through the wire at them, I imagined myself in Nazi Germany, the policemen Nazi soldiers. They couldn't have been any rougher than these cops. Yet this was America, "the land of the free and the home of the brave."

About five-thirty we were told that dinner was ready. We were lined up single file and marched out of the compound. They had the cook from the city jail there. He was standing over a large garbage can stirring something in it with a stick. The sight of it nauseated me. No one was eating, girls or boys. In the next few days, many were taken from the fairgrounds sick from hunger.

When I got out of jail on Saturday, the day before Medgar's funeral, I had lost about fifteen pounds. They had prepared a special meal on campus for the Tougaloo students, but attempts to eat made me sicker. The food kept coming up. The next morning I pulled myself together enough to make the funeral services at the Masonic Temple. I was glad I had gone in spite of my illness. This was the first time I had ever seen so many Negroes together. There were thousands and thousands of them there. Maybe Medgar's death had really brought them to the Movement, I thought. Maybe his death would strengthen the ties between Negroes and Negro organizations. If this resulted, then truly his death was not in vain.

The Sunday following Medgar's funeral, Reverend Ed King organized an integrated church-visiting team of six of us from the college. Another team was organized by a group in Jackson. Five or six churches were hit that day, including Governor Ross Barnett's. At each one they had prepared for our visit with armed policemen, paddy wagons, and dogs—which would be used in case we refused to leave after "ushers" had read us the prepared resolutions. There were about eight of these ushers at each church, and they were never exactly the usherly type. They were more on the order of Al Capone. I think this must have been the first time any of these men had worn a flower in his lapel. When we were asked to leave, we did. We were never even allowed to get past the first step.

A group of us decided that we would go to church again the next Sunday. This time we were quite successful. These visits had not been publicized as the first ones were, and they were not really expecting us. We went first to a Church of Christ, where we were greeted by the regular ushers. After reading us the same resolution we had heard last week, they offered to give us cab fare to the Negro extension of the church. Just as we had refused and were walking away, an old lady stopped us. "We'll sit with you," she said.

We walked back to the ushers with her and her family. "Please let them in, Mr. Calloway. We'll sit with them," the old lady said.

"Mrs. Dixon, the church has decided what is to be done. A resolution has been passed, and we are to abide by it."

"Who are we to decide such a thing? This is a house of God, and God is to make all of the decisions. He is the judge of us all," the lady said.

The ushers got angrier then and threatened to call the police if we didn't leave. We decided to go.

"We appreciate very much what you've done," I said to the old lady.

As we walked away from the church, we noticed the family leaving by a side entrance. The old lady was waving to us.

Two blocks from the church, we were picked up by Ed King's wife, Jeanette. She drove us to an Episcopal church. She had previously left the other two girls from our team there. She circled the block a couple of times, but we didn't see them anywhere. I suggested that we try the church. "Maybe they got in," I said. Mrs. King waited in the car for us. We walked up to the front of the church. There were no ushers to be seen. Apparently, services had already started. When we walked inside, we were greeted by two ushers who stood at the rear.

"May we help you?" one said.

"Yes," I said. "We would like to worship with you today."

"Will you sign the guest list, please, and we will show you to your seats," said the other.

I stood there for a good five minutes before I was able to compose myself. I had never prayed with white people in a white church before. We signed the guest list and were then escorted to two seats behind the other two girls in our team. We had all gotten in. The church service was completed without one incident. It was as normal as any church service. However, it was by no means normal to me. I was sitting there thinking any moment God would strike the life out of me. I recognized some of the whites, sitting around me in that church. If they were praying to the same God I was, then even God, I thought, was against me.

When the services were over the minister invited us to visit again. He said it as if he meant it, and I began to have a little hope.

Woolworth sit-in, May 28, 1963. White youths shower abuse and food on a Tougaloo College professor and students staging a sit-in at a segregated lunch counter in Jackson, Mississippi. After soda, ketchup, mustard, and sugar failed to deter them, the civil rights demonstrators were doused with spray paint and beaten.

# Rev. Edwin King

## Christianity in Mississippi

*Edwin King, a white native Mississippian, was chaplain of Tougaloo College and a leader in the civil rights movement in the state.*

### Mourners in Prison

After the funeral of Medgar Evers [a prominent civil rights leader murdered in Jackson, Mississippi, in 1963], over 5,000 black people from all parts of Mississippi walked behind his casket through the streets of Jackson in a protest funeral march. The last mourners in the long line began singing hymns and freedom songs in civil disobedience of the police order for silence. Soon there was confrontation between the young demonstrators and the nervous, confused, and angry white police. Officers beat, then arrested many mourners in the streets and even entered a Farish Street building and rushed to the second floor to strike and seize John Salter and myself. We were taken to the Fairgrounds prison.

John Salter and I began to understand what was happening on the Jackson streets as other prisoners were put into our police truck. Two more of them had bloody heads from police beatings. Finally, we were taken to the Fairgrounds prison. The ride was punctuated with deliberate stops and jerks by the driver which threw us around the vehicle for further battering. We were among the first adults in the new jail which had already held over five hundred students and children. (The children's stories were true; the children's nightmares were true.) It was like a concentration camp and the police, no doubt frightened and shaken by the near

*Source:* The first selection appeared in a slightly different form in *Mississippi Writers*, Vol II: *Nonfiction* (Jackson: University Press of Mississippi, 1987). A slightly different version of the final piece appeared in the United Methodist Church, *Journal of Commission on Religion and Race*, 1989. Mr. King supplied the manuscript material.

riot after the funeral of Medgar Evers, were now ready to punish, even torture, those of us in their hands.

We arrived at the compound and the back doors of the truck were opened. We could see the famous prison. We had passed through a series of gates and were now inside the wire enclosed area. An officer looked into the truck and asked if King and Salter were there. He then instructed the guard, "Close the doors, and let them sweat awhile." We trembled as we thought of Anne Moody's report earlier that week of the horrors of this sweat box, so like Nazi railway cars crammed with victims, when Jackson children had been so near suffocation some had passed out. John Salter had been held this way only two days earlier while still bleeding from the police assault on the demonstrators on Rose Street, and he too, had almost fainted that day. We were kept in this hot, closed truck about ten more minutes, taken out, and booked.

Soon we were sent to join a line of prisoners and forced to lean against a wall with our hands outstretched about our heads, braced against the wall at an almost straight angle. We had to stay in this position of terrible tension and severe pain for about twenty minutes. There were other prisoners present who had been there already more than half an hour. Whenever any one of us would groan or cry and begin to drop our arms or shift the position of our bodies, the armed guards would walk up, curse us, and sometimes poke people with their guns or clubs—an act almost as painful as being struck with force.

"Hey, you bastard," an officer would say, "what do you think this is? Straighten out your damn arms. Reach higher, higher on that wall." Although I wanted to scream and drop to the ground, to twist and curl my body to relieve the agony and pain of the position, I would respond to the order and stiffen my body again. I never saw any other prisoner dare to drop out of the position, although I didn't know how those who had been there longer could stand the pain without fainting. Since I was already bruised from being dragged down the stairs when captured, I felt the intended pain of this "magnolia torture" quickly. There was absolutely no reason for being forced to stand like this. We were inside the compound, surrounded by wire—and dogs—and heavily outnumbered by the police. And we, of course, had no weapons.

The man standing next to me, about four feet away, was a stranger, a white person. I wondered how someone I did not even recognize could be in this place and in his bloody condition. I whispered to him. He told me his name was Peter Nemene. He had come down from New York to be interviewed for a math teaching job at Tougaloo College and had stayed an extra day to attend the funeral. He had been badly beaten by the police. On the back of his head was an ugly patch of blood, almost black. His shirt collar showed bright red blood marks and the back of his coat had deep maroon stains. Flecks of bright, fresh blood oozed out of the head wound. Big horseflies were buzzing around, crawling on his bloody, sweaty coat. Some flies even crawled in his hair and in the wound on his scalp. The police had ordered me to keep face forward, towards the wall, but I had noticed this man's injuries when they brought me from the truck to stand next to him. I found what little courage I still had and slowly turned my head in his direction as we whispered, hoping the police would not notice. Soon I turned far enough so I could see clearly the filthy, bloody wound on his head. Then I saw the flies crawling in it. I was sick; I no longer cared about the police. I dropped my arms, pulled a handkerchief from my pocket, and stepped over to the wounded man. An officer shouted and ran up to us. "Hey, King, what the hell are you doing out of line?"

What I was doing was obvious, but I tried to reason with the officer. Although my clothes were torn, I still wore part of my clerical collar and looked like some sort of ragged priest. "I want to wipe off his wound, and chase the flies out of the blood, away from his head."

The policeman looked at me. He raised his rifle in the air, holding the butt end ready. "You nigger-loving son of a bitch. What the hell you think this is, a damn hospital? I know you ain't no damn doctor. Shit, you ain't no preacher either. You touch his head, and you get one just like it."

I hesitated. In the moment of silence a fly made a filthy buzzing noise. I moved one step closer towards the injured man. "My god," shouted the policeman, "You don't think I'll do it, do you? I'll beat the hell out of you. It's time somebody did!"

I stared at the rifle butt, and then at the man's eyes. I knew he wanted to kill me. I was afraid. Afraid, not so much of death, but just afraid of pain. I did not want the rifle butt crashing into my skull—and the blood, and the dirt, and the flies, those damned flies, but, mostly, the pain. My head had never stopped aching for the past hour since the police had bounced my head on the stairs, sidewalk, curbs and gutter when they had captured me and dragged me feet first. My whole body ached from stretching against the wall. Now this man was ready to club me, beat me, perhaps shoot me. I was afraid I could stand no more pain. . . .

Slowly, I turned away from the injured man. I would not bind up his wounds. I turned away from the sweat and the filth, from the flies and the blood. I turned towards the policeman. I saw only the danger to myself; I heard only the threat to me, to me . . . If the injured man at my side had screamed, I would not let myself hear. If the man was dying at my feet, I would not look down. There was no courage, no goodness, no decency left, only fear. I spoke to the policeman, "I understand you, sir. I know what you can do."

He lowered the gun, grabbed me by one arm, and jerked me away. He led me to the opposite end of the line of prisoners and forced me to resume the same position. I felt some shame about my own weakness but I had become so conscious of my own pain, my thoughts were so centered on my own body, that I was also quite aware that it had been helpful to walk that short distance and move my limbs. I would have stumbled and fallen to the ground several times had the policeman not held my arm; but it was a chance to move most of my bones and muscles. Now the pain was not as bad. I never once looked back at the bloody man with the flies.

But after a few minutes in the tense position again the pain returned. Making the pain even worse was the terrible thirst. The temperature was 103 degrees. The police never allowed the prisoners a taste of water. But the officers enjoyed making jokes about the heat; they made a point of stirring the ice in a water cooler nearby so vigorously that we could hear the splash of water and clink of ice. They talked to each other about how good the cool water was.

I lost track of time. Eventually, John Salter and I and a few others were ordered away from the wall, and told we were being taken out of the prison compound and up to the city jail. This time we were told to stand in a new position. We had to place our hands flat atop our head, elbows painfully extended to the sides. Again there was no reason for this except punishment. We waited like this perhaps ten minutes to be loaded into another truck for another battering ride to the city jail.

I looked at the policemen and I knew that if they did this work more than one day they could invent torture worthy of the Huns. And I knew these ordinary folk could administer death camps and ovens as easily as any Nazis in time if the Movement did not change things. I thought that if I was ever in an American death camp I might be so afraid, so broken down in spirit, that I might be a docile prisoner tool of the guards. I had always wondered why the prisoners of the Germans did not organize themselves and revolt. Now I knew. Any of us could be good Mississippians, good Germans, good Americans.

These were the thoughts I had part of the time as I stood in the line. Most of the thoughts just centered on my own pain. Sometimes I moved from thoughts of self and pain to intense hatred for the white guards.

"Hey, King. Rev. King," a voice whispered. I was startled because this was not the voice of either prisoner next to me. It was a policeman, a hated white policeman. I was afraid. Even the jokes about water now hurt. I did not want any more pain. I thought I might suddenly begin crying. I could not take anything else. I pretended I did not hear the voice.

The policeman, one of the guards standing on the outside of the wire enclosure, came closer to the fence and looked at me. Then he whispered again—and I understood the words. "I hope ya'll win," he said. "Some of us think the niggers oughta get a better break. We know things ain't right like it is in Miss'ssippi. Don't you give up now."

Before I could whisper a reply, had I dared, he was gone. Rifle on his shoulder, he marched on down the fence, looking like a proper concentration camp guard. A moment ago, I had wanted to kill all these Nazis. I hated every white policeman that existed. And now I couldn't even be sure whom to hate—or kill. This was just too much to think about. I was almost glad to shift my attention back to my physical pain. . . .

## Fall 1963, Mississippi Life: Church

The White Church was the guardian of the soul of the Closed Society. The White Church gave strength to the segregation system yet the white church was also the place where the white moderates might have had the best chance to stand and support change. The Church, in both white and Black communities, had more status and influence in Mississippi than any other state in the land. Here the failure of the white moderates is most clearly seen. In the fall of 1963 it became clear that there was almost no hope for support for moderate, gradual change towards an interracial society, towards justice, towards decency even in the white church. If there was no hope in the white church—then there was no hope in the society.

Many white ministers had left the state voluntarily to avoid "causing" trouble. Others who became too moderate in their sermons or conversations were advised to leave—and most did so quietly. Some (in every denomination, Jewish to Southern Baptist) refused to leave "graciously" and were removed from their pulpits by their congregations or church authorities and forced to leave the state. In January of 1963 a group of 28 young Methodist ministers signed a "Statement of Conscience" in the wake of conversations and examination after the Ole Miss riots. Within a few months over half of these had been forced to leave the state; most of the rest soon followed. Yet their statement had been one of great moderation but did question the sacredness of segregation.

On the Sunday before the murder of Medgar Evers in June, a group of Jackson blacks and Tougaloo students had attempted to attend the morning worship services at several Jackson white churches. Every church turned them away. (Several prominent white ministers tried to persuade their congregations to open the church doors. Persuasion failed and several ministers resigned or were forced to leave their pulpits.) These church visits had been attempted several times during the rest of the summer. On the Sunday night after the Birmingham Church bombing a group of Tougaloo Movement students thought that this would be a good time to worship at a "white" church; thinking that if white Christians were ever going to respond to their consciences and the teachings of their churches it would be at such an hour. Again the church doors were closed.

Two weeks later another attempt was made by an interracial group of three coeds from Tougaloo to attend the Sunday morning service at the Capitol Street Methodist Church on "World-Wide Communion Sunday," a time the Methodist Church stresses openness. The students were convinced that if black and white people in Mississippi were ever going to start talking to each other about the problems of the state, it could never start unless some white moderates made the beginning. The students assumed that these moderates might be reached at their churches—since there was no other way to communicate with them. The white moderates would never see mass demonstrations. Their press and TV distorted all black news. And there were no interracial meetings of any sort at which the hint of communication was possible. On this particular Sunday the students were followed to the church by a Jackson police car. At the church they were, once again, turned away as ushers blocked the door. But the students started conversations with the guards and other church members, asking why the Christian church was not open to all Christians, asking why Christians could not worship together, beginning to talk about why black people in Mississippi were now protesting so many things, always appealing to the religious teachings and conscience of the whites they faced. And on the steps of that closed church the closed society began to experience some honest interracial conversation and communication.

The students did not try to argue the whites into opening the church doors—but the students did ask many questions for which there were no easy answers. A Black coed and long-time Movement leader, Bette Poole, asked a white man a question right out of Mississippi Sunday School teachings, "But what would Jesus do?" And the poor man replied, "Leave Christ out of this. What does he have to do with it, . . ." and then his voice trailed off into mumbling as he realized what he was saying. But still he stood fast, blocking the doorway to the church of Christ. Before such communication could continue the white police moved in and stopped the conversation. Although the white church did not ask for police help, the officers arrested the three coeds, and jailed them.

There had never been any question of blacks forcing their way literally into a segregated white church. But their persistent presence and attitude were forcing their way into the white conscience. The police state responded by direct intervention into the business of the church. The local minister and the white Methodist church officials of the state always maintained that they had never asked for anyone to be arrested at their church. But they were too frightened of the state to condemn or even protest what the police had done and perhaps satisfied that the police had removed the troubling presence for them.

Bette Poole and the other two girls, Ida Hannah, black, and Julia Zaugg, white, were held in the jail without bond and then given a quick, secret trial early the next morning before we could get any vital legal help to them. They were convicted of "trespassing" and "disturbing public worship" and given a total fine of $1,000.00 and twelve months at hard labor on the county prison farm. This was the heaviest punishment given in Mississippi for any civil rights offense—and just stressed the importance of the closed church for the closed society. No white church officials from Mississippi even appeared to beg for a more lenient sentence.

But the national Methodist Church was informed of the affair. The Board of Missions and the Women's Division of the church sent the three thousand dollars of bond money needed to release the coeds so their cases might be appealed. Ministerial friends of mine in Chicago contacted me and offered to help. The church visits were resumed, with two northern ministers walking up to the doors of the same church with the same three coeds. This time all five were arrested. The matter of the police actually jailing blacks for just knocking on the doors of white churches became a topic of conversation and soul searching for white church people throughout the city and many parts of the state. This was a heavier price than most people expected to see paid for the preservation of their white churches. . . .

One extreme symbol of the police state that had been built in this Bible Belt country was the attitude of white police towards black churches. One late October morning the police marched into the Tougaloo College chapel building during the worship service. Two brown-shirted deputy sheriffs came up to the chapel doors and demanded to see President Beittel and me. The student ushers explained that the service had already begun and asked the police to wait and see us when the service ended, only about twenty more minutes. One usher invited the officers to be seated in a pew and worship with us. The men pushed open the church doors and noisily entered the sanctuary. I was reading a scripture lesson and could see the police in the back of the church. I then asked the congregation to bow their heads and began leading the morning prayers.

The officers obviously recognized me behind the pulpit—but they headed first for Dr. Beittel. He was also easily recognized because of his bright white hair and his seat in the very first pew. The church was silent except for my voice so the heavy steps of the police rushing down the aisle were heard by every one of the several hundred students and teachers present. The startled Dr. Beittel was brusquely handed a piece of paper by the police; then one of them began moving towards the pulpit, waving his paper, ignoring my prayer and loudly saying, "Hey, King, take this summons!" I ended the prayer as the policeman cast his document down on the open pulpit Bible. The paper slid off the Bible and down to the floor. The congregation was shocked and now beginning to buzz with whispers. I nodded to the organist and announced a hymn. The choir began to sing, the congregation stood and joined the hymn of faith as the storm troopers walked back down the central aisle. The officers left off the final touch—all they needed to do was click their heels, extend their arms, and shout "Seig, Heil!"

(The legal papers the police had brought were orders for the two of us to appear in county court that very day, immediately. We both ignored the summons because of the style in which it was delivered. For some reason we were not arrested. And, naturally, although our own students and sympathetic outside ministers were being arrested weekly and convicted of things like "disturbing worship" and "trespassing" on church property, neither of the storm troopers, the only ones who had literally disrupted a church service, was worried about arrest.)

The power and essence of what remained of the faith of the white Christians of Mississippi were manifest in the locked churches, the jailed blacks who attempted to worship there, and the contempt white police showed for black churches. In such a situation there is no place for the moderate. And within a few months, Mississippi became the church burning center of the world. Starting in the spring of 1964 black churches were bombed and burned at the rate of at least one church a week for over a full year. Thus did white Mississippi fight the powers of "atheistic communism" which was always seen by them as the true source of the Civil Rights Movement. . . .

## Testimony from Mt. Zion

In the all Black Longdale Community, far out in an isolated rural part of Neshoba, Dr. [Martin Luther] King commented at the ruined church, "I feel sorry for those who were hurt by this . . . I rejoice that there are churches relevant enough that people of ill will will be willing to burn them. This church was burned because it took a stand."

After prayers at the church site we went further down the dirt road to the home of Mr. and Mrs. Roosevelt "Bud" Cole. They told their story to Dr. King, just as they had told it a few weeks earlier to James Chaney, Andrew Goodman, and Mickey Schwerner, as told to other COFO workers, and, as told, in full detail, to FBI agents, several days before the three men had disappeared. The men had interviewed them then headed home—and disappeared. Mrs. Beatrice Cole did most of the talking. Bud Cole still suffered from injuries, including a broken jaw, received in the klan beating. This church was the only church in the county open to the Movement. Bishop Charles Golden a few months earlier had called for all Methodist churches to be open to the Civil Rights Movement— that is, the Black churches of the Central Jurisdiction of the Methodist Church. Mt. Zion accepted the Bishop's call and the call of the Movement and had agreed to host both a Freedom School and voter registration meetings and mass meetings. Chaney and Schwerner had visited there several times that spring and Mickey had made an impassioned appeal at the Sunday service at the end of May. Bud Cole was a church officer and Beatrice Cole was a voter registration worker. On June 16 after a routine Board of Stewards meeting ended around 9:00 p.m. a mob of white men had blocked all road exits from the church. Several men were terribly beaten and Bud Cole was beaten unconscious. Beatrice Cole told us the story. Dr. King and the rest of us listened to her words which sounded like Scripture:

> They (white men) stopped us not far from the church and one of the men had some words with my husband. There was at least 20 of them there. Then one of them pulled my husband out of the car and beat him, I couldn't see what with but it looked like an iron object. Then they kicked him while he was lying on the ground. Then they said to him, "Better say something or we'll kill you."
>
> I said, "He can't say nothing, he's unconscious." Then I began to pray ... I was praying very hard. I was just praying saying "Lord have mercy, Lord have mercy, don't let them kill my husband." And then I heard a voice sound like a woman scream down the road just a little piece below me and then a man walked up with a club and I was continue saying, "Lord have mercy," and he drew back to hit me and I asked this policeman that was standing by him would he allow me to pray and this one was on the right and one was on the left. The one on the right says if you think it will do you any good you had better pray. The one on the left says it is too late to pray ... They told me to shut my mouth. But I said, "Let me pray."
>
> I stretched out my hands. I fell on my knees and I began to pray, and as I prayed I just said, "Father I stretch my hands to Thee, I stretch my hands to Thee, no other help I know. If Thou withdraw Thyself from me, whither can I go?" That struck the hearts of those men. The Lord was there. Because then the man said, "Let her alone," and he looked kind of sick about it.

Mrs. Cole's husband had not regained consciousness during this. She then told of one of the white men raising the butt of his gun to hit her and another white man interjecting, "Don't touch her ... You might as well let them live." She was finally able to arouse her husband and the white men let them get in their car and leave. The white men stayed at the church. From her home down the road and out of sight of the church she looked back at a terrible sight, a red glow in the night sky, "a lot of light coming up from around the church." She did not dare leave her husband or return to the church. The next morning she did visit the still smoking ruins.

She also told us of two very important earlier visits:

Those three boys ... the same ones that are missing, came here on Sunday, June 21, ... They stayed about 20 minutes and left in the middle of the afternoon. The white boy with the beard I saw at that meeting at the church a couple of weeks ago when they talked about setting up a special school ... The FBI was here the Friday after the church burned down and asked us questions about it.

We had come to comfort her, to show that we stood with the local people. But this Christian woman, with her powerful testimony of faith, had brought comfort and strength to us. And we were blessed.

Beatrice Cole later told a friend, Florence Mars, that the words of her prayer were from an old Methodist hymn. "That song always have cherished me. The Devil was sponsoring that group but the Lord was there."

# Benjamin Van Clark

## Nonviolence in Savannah, Georgia

*Events in Savannah illustrate the difficulty of maintaining nonviolence.*

We could never have accomplished what we did without the SCLC. Without the help of SCLC staff members we could not have come this far in such a short space of time. Hosea Williams is in jail as I write and I know how he feels because I was there for fifteen long days myself with the roaches, the rats and chinches. The food is horrible; the mattresses, the sheets, everything is dirty. Everything is—how do I say this—well, there is an odor one usually associates with things not being very clean. So I know that Hosea is undergoing tremendous agony and pain simply because the jail house is not what some people think it is. The demonstrators are treated far worse than the criminals.

Now I want to describe the events that led to these jailings. Mr. Williams had appeared on a TV show on July 8, 1963. He was to explain the good points of our movement in order to try to win some of the white moderates over to our side. After the TV show that Wednesday, he moved into the area of public relations work for the movement, mainly the publishing of a newspaper called *The Crusader*. When I was released from jail, I discussed the movement with Mr. Williams. At two a.m. the Chatham County deputy sheriff walked into his house and arrested him on a "good behavior" warrant, in effect, a peace bond taken out by an individual fearful for his life. Under a "good behavior" bond, one can post bail of two hundred dollars and get out of jail. But that night the bond was set at $2500. *The warrant was taken out by a white woman who said she had seen Hosea Williams on TV and heard he was a leader of the movement and she was "afraid" of what the Negroes might do. She did not know Mr. Williams personally.*

---

*Source:* Benjamin Van Clark, "Siege at Savannah," *Freedomways,* 4 (Winter 1964).

*To our knowledge, the last time a "good behavior" warrant was used in Savannah was just before the Reconstruction period against some slaves. The law is over one hundred years old and entirely unknown in the community.*

We went down to bail Williams out; we had to see the solicitor-general but were told to come back the next day. When we went down the next day we found that the bond had been upped to $3,000. Each time we got the necessary bail, we found that it had been upped again. Eighteen days later the bail was $70,000. A writ of *habeas corpus* was set on the fourth day and denied by the judge on the eighth day. Reverend Wyatt T. Walker of the Southern Christian Leadership Conference had just arrived in town. We were asking for total desegregation of everything— jobs, movies, bowling alleys. Reverend Walker had come at our request. After speaking before 1,800 Negroes, Reverend Walker and the crowd started walking toward the City Hall. At City Hall, we called upon the mayor to arrest us. But Mayor McClain backed up and we left City Hall and went around to the county jail to see Williams and we were singing freedom songs and talking to him. One white fellow ran out of his house with a shotgun and the police got to him before he could get a good aim. They took the shotgun away from him and one of the girls in the crowd said that they had better unload the gun. When they did they found that the gun was unloaded.

We are a large minority in Savannah. Brutality is an every-day thing and when it happens it is usually so tragic that one cannot help but remember. If a Negro isn't killed, his head is beaten so that he might just as well be dead. I knew a young fellow about 23 years old, Artie James. One night a group decided to go down to a new restaurant that had been opened—the "Safari." Artie had some car trouble in front of the restaurant and when Artie went into the restaurant a policeman came up behind him and shot him. When he was shot, Artie threw up his hands and said, "Please don't kill me," and those were his last words. The Justice Department did send down a representative but we never heard any more about it.

I could cite many other cases of police brutality in recent months during our demonstrations. At first the police stood by, supposedly to protect the demonstrators. Then the white community, the White Citizens Council and the Ku Klux Klan elements, demanded that the Negro demonstrators be arrested. The police began to pick up Negro citizens and beat them on their heads with gun butts. One lady was hit in the stomach with a tear gas bomb.

All this was done to nonviolent demonstrators. Jail cells that normally held ten persons were jammed with seventy-five. Savannah outwardly presents a very beautiful picture but it is terror and nightmare.

The community's reaction to these events is a very mixed one with one element saying "be nonviolent" and the other saying "you will get nothing without violence." We tried to make them demonstrate nonviolently and we finally convinced them that nonviolence would get them what they wanted, and they agreed. Two weeks later a tear gas bomb was thrown into a crowd of 1500 demonstrators. This was the night Hosea Williams and I were arrested. On the march from the segregated hotel, another tear gas bomb was thrown at us. One business, worth three million dollars, was burned to the ground during the night. We have been blamed for the violence but everyone in Savannah knows that every act of violence has been perpetrated by the riot squad. *The riot squad is trained to use police dogs and riot guns and the dogs are trained to attack only Negroes.*

Police dogs attack a civil rights demonstrator in Birmingham, Alabama, 1963.

# Rev. Joseph Lowery

## The Persuasive Power of Nonviolence

*Joseph Lowery, an official of the Southern Christian Leadership Conference and present at many of the demonstrations of the era, here considers both the tactical effectiveness and the ethical rightness of nonviolence. Like other commentators on nonviolence, he also speaks of the difficulty of practicing it.*

LOWERY: . . . Most of us were preachers and as disciples of Jesus Christ we were committed to the ethic, you know, the love ethic. . . . Jesus himself was non-violent. He rebuked Peter for reaching for the sword and using the sword. He practiced passive resistance, if you want to call it that. And he engaged in non-violent resistance to evil. And so it was rather easy for ministers to apply this to the civil rights movement. Plus the fact that Martin was a student at Gandhi and Gandhi of course had been very successful and very effective in the use of non-violence in his struggle against the British Empire. And so it grew to be an acceptable technique. . . . [I]t became very effective, too, in Montgomery. It was so successful in the boycott that even those who might have questioned it philosophically or theologically could hardly question it technically. . . . It involved 50,000 black people in a year long campaign unprecedented in this nation or in the world for that matter I assume. . . . It exposed the cruelty that was inherent in a system [of] segregation. And it compelled the courts to rule, finally, a lawsuit. . . . The significant thing, it had become a means of pulling together 50,000 people over here to walk and protest. And nobody could question that. So that even those that had trouble with it as I said from a philosophic point of view could hardly question it.

WRIGHT: What was your view on it?

*Source:* Transcript of the Rev. Joseph Lowery, oral history interview, Moorland-Spingarn Research Center, Howard University. Interview on October 19, 1970; interviewer Robert Wright.

**149**

LOWERY: Well as I said as a preacher I had no problem with it because the Christian has always been challenged to use weapons that were more spiritual than physical. And it was a very practical thing as far as I was concerned. . . .

. . . So it was a wise tactic and had a power in the field of moral persuasion because the Christian ethic is the prevalent ethic in America theoretically anyway. . . .

I've been really frightened three times in the civil rights movement. I guess the first one was when we tested the buses in Mobile, which was my first test of non-violence. I had been in non-violent clinics, I had even led a couple. But I hadn't really been tested. And so when we got ready to ride the buses that morning the tough place we would be is Pritchard. It's a community called Pritchard, still is. There's no tougher community in Alabama than Pritchard unless it's Bessemer. Pritchard is right on the edge of Mobile like Bessemer's on the edge of Birmingham. And they said, "Well you ride the Pritchard bus." I said, "Okay." I got in, Sam McCree and I rode the Pritchard bus, a Baptist preacher. And we were doing fine until we almost got to the end of the line. Some guy got on half drunk, a white guy. He had his bottle with him. And he didn't see us for a while. And then finally he noticed we were sitting on the front seat. . . . And he looked at the bus driver and he got up and said something to the bus driver. And we heard the bus driver say he didn't have anything to do with it. What he was telling the bus driver was to make the niggers get back. So the bus driver wouldn't do anything so he tells us, he says, "You niggers get back." So Mac says, "Now you handle it because I'm not sure I can be non-violent." So I said nothing. So he said _____ again. So we ignored him three times. Finally he came to us. I said, "Wait a minute." I said, "Now you sit down. In the first place you're drinking and you're not at yourself. In the second place the bus driver's in charge of the bus. Sit down." So he sat down. And didn't realize that he had sat down at the orders of a nigger. So he got up with the bottle handle in his hand and came toward us. And I really—you know, that was my test. And I had within a flash, I guess, to decide whether, . . . if he swung the handle to duck, grab it, grab his arm, or hit him before he could swing it. And I decided again to use initiative. And I said to him in a very stern and loud voice, "Wait, you are not the sponsor of this bus. Sit down." I said, "Driver, make this man sit down." And the driver hollered at him, "Sit down." And he sat down and that was the end of that. Now I don't know what I would have done if the guy had hit me with the bottle. But I was afraid.

The second time was in Selma that we went back across that bridge. . . .

. . . Anyway we decided to march. And we left the church, I don't know, I guess they had all their game wardens, all their dog catchers, everything they could find from all over the state they had lined up on both sides of the street from the time we left the church all the way up to the bridge. And as soon as the march would pass them they would close in behind us. . . . And that really frightened me because I didn't want to fall in that river. That was a really frightening experience, a very frightening experience. Of course we made it through.

And I guess the other time was, well I wasn't frightened. A guy threw some tea on me once in a restaurant in Birmingham, but I didn't frighten. And again I passed the test of non-violence. He was a little old man.

But I guess the other time was a truck. . . . See, we knelt down and sat on the ground in front of garbage trucks out here. Right after I came to Atlanta. I came in June of '68 and this must have been in July or August of '68. And we weren't sure the trucks were going to stop. And I remember a guy got killed in Cleveland you know, on a construction job. But they drove right up to us and stopped. I was trying to get in the middle. They fellows thought I was brave but I wasn't. The wheels were on the end you see. And if they hadn't stopped somebody in the middle might not have gotten hit. But it stopped and put us in arrest. But there have been many frightening moments.

# Robert S. Browne

## The Civil Rights Movement and Vietnam

*Robert S. Browne, a Vietnamese-speaking black American,
published in 1965 the article from which these passages
come. The essay is an early indication of the fusion between the civil rights movement and resistance to the war.
Browne assumed that the component of nonviolence in the
rights movement would lend itself to the quest for peace.
Later, a portion of the forces in opposition to the war
would turn to a vocabulary of violence.*

The Vietnam war is gradually replacing civil rights as the top
story of the mid-sixties, and because the protest against the United
States policy in Vietnam has been primarily made on moral
grounds, as was the demand for civil rights, there has been an inevitable coincidence of the two movements on various levels. This
has been particularly noticeable on the organizational circuit,
where many of the groups which have been most vocal in their
support of civil rights are the same ones which are most outspoken
against the worst aspects of United States involvement in Vietnam. Especially prone to this double involvement have been the
northern-based student movements, the pacifist organizations,
and the more militant religious institutions. Inevitably, this dual-
ity of interests led to growing pressure upon the major civil rights
organizations to extend their scope sufficiently to encompass a
position on the vital Vietnam question. Martin Luther King, as a
Nobel Peace Prize winner and world symbol of non-violent resolution of conflicts, was particularly urged to take a public position on
Vietnam. As the personification of America's moral conscience, his
endorsement was viewed as especially significant for the moral
protest against United States atrocities in Vietnam.

*Source:* Robert S. Browne, "The Freedom Movement and the War in Vietnam,"
*Freedomways,* 5 (Autumn 1965).

These pressures introduced a new and potentially revolutionary dimension into the civil rights movement, and perhaps into Negro thinking generally. Traditionally, the American Negro has been single-minded to a fault insofar as his social consciousness was concerned. He has bestirred himself solely about problems directly involving his welfare *as a Negro*. Issues involving him only as a citizen, but not as an ethnic group, were of little interest to him; and certainly foreign policy, one of the most sophisticated of public affairs, was generally beyond his sphere of interest. No wonder then that the effort to involve the civil rights movement in the Vietnam crisis met strong resistance. Roy Wilkins, the leader of the National Association for the Advancement of Colored People, adopted the curious position that foreign policy was not a proper sphere for public analysis and criticism. On the other hand, James Farmer of the Congress of Racial Equality was willing to offer his critical judgment of the Administration's foreign policy, but insisted on doing it as an individual, vigorously opposing his organization's taking a public stand on Vietnam. The Southern Christian Leadership Conference and the Student Non-Violent Coordinating Committee have openly supported efforts to seek a peaceful solution to America's involvement in the Vietnam conflict and perhaps the most durable tie between the civil rights and the peace movements is the growing tendency for the peace movement to adopt the non-violent techniques perfected by the latter two organizations. Following publication of a moving "open letter to Martin Luther King" from the Vietnamese Buddhists, a letter in which he was urged not to remain silent in this moment of great "suffering caused by this unnecessary war," Dr. King publicly added his great prestige to the burgeoning nationwide moral condemnation of the ungodly American activities in Vietnam. . . .

. . . [T]here are strong arguments favoring a civil rights alliance with the Vietnam protest, or with the peace movement generally. These . . . fall under four headings:

(1) the recognition that the civil rights movement represents the moral conscience of America and therefore naturally belongs in the vanguard of the Vietnam protest, felt now to be the number one moral issue confronting American society.

(2) the argument that the billions of dollars being diverted to the Vietnam war represent funds which might otherwise be available for giving substance to the programs necessary for raising the Negro to a level of real equality in American life.

(3) the belief that the civil rights objectives are unachievable under the present organization of American society and therefore

must necessarily be fought for as part of a larger effort to remake American society, including its foreign policy.

(4) the view that the Vietnam war is intimately involved in American racist attitudes generally, and therefore falls naturally within the range of American Negroes' direct sphere of interest.

That the civil rights movement has reinvigorated and restored a strain of morality to an increasingly purposeless and alienated American society is generally conceded, and it is also probably safe to predict that as the American public becomes aware of the true nature of its government's role and activities in Vietnam, the Vietnam involvement may well become the leading moral issue in America. . . .

The argument that funds spent in Vietnam can be used for constructive projects at home is indisputable. The only matter for question here is whether the funds would, in fact, be used for the poverty program if they were not being used in Vietnam. Our Congress is notoriously more generous in voting funds for military purposes than for programs of social welfare.

The viewpoint that achievement of full civil rights for the Negro requires ultimately a thorough going revision in American society has a variety of rationalizations. . . .

It is not primarily the dollar which is sending 125,000 American troops to Vietnam: it is fear of a strong, independent China, and although the basis of this fear may be partly in the ultimate economic threat which a revitalized China portends, one suspects that America's racist obsession—in this case, with the "yellow peril"—plays the significant role in the anti-Chinese hysteria.

We are thus brought to the final consideration: whether or not there is a racist aspect to the Vietnam war, and if so what implications this has for American Negroes. . . .

To see innocent, uprooted American youths being incited to maim and murder women and children in Vietnam last summer was indescribably depressing to me, but to see American Negroes forced to engage in such atrocities absolutely enraged me. I was further appalled by what seemed to be a disproportionately large number of Negro faces among the United States troops and I could only wonder if this were the Pentagon's way of attempting to deflect the accusations of whites killing non-whites—and at the same time a way of driving a wedge between American Negroes and the colored people of Asia. . . .

Whether or not the time has come to utilize Negro power in this way promises to become a major topic of controversy. When I first read of the Mississippi statement urging Negroes not to fight in Vietnam I greeted it as a worthy first step toward bringing the beleaguered Vietnamese people the peace and self-determination which they so desperately want. A moment's reflection, however, caused me to realize that the implications of the proposed military service boycott were much broader in scope than a simple moral objection to the wanton murder which we are committing in Vietnam. Although such a boycott, if it caught hold amongst both whites and Negroes, might well offer some relief to the Vietnamese peoples, it holds equally the potential for creating of America a true force for peace at this critical moment for human survival. It could become the first step in promoting a genuine human community surpassing the narrow boundaries of the nation-state, which is basically a European concept in any case. By the same token, however, so drastic a step poses a severe risk to the entire Negro struggle to win acceptance into the "Great Society" of President Johnson and obviously should not be taken without sober thought.

James Baldwin has bemoaned the fact that the Negro is working so hard to gain acceptance into a society which is basically sick and in decline, an observation with which many will agree. But certainly our glorious struggle is for something greater, something more substantial than merely to win for Negroes an opportunity to imitate their white compatriots—to immerse themselves in a color television or to kill themselves in an overpowered automobile. Hopefully, our vision of a better world relies as much on the spiritual values as on the material ones. Is it not conceivable, then, that the Negro people, who understand the white man's hypocrisy better than any one else and who are already applying an enema to the rot which has for so long contaminated America's domestic social organization, may spark an international purification as well?

Whether we are indeed ready to undertake this ambitious task or not, there should be no disagreement regarding the urgency of ensuring that, as non-whites, we are not being inadvertently manipulated into an untenable position within the global framework. We must amass all of our wits so as to steer a careful course between the Scylla of American racism and the Charybdis of foreign intrigue. We intend to be tools of neither. Rather, Afro-Americans can perform no greater service to their country and to humanity than to use their unique position to encourage international racial amity and to prevent international racial conflict. They can do mankind no greater disservice than to allow themselves to be used as tools in precipitating such a catastrophe.

A VISTA volunteer, one of thousands of recruits in the War on Poverty, talks to a child in Alabama.

# Part 4

# LIBERALS

*We have in mind here those figures, most of them white, who supported the civil rights movement and even in some cases faced a political backlash, but stood to some degree outside or at the borders of the movement. The category includes major political figures, notably Presidents Kennedy and Johnson. The liberals were ambivalently related to the movement. Conservative elements in Congress and throughout the electorate thought the liberals to be the major sources—the major villains, they might insist—of civil rights advocacy, pressing legislative and administrative measures of integration on an unwilling white population and disrupting longstanding social arrangements. Daily participants in the rights movement itself, particularly the voter registration workers who faced constant danger in Mississippi, grew to dislike liberals even more, if that is possible, than did the conservatives. By the mid-sixties rights activists were viewing liberals in general as merely flirting with civil rights out of a self-stroking desire to do good. And they decided that liberal politicians were manipulators willing to curry African American support but not at risk of alienating large numbers of white racists.*

*Understanding how liberals won the anger of white supremacists and social conservatives is easy enough. Why the left and the rights activists came to scorn them is partly a matter of the liberal temperament. Liberals like orderly procedures; they prefer discussion to confrontation; they distrust display of emotions. This mentality made liberals admirable enemies of white racism with its primitive passions. But it also made them uncomfortable with the black and white insurgents of the Mississippi Freedom Democratic Party, these shock troops of the rights movement who, having braved the police and the thugs of Mississippi, came to the Democratic Convention in 1964 demanding seats in the state's delegation. Liberals could not anticipate the anger, the conviction of having been betrayed, that pos-*

*sessed the Freedom Democrats on discovering that in the interests of party harmony the liberals were smoothly maneuvering them into a corner of the Convention. By the late 1960s, moreover, the civil rights movement had largely joined the opposition to the American involvement in Vietnam, an involvement that continued the policies of cold-war liberals from the time of President Truman into that of President Johnson. Any rapprochement between establishment liberalism and the left wing of the rights movement was now impossible.*

*It was, of course, from the point of view of the civil rights activists that the liberals seemed cautious and obstructionist. Within American politics in general, liberals were at the forefront of the struggle for equal rights, joined by some conservatives at crucial moments. They ended up as bedraggled survivors of the 1960s, resented by white racists for championing integration, by affluent taxpayers for putting money into social programs, and by radicals for pursuing the war in Vietnam. Liberalism is still attempting to rediscover its core of beliefs.*

*Included in the selections here are illustrative major liberal pronouncements, along with commentaries by James Baldwin and Jerome Smith, each of whom without rejecting liberalism argued for going beyond its spiritual limits.*

In Edwards, Mississippi, a young black man urges his elder to register to vote.

# Harry S Truman

## Equality in the Armed Services

*The armed forces, by nature socially conservative, had maintained segregation and in general assigned black servicemen subordinate positions. President Truman, from the border state of Missouri and himself conservative in racial issues, was nonetheless close enough to the liberal wing of his Democratic party to issue on July 26, 1948, an executive order commanding equality in the military.*

WHEREAS it is essential that there be maintained in the armed services of the United States the highest standards of democracy, with equality of treatment and opportunity for all those who serve in our country's defense:

NOW, THEREFORE, by virtue of the authority vested in me as President of the United States, by the Constitution and the statutes of the United States, and as Commander in Chief of the armed services, it is hereby ordered as follows:

1. It is hereby declared to be the policy of the President that there shall be equality of treatment and opportunity for all persons in the armed services without regard to race, color, religion or national origin. This policy shall be put into effect as rapidly as possible, having due regard to the time required to effectuate any necessary changes without impairing efficiency or morale.

2. There shall be created in the National Military Establishment an advisory committee to be known as the President's Committee on Equality of Treatment and Opportunity in the Armed Services, which shall be composed of seven members to be designated by the President.

3. The Committee is authorized on behalf of the President to examine into the rules, procedures and practices of the armed ser-

*Source: Blacks in the United States Armed Forces: Basic Documents,* edited by Morris J. MacGregor and Bernard C. Nalty, Vol. 8, *Segregation Under Siege* (Wilmington, Delaware: Scholarly Resources, 1977).

vices in order to determine in what respect such rules, procedures and practices may be altered or improved with a view to carrying out the policy of this order. The Committee shall confer and advise with the Secretary of Defense, the Secretary of the Army, the Secretary of the Navy, and the Secretary of the Air Force, and shall make such recommendations to the President and to said Secretaries as in the judgment of the Committee will effectuate the policy hereof.

4. All executive departments and agencies of the Federal Government are authorized and directed to cooperate with the Committee in its work, and to furnish the Committee such information or the services of such persons as the Committee may require in the performance of its duties.

5. When requested by the Committee to do so, persons in the armed services or in any of the executive departments and agencies of the Federal Government shall testify before the Committee and shall make available for the use of the Committee such documents and other information as the Committee may require.

6. The Committee shall continue to exist until such time as the President shall terminate its existence by Executive order.

# Robert S. McNamara

## Pressing for Equality

*The question of how liberal was the administration of Democratic President John F. Kennedy is still debated. While defenders of segregation saw him as an enemy, civil rights workers were disappointed with what they perceived to be hesitancy on the part of the administration to support and protect rights activities in the South. But the administration made a number of significant decisions. This memorandum of July 24, 1963, to Kennedy, sent by Secretary of Defense Robert S. McNamara, reflects one of them.*

MEMORANDUM FOR THE PRESIDENT:

On June 21 you sent me a copy of the initial report of your Committee on Equal Opportunity in the Armed Forces and asked that I review the document and report on the recommendations within thirty days. This memorandum responds to that request.

In its year of work the Committee observed racial imbalances and vestiges of racial discrimination within the Armed Forces themselves. Nevertheless, the Committee found that in the main, racial equality is a reality on military bases today. The Department of Defense will eliminate the exceptions and guard the continuing reality.

It is to the Department's off-base responsibilities that the Committee has devoted the bulk of its report. In eloquent terms the Committee has described the nature and pervasiveness of off-base discrimination against Negro servicemen and their families, the divisive and demoralizing impact of that discrimination, and the general absence of affirmative, effective action to ameliorate or end the off-base practices affecting nearly a quarter of a million of our servicemen.

Source: *Blacks in the United States Armed Forces: Basic Documents*, edited by Morris J. MacGregor and Bernard C. Nalty, Vol. 13, *Equal Treatment and Opportunity: The McNamara Doctrine* (Wilmington, Delaware: Scholarly Resources, 1977).

Our military effectiveness is unquestionably reduced as a result of civilian racial discrimination against men in uniform. The Committee report has made this point with great clarity. With equal clarity it demonstrates that the Department of Defense has in the past only imperfectly recognized the harm flowing from off-base discrimination. That imperfect recognition has in turn meant the lack of a program to correct the conditions giving rise to the harm.

The Committee report contained recommendations for such a program. Consistently therewith I have issued a directive explicitly stating Department of Defense policy with respect to off-base discrimination and requiring:

—preparation of detailed directives, manuals and regulations making clear the leadership responsibility both on and off-base and containing guidance as to how that responsibility is to be discharged.

—institution in each service of a system for regularly monitoring and measuring progress in this field.

We are in the process of establishing a staff element within my office to give full time to such matters.

While the foregoing is in accord with the recommendations of the Committee, the details of the program necessarily will be found in the manuals and regulations to be issued as a result of my directive.

The initial Committee report contained many specific recommendations on recruitment, assignment, promotion, techniques for eliminating on and off-base discrimination, housing, education and recording of racial data. Many of these have been or will be put into effect, but some require more study and on a few we have reservations. These will be discussed further with the Committee.

The recommendations on sanctions do require special comment. The Committee suggests using a form of the off-limits sanction when, despite the commander's best efforts with community leaders, relentless discrimination persists against Negro servicemen and their families.

Certainly the damage to military effectiveness from off-base discrimination is not less than that caused by off-base vice, as to which the off-limits sanction is quite customary. While I would hope that it need never be put in effect, I agree with the Committee that a like sanction against discrimination must be available. It should be applied, however, only with the prior approval of the Secretary of the Military Department concerned.

The Committee also suggested the possibility of closing bases near communities where discrimination is particularly prevalent. I do not regard this as a feasible action at this time.

In your letter transmitting the Committee report you wrote that "Discriminatory practices are morally wrong wherever they occur—they are especially inequitable and iniquitous when they inconvenience and embarrass those serving in the Armed Services and their families."

Guided by those words and the report of your Committee on Equal Opportunity in the Armed Forces, the military Departments will take a leadership role in combatting discrimination wherever it affects the military effectiveness of the men and women serving in defense of this country.

# John F. Kennedy

## Facing the Issues

*These passages from President Kennedy's radio and tele-
vision address of June 11, 1963, at a time of massive and
massively opposed demonstrations in Birmingham, defined a new direction for the government in racial policy.*

[T]his Nation, for all its hopes and all its boasts, will not be
fully free until all its citizens are free.

We preach freedom around the world, and we mean it, and
we cherish our freedom here at home, but are we to say to the
world, and much more importantly, to each other that this is the
land of the free except for the Negroes; that we have no second-
class citizens except Negroes; that we have no class or cast[e] system, no ghettoes, no master race except with respect to Negroes?

Now the time has come for this Nation to fulfill its promise.
The events in Birmingham and elsewhere have so increased the
cries for equality that no city or State or legislative body can pru-
dently choose to ignore them.

The fires of frustration and discord are burning in every city,
North and South, where legal remedies are not at hand. Redress
is sought in the streets, in demonstrations, parades, and protests
which create tensions and threaten violence and threaten lives.

We face, therefore, a moral crisis as a country and as a people.
It cannot be met by repressive police action. It cannot be left to
increased demonstrations in the streets. It cannot be quieted by
token moves or talk. It is time to act in the Congress, in your State
and local legislative body and, above all, in all of our daily lives.

It is not enough to pin the blame on others, to say this is a
problem of one section of the country or another, or deplore the

*Source:* Radio and Television Report to the American People on Civil Rights, June
11, 1963. U.S. President, *Public Papers of the Presidents of the United States* (Washington, D.C.: United States Government Printing Office, 1964), John F. Kennedy,
1963, pp. 468–71.

fact that we face. A great change is at hand, and our task, our obligation, is to make that revolution, that change, peaceful and constructive for all.

Those who do nothing are inviting shame as well as violence. Those who act boldly are recognizing right as well as reality.

Next week I shall ask the Congress of the United States to act, to make a commitment it has not fully made in this century to the proposition that race has no place in American life or law. The Federal judiciary has upheld that proposition in a series of forthright cases. The executive branch has adopted that proposition in the conduct of its affairs, including the employment of Federal personnel, the use of Federal facilities, and the sale of federally financed housing.

But there are other necessary measures which only the Congress can provide, and they must be provided at this session. The old code of equity law under which we live commands for every wrong a remedy, but in too many communities, in too many parts of the country, wrongs are inflicted on Negro citizens and there are no remedies at law. Unless the Congress acts, their only remedy is the street.

I am, therefore, asking the Congress to enact legislation giving all Americans the right to be served in facilities which are open to the public—hotels, restaurants, theaters, retail stores, and similar establishments.

This seems to me to be an elementary right. Its denial is an arbitrary indignity that no American in 1963 should have to endure, but many do.

I have recently met with scores of business leaders urging them to take voluntary action to end this discrimination and I have been encouraged by their response, and in the last 2 weeks over 75 cities have seen progress made in desegregating these kinds of facilities. But many are unwilling to act alone, and for this reason, nationwide legislation is needed if we are to move this problem from the streets to the courts.

I am also asking Congress to authorize the Federal Government to participate more fully in lawsuits designed to end segregation in public education. We have succeeded in persuading many districts to desegregate voluntarily. Dozens have admitted Negroes without violence.

# James Baldwin

## An Impassioned Criticism

*In 1963 the black novelist and essayist James Baldwin published a book-length essay,* The Fire Next Time. *Without rejecting the liberal integrationist faith, Baldwin demanded a moral regeneration, and more especially a radical self-scrutiny on the part of whites, that would go beyond the normal limits of liberal reformism. In the opening passage here, he is addressing his nephew.*

This innocent country set you down in a ghetto in which, in fact, it intended that you should perish. Let me spell out precisely what I mean by that, for the heart of the matter is here, and the root of my dispute with my country. You were born where you were born and faced the future that you faced because you were black and *for no other reason*. The limits of your ambition were, thus, expected to be set forever. You were born into a society which spelled out with brutal clarity, and in as many ways as possible, that you were a worthless human being. You were not expected to aspire to excellence: you were expected to make peace with mediocrity. Wherever you have turned, James, in your short time on this earth, you have been told where you could go and what you could do (and *how* you could do it) and where you could live and whom you could marry. I know your countrymen do not agree with me about this, and I hear them saying, "You exaggerate." They do not know Harlem, and I do. So do you. Take no one's word for anything, including mine—but trust your experience. Know whence you came. If you know whence you came, there is really no limit to where you can go. The details and symbols of your life have been deliberately constructed to make you believe what white people say about you. Please try to remember that what they believe, as well as what they do and cause you to endure, does not

*Source:* James Baldwin, *The Fire Next Time* (New York: The Dial Press, 1963).

testify to your inferiority but to their inhumanity and fear. Please try to be clear, dear James, through the storm which rages about your youthful head today, about the reality which lies behind the words *acceptance* and *integration*. There is no reason for you to try to become like white people and there is no basis whatever for their impertinent assumption that *they* must accept *you*. The really terrible thing, old buddy, is that *you* must accept *them*. And I mean that very seriously. You must accept them and accept them with love. For these innocent people have no other hope. They are, in effect, still trapped in a history which they do not understand; and until they understand it, they cannot be released from it. They have had to believe for many years, and for innumerable reasons, that black men are inferior to white men. Many of them, indeed, know better, but, as you will discover, people find it very difficult to act on what they know. To act is to be committed, and to be committed is to be in danger. In this case, the danger, in the minds of most white Americans, is the loss of their identity. Try to imagine how you would feel if you woke up one morning to find the sun shining and all the stars aflame. You would be frightened because it is out of the order of nature. Any upheaval in the universe is terrifying because it so profoundly attacks one's sense of one's own reality. Well, the black man has functioned in the white man's world as a fixed star, as an immovable pillar: and as he moves out of his place, heaven and earth are shaken to their foundations. You, don't be afraid. I said that it was intended that you should perish in the ghetto, perish by never being allowed to go behind the white man's definitions, by never being allowed to spell your proper name. You have, and many of us have, defeated this intention; and, by a terrible law, a terrible paradox, those innocents who believed that your imprisonment made them safe are losing their grasp of reality. But these men are your brothers—your lost, younger brothers. And if the word *integration* means anything, this is what it means: that we, with love, shall force our brothers to see themselves as they are, to cease fleeing from reality and begin to change it. For this is your home, my friend, do not be driven from it; great men have done great things here, and will again, and we can make America what America must become. It will be hard, James, but you come from sturdy, peasant stock, men who picked cotton and dammed rivers and built railroads, and, in the teeth of the most terrifying odds, achieved an unassailable and monumental dignity. You come from a long line of great poets, some of the greatest poets since Homer. One of them said, *The very time I thought I was lost, My dungeon shook and my chains fell off.*

You know, and I know, that the country is celebrating one hundred years of freedom one hundred years too soon. We cannot be free until they are free. God bless you, James, and Godspeed.

Your uncle,
James. . . .

When we were told to love everybody, I had thought that that meant *everybody*. But no. It applied only to those who believed as we did, and it did not apply to white people at all. I was told by a minister, for example, that I should never, on any public convey-ance, under any circumstances, rise and give my seat to a white woman. White men never rose for Negro women. Well, that was true enough, in the main—I saw his point. But what was the point, the purpose, of *my* salvation if it did not permit me to behave with love toward others, no matter how they behaved toward me? What others did was their responsibility, for which they would answer when the judgment trumpet sounded. But what *I* did was *my* re-sponsibility, and I would have to answer, too—unless, of course, there was also in Heaven a special dispensation for the benighted black, who was not to be judged in the same way as other human beings, or angels. It probably occurred to me around this time that the vision people hold of the world to come is but a reflection, with predictable wishful distortions, of the world in which they live. And this did not apply only to Negroes, who were no more "simple" or "spontaneous" or "Christian" than anybody else— who were merely more oppressed. In the same way that we, for white people, were the descendants of Ham, and were cursed for-ever, white people were, for us, the descendants of Cain. And the passion with which we loved the Lord was a measure of how deeply we feared and distrusted and, in the end, hated almost all strangers, always, and avoided and despised ourselves. . . .

I cannot accept the proposition that the four-hundred-year travail of the American Negro should result merely in his attain-ment of the present level of the American civilization. I am far from convinced that being released from the African witch doctor was worthwhile if I am now—in order to support the moral con-tradictions and the spiritual aridity of my life—expected to become dependent on the American psychiatrist. It is a bargain I refuse. The only thing white people have that black people need, or should want, is power—and no one holds power forever. White people cannot, in the generality, be taken as models of how to live. Rather, the white man is himself in sore need of new standards, which will release him from his confusion and place him once again in fruitful communion with the depths of his own being. And I repeat: The price of the liberation of the white people is the liberation of the blacks—the total liberation, in the cities, in the towns, before the law, and in the mind. Why, for example—especially knowing the family as I do—I should *want* to marry your sister is a great mystery to me. But your sister and I have every right to marry if we wish to, and no one has the right to stop us. If she cannot raise me to her level, perhaps I can raise her to mine.

In short, we, the black and the white, deeply need each other here if we are really to become a nation—if we are really, that is, to achieve our identity, our maturity, as men and women.... If we—and now I mean the relatively conscious whites and the relatively conscious blacks, who must, like lovers, insist on, or create, the consciousness of the others—do not falter in our duty now, we may be able, handful that we are, to end the racial nightmare, and achieve our country, and change the history of the world. If we do not now dare everything, the fulfillment of that prophecy, recreated from the Bible in song by a slave, is upon us: *God gave Noah the rainbow sign, No more water, the fire next time!*

# Norman Podhoretz

## Memories of a White Childhood

*In these portions of Podhoretz's essay of 1963, a white
intellectual reflects on the conflicting feelings toward race
that went back to his childhood.*

Two ideas puzzled me deeply as a child growing up in Brooklyn during the 1930's in what today would be called an integrated
neighborhood. One of them was that all Jews were rich; the other
was that all Negroes were persecuted. These ideas had appeared
in print; therefore they must be true. My own experience and the
evidence of my senses told me they were not true, but that only
confirmed what a day-dreaming boy in the provinces—for the
lower-class neighborhoods of New York belong as surely to the
provinces as any rural town in North Dakota—discovers very
early: *his* experience is unreal and the evidence of his senses is not
to be trusted. Yet even a boy with a head full of fantasies incon-
gruously synthesized out of Hollywood movies and English novels cannot altogether deny the reality of his own experience—
especially when there is so much deprivation in that experience.
Nor can he altogether gainsay the evidence of his own senses—
especially such evidence of the senses as comes from being repeatedly beaten up, robbed, and in general hated, terrorized, and
humiliated.

And so for a long time I was puzzled to think that Jews were
supposed to be rich when the only Jews I knew were poor, and that
Negroes were supposed to be persecuted when it was the Negroes
who were doing the only persecuting I knew about—and doing it,
moreover, to *me*. During the early years of the war, when my older
sister joined a left-wing youth organization, I remember my aston-
ishment at hearing her passionately denounce my father for think-

*Source:* Norman Podhoretz, *Doings and Undoings* (New York: Farrar, Straus and
Giroux, 1963).

ing that Jews were worse off than Negroes. To me, at the age of twelve, it seemed very clear that Negroes were better off than Jews—indeed, than *all* whites. A city boy's world is contained within three or four square blocks, and in my world it was the whites, the Italians and Jews, who feared the Negroes, not the other way around. The Negroes were tougher than we were, more ruthless, and on the whole they were better athletes. What could it mean, then, to say that they were badly off and that we were more fortunate? Yet my sister's opinions, like print, were sacred, and when she told me about exploitation and economic forces I believed her. I believed her, but I was still afraid of Negroes. And I still hated them with all my heart. . . .

What kind of feelings do I have about Negroes today? What happened to me, from Brooklyn, who grew up fearing and envying and hating Negroes? Now that Brooklyn is behind me, do I fear them and envy them and hate them still? The answer is yes, but not in the same proportions and certainly not in the same way. I now live on the upper west side of Manhattan, where there are many Negroes and many Puerto Ricans, and there are nights when I experience the old apprehensiveness again, and there are streets that I avoid when I am walking in the dark, as there were streets that I avoided when I was a child. I find that I am not afraid of Puerto Ricans, but I cannot restrain my nervousness whenever I pass a group of Negroes standing in front of a bar or sauntering down the street. I know now, as I did not know when I was a child, that power is on my side, that the police are working for me and not for them. And knowing this I feel ashamed and guilty, like the good liberal I have grown up to be. Yet the twinges of fear and the resentment they bring and the self-contempt they arouse are not to be gainsaid.

But envy? Why envy? And hatred? Why hatred? Here again the intensities have lessened and everything has been complicated and qualified by the guilts and the resulting over-compensations that are the heritage of the enlightened middle-class world of which I am now a member. Yet just as in childhood I envied Negroes for what seemed to me their superior masculinity, so I envy them today for what seems to me their superior physical grace and beauty. I have come to value physical grace very highly, and I am now capable of aching with all my being when I watch a Negro couple on the dance floor, or a Negro playing baseball or basketball. They are on the kind of terms with their own bodies that I should like to be on with mine, and for that precious quality they seem blessed to me. . . .

The Black Muslims, like their racist counterparts in the white world, accuse the "so-called Negro leaders" of secretly pursuing miscegenation as a goal. The racists are wrong, but I wish they were right, for I believe that the whole-sale merging of the two races is the most desirable alternative for everyone concerned. I am not claiming that this alternative can be pursued programmatically or that it is immediately feasible as a solution; obviously there are even greater barriers to its achievement than to the achievement of integration. What I am saying, however, is that in my opinion the Negro problem can be solved in this country in no other way.

I have told the story of my own twisted feelings about Negroes here, and of how they conflict with the moral convictions I have since developed, in order to assert that such feelings must be acknowledged as honestly as possible so that they can be controlled and ultimately disregarded in favor of the convictions. It is *wrong* for a man to suffer because of the color of his skin. Beside that clichéd proposition of liberal thought, what argument can stand and be respected? If the arguments are the arguments of feeling, they must be made to yield; and one's own soul is not the worst place to begin working a huge social transformation. Not so long ago, it used to be asked of white liberals, "Would you like your sister to marry one?" When I was a boy and my sister was still unmarried, I would certainly have said no to that question. But now I am a man, my sister is already married, and I have daughters. If I were to be asked today whether I would like a daughter of mine "to marry one," I would have to answer: "No, I wouldn't *like* it at all. I would rail and rave and rant and tear my hair. And then I hope I would have the courage to curse myself for raving and ranting, and to give her my blessing. How dare I withhold it at the behest of the child I once was and against the man I now have a duty to be?"

# Lyndon B. Johnson

## The Right to Vote

*This President from the state of Texas, which has an identity embracing both South and West, got through Congress the civil rights bill that President Kennedy had proposed. Johnson also put through the national legislature the voting rights measure described in an address to a joint session of Congress on March 15, 1965, which includes these passages.*

Many of the issues of civil rights are very complex and most difficult. But about this there can and should be no argument. Every American citizen must have an equal right to vote. There is no reason which can excuse the denial of that right. There is no duty which weighs more heavily on us than the duty we have to insure that right.

Yet the harsh fact is that in many places in this country men and women are kept from voting simply because they are Negroes.

Every device of which human ingenuity is capable has been used to deny this right. The Negro citizen may go to register only to be told that the day is wrong, or the hour is late, or the official in charge is absent. And if he persists, and if he manages to present himself to the registrar, he may be disqualified because he did not spell out his middle name or because he abbreviated a word on the application.

And if he manages to fill out an application he is given a test. The registrar is the sole judge of whether he passes this test. He may be asked to recite the entire Constitution, or explain the most complex provisions of State law. And even a college degree cannot be used to prove that he can read and write.

*Source:* Special Message to the Congress: The American Promise, March 15, 1965. U.S. President, *Public Papers of the Presidents of the United States* (Washington, D.C.: United States Government Printing Office, 1966), Lyndon B. Johnson, 1965, pp. 281–87.

For the fact is that the only way to pass these barriers is to show a white skin.

Experience has clearly shown that the existing process of law cannot overcome systematic and ingenious discrimination. No law that we now have on the books—and I have helped to put three of them there—can insure the right to vote when local officials are determined to deny it.

In such a case, our duty must be clear to all of us. The Constitution says that no person shall be kept from voting because of his race or his color. We have all sworn an oath before God to support and to defend that Constitution. We must now act in obedience to that oath.

Wednesday I will send to Congress a law designed to eliminate illegal barriers to the right to vote.

The broad principles of that bill will be in the hands of the Democratic and Republican leaders tomorrow. After they have reviewed it, it will come here formally as a bill. I am grateful for this opportunity to come here tonight at the invitation of the leadership to reason with my friends, to give them my views, and to visit with my former colleagues.

I have had prepared a more comprehensive analysis of the legislation which I had intended to transmit to the clerk tomorrow but which I will submit to the clerks tonight. But I want to really discuss with you now briefly the main proposals of this legislation.

This bill will strike down restrictions to voting in all elections—Federal, State, and local—which have been used to deny Negroes the right to vote.

This bill will establish a simple, uniform standard which cannot be used, however ingenious the effort, to flout our Constitution.

It will provide for citizens to be registered by officials of the United States Government if the State officials refuse to register them. . . .

But even if we pass this bill, the battle will not be over. What happened in Selma is part of a far larger movement which reaches into every section and State of America. It is the effort of American Negroes to secure for themselves the full blessings of American life.

Their cause must be our cause too. Because it is not just Negroes, but really it is all of us, who must overcome the crippling legacy of bigotry and injustice.

And we shall overcome.

As a man whose roots go deeply into Southern soil I know how agonizing racial feelings are. I know how difficult it is to reshape the attitudes and the structure of our society.

But a century has passed, more than a hundred years, since the Negro was freed. And he is not fully free tonight.

It was more than a hundred years ago that Abraham Lincoln, a great President of another party, signed the Emancipation Proclamation, but emancipation is a proclamation and not a fact.

A century has passed, more than a hundred years, since equality was promised. And yet the Negro is not equal.

A century has passed since the day of promise. And the promise is unkept.

The time of justice has now come. I tell you that I believe sincerely that no force can hold it back. It is right in the eyes of man and God that it should come. And when it does, I think that day will brighten the lives of every American.

For Negroes are not the only victims. How many white children have gone uneducated, how many white families have lived in stark poverty, how many white lives have been scarred by fear, because we have wasted our energy and our substance to maintain the barriers of hatred and terror?

So I say to all of you here, and to all in the Nation tonight, that those who appeal to you to hold on to the past do so at the cost of denying you your future.

This great, rich, restless country can offer opportunity and education and hope to all: black and white, North and South, sharecropper and city dweller. These are the enemies: poverty, ignorance, disease. They are the enemies, not our fellow man, not our neighbor. And these enemies, too, poverty, disease and ignorance, we shall overcome.

Now let none of us in any sections look with prideful righteousness on the troubles in another section, or on the problems of our neighbors. There is really no part of America where the promise of equality has been fully kept. In Buffalo as well as in Birmingham, in Philadelphia as well as in Selma, Americans are struggling for the fruits of freedom.

This is one Nation. What happens in Selma or in Cincinnati is a matter of legitimate concern to every American. But let each of us look within our own hearts and our own communities, and let each of us put our shoulder to the wheel to root out injustice wherever it exists.

# Summary of the Report of the National Advisory Commission on Civil Disorders, 1968

*The report from which these materials are taken, often known as the Kerner Commission Report after Governor Otto Kerner, Illinois, who was chair of the Commission, gives a grim appraisal of the state of race relations in 1968. Its findings were highly influential in subsequent national discussions of racial questions. It is an illustration of the kind of fact-finding to which liberals have often trusted.*

The "typical" riot did not take place. The disorders of 1967 were unusual, irregular, complex and unpredictable social processes. Like most human events, they did not unfold in an orderly sequence. However, an analysis of our survey information leads to some conclusions about the riot process.

In general:

The civil disorders of 1967 involved Negroes acting against local symbols of white American society, authority and property in Negro neighborhoods—rather than against white persons.

Of 164 disorders reported during the first nine months of 1967, eight (5 percent) were major in terms of violence and damage; 33 (20 percent) were serious but not major; 123 (75 percent) were minor and undoubtedly would not have received national attention as "riots" had the nation not been sensitized by the more serious outbreaks.

In the 75 disorders studied by a Senate subcommittee, 83 deaths were reported. Eighty-two percent of the deaths and more than half the injuries occurred in Newark and Detroit. About 10 percent of the dead and 38 percent of the injured were public employees, primarily law officers and firemen. The overwhelming majority of the persons killed or injured in all the disorders were Negro civilians.

Initial damage estimates were greatly exaggerated. In Detroit, newspaper damage estimates at first ranged from $200 million to $500 million; the highest recent estimate is $45 million. In Newark, early estimates ranged from $15 to $25 million. A month later damage was estimated at $10.2 million, over 80 percent in inventory losses.

## In the 24 disorders in 23 cities which we surveyed:

The final incident before the outbreak of disorder, and the initial violence itself, generally took place in the evening or at night at a place in which it was normal for many people to be on the streets.

Violence usually occurred almost immediately following the occurrence of the final precipitating incident, and then escalated rapidly. With but few exceptions, violence subsided during the day, and flared rapidly again at night. The night-day cycles continued through the early period of the major disorders.

Disorder generally began with rock and bottle throwing and window breaking. Once store windows were broken, looting usually followed.

Disorder did not erupt as a result of a single "triggering" or "precipitating" incident. Instead, it was generated out of an increasingly disturbed social atmosphere, in which typically a series of tension-heightening incidents over a period of weeks or months became linked in the minds of many in the Negro community with a reservoir of underlying grievances. At some point in the mounting tension, a further incident—in itself often routine or trivial—became the breaking point and the tension spilled over into violence.

"Prior" incidents, which increased tensions and ultimately led to violence, were police actions in almost half the cases; police actions were "final" incidents before the outbreak of violence in 12 of the 24 surveyed disorders.

No particular control tactic was successful in every situation. The varied effectiveness of control techniques emphasizes the need for advance training, planning, adequate intelligence systems, and knowledge of the ghetto community.

Negotiations between Negroes—including young militants as well as older Negro leaders—and white officials concerning "terms of peace" occurred during virtually all the disorders surveyed. In many cases, these negotiations involved discussion of underlying grievances as well as the handling of the disorder by control authorities.

The typical rioter was a teenager or young adult, a life-long resident of the city in which he rioted, a high school dropout; he was, nevertheless, somewhat better educated than his nonrioting Negro neighbor, and was usually underemployed or employed in a menial job. He was proud of his race, extremely hostile to both whites and middle-class Negroes and, although informed about politics, highly distrustful of the political system.

A Detroit survey revealed that approximately 11 percent of the total residents of two riot areas admitted participation in the rioting, 20 to 25 percent identified themselves as "bystanders," over 16 percent identified themselves as "counter-rioters" who urged rioters to "cool it," and the remaining 48 to 53 percent said they were at home or elsewhere and did not participate. In a survey of Negro males between the ages of 15 and 35 residing in the disturbance area in Newark, about 45 percent identified themselves as rioters, and about 55 percent as "noninvolved."

Most rioters were young Negro males. Nearly 53 percent of arrestees were between 15 and 24 years of age; nearly 81 percent between 15 and 35.

In Detroit and Newark about 74 percent of the rioters were brought up in the North. In contrast, of the noninvolved, 36 percent in Detroit and 52 percent in Newark were brought up in the North.

What the rioters appeared to be seeking was fuller participation in the social order and the material benefits enjoyed by the majority of American citizens. Rather than rejecting the American system, they were anxious to obtain a place for themselves in it.

Numerous Negro counter-rioters walked the streets urging rioters to "cool it." The typical counter-rioter was better educated and had higher income than either the rioter or the noninvolved.

The proportion of Negroes in local government was substantially smaller than the Negro proportion of population. Only three of the 20 cities studied had more than one Negro legislator; none had ever had a Negro mayor or city manager. In only four cities did Negroes hold other important policy-making positions or serve as heads of municipal departments.

Although almost all cities had some sort of formal grievance mechanism for handling citizen complaints, this typically was regarded by Negroes as ineffective and was generally ignored.

Although specific grievances varied from city to city, at least 12 deeply held grievances can be identified and ranked into three levels of relative intensity:

*First Level of Intensity*

1. Police practices
2. Unemployment and underemployment
3. Inadequate housing

*Second Level of Intensity*

4. Inadequate education
5. Poor recreation facilities and programs
6. Ineffectiveness of the political structure and grievance mechanisms

*Third Level of Intensity*

7. Disrespectful white attitudes
8. Discriminatory administration of justice
9. Inadequacy of federal programs
10. Inadequacy of municipal services
11. Discriminatory consumer and credit practices
12. Inadequate welfare programs

The results of a three-city survey of various federal programs—manpower, education, housing, welfare and community action—indicate that, despite substantial expenditures,
the number of persons assisted constituted only a fraction of
those in need.

The background of disorder is often as complex and difficult
to analyze as the disorder itself. But we find that certain general
conclusions can be drawn:

Social and economic conditions in the riot cities constituted a clear pattern of severe disadvantage for Negroes compared with whites, whether the Negroes lived in the area
where the riot took place or outside it. Negroes had completed
fewer years of education and fewer had attended high school.
Negroes were twice as likely to be unemployed and three times
as likely to be in unskilled and service jobs. Negroes averaged
70 percent of the income earned by whites and were more than
twice as likely to be living in poverty. Although housing cost
Negroes relatively more, they had worse housing—three times
as likely to be overcrowded and substandard. When compared
to white suburbs, the relative disadvantage is even more pro-
nounced.

A study of the aftermath of disorder leads to disturbing conclusions. We find that, despite the institution of some post-riot
programs:

Little basic change in the conditions underlying the outbreak of disorder has taken place. Actions to ameliorate Negro
grievances have been limited and sporadic; with but few exceptions, they have not significantly reduced tensions.
In several cities, the principal official response has been
to train and equip the police with more sophisticated weapons.
In several cities, increasing polarization is evident, with
continuing breakdown of inter-racial communication, and
growth of white segregationist or black separatist groups. . . .

One of the first witnesses to be invited to appear before this
Commission was Dr. Kenneth B. Clark, a distinguished and per-

ceptive scholar. Referring to the reports of earlier riot commissions, he said:

> I read that report . . . of the 1919 riot in Chicago, and it is as if I were reading the report of the investigating committee on the Harlem riot of '35, the report of the investigating committee on the Harlem riot of '43, the report of the McCone Commission on the Watts riot.
> I must again in candor say to you members of this Commission—it is a kind of Alice in Wonderland—with the same moving picture re-shown over and over again, the same analysis, the same recommendations, and the same inaction.

These words come to our minds as we conclude this report.

We have provided an honest beginning. We have learned much. But we have uncovered no startling truths, no unique insights, no simple solutions. The destruction and the bitterness of racial disorder, the harsh polemics of black revolt and white repression have been seen and heard before in this country.

It is time now to end the destruction and the violence, not only in the streets of the ghetto but in the lives of people.

# Jerome Smith

## Beyond Reform

*This portion of an article of 1964 by Jerome Smith, field secretary for the Congress of Racial Equality in Louisiana, like Baldwin's writing calls for a spiritual and mental re-making of American society that reaches beyond conventional reform.*

I, Jerome Smith, want to be free, but I want a freedom that is much greater than the type of freedom that I can get from the White House; because if I accept the freedom that is going to be given to me from the White House I will not do anything that will save my country. In effect, I must want something that is better than what is being offered. I can't "integrate" into the situation as is, and I can't integrate into quicksand. I must use myself if the country is going to be saved. The black people in America must use themselves to save the country, and the only way they can do that is not to integrate into the country *as it is*. We must make this country recognize the fact that *people are more important than dollars*. This must be the real important thing in the country, because if the country does not recognize that people are more important than dollars (which has nothing to do with my being *black* but has to do with the fact that I am a human being), the country will ultimately be destroyed; and it is dying now, with the activities in Panama, South America, Vietnam and other parts of the world, saying "Amen." These are signs to watch, and it has a lot to do with the country's placing more value on *dollars* than value it has for *people*. We must make the country recognize this. The fact that I can eat at some lunch counter with some white fellow, is not *really* bringing any great change for the country *or* for me. We need some great changes in this country. We need changes in depth, and to get the country to do this we must stand on the outside and say

*Source:* Jerome Smith, "Louisiana Story," *Freedomways*, 4 (Spring 1964).

that "these changes must be made." This is the only way America can become America. The America of today, as defined, is not the America we live in. If the words in the Constitution mean anything they mean that I must love my next door neighbor and that I must love or have real concern for some poor fellow who has no shoes on in other parts of the world; in Cuba or Panama, or Africa, and must be willing to tell the truth about my country's relationship with other countries.

# Part 5

# POWER

*In one way or another, every strand of civil rights policy and thinking relates to the question of power: how to resist it, how to get it, how to discover and cultivate it as a condition of mind and character, how to distinguish legitimate from illegitimate power. But the appearance of the black power movement in its many phases late in the sixties has given the issue a definiteness and centrality that it might not otherwise have achieved.*

*Power as people commonly understand it lodges especially in political and economic conditions. The Mississippi voter-registration project aimed directly at achieving the power of the vote. But beyond that, the project workers sought to awaken in individual black Mississippians an awareness of their own potential power, and of the empowerment that comes of action in concert with others. The pursuit of economic power, either through the integrationist goal of winning entrance into the white economy or through the creation of separate black communal institutions, also had that objective of transforming minds and spirits. Booker T. Washington, despised by radicals, had himself possessed a sense of the relationship between learning a skill and acquiring a sense of independence and power.*

*The question of power is so pervasively present that selecting materials for special inclusion in this category had to be arbitrary. Our choices were determined by how explicitly a particular statement addresses itself to the issue. Advocates of black power are therefore prominently included here, but a reader should notice the varieties of thinking among them. The Black Panthers, as an illustration, might seem from their revolutionary rhetoric the most militantly self-isolating of African American groups. Yet the Panthers, while insisting that the black population has its distinct role in the remaking of society, looked beyond black separatism to an essentially traditional left vision of a future in which power has been transferred into the hands of the dispossessed of all races.*

Union rights and civil rights. Malcolm X and trade union leader A. Philip Randolph share a platform during a 1962 rally celebrating a successful hospital workers' strike.

# Elijah Muhammad

## The Nation of Islam

*Elijah Muhammad's sect, popularly known as the Black
Muslims and identifying itself with the Moslem faith, has
had a complex set of beliefs including the conviction that
the white race is the degenerate offspring of black people
in ancient times. Elijah Muhammad, born Elijah Poole,
assumed control of the Nation of Islam in 1934. Based primarily in northern cities, the organization, which enjoyed
its greatest strength in the 1960s, had a membership vari-
ously estimated from 50,000 to 250,000. Elijah Muhammad
sought power for his followers through faith, a rigorous
personal discipline, a close community bonding among believers, and in time a separate nation.*

## What Do the Muslims Want?

This is the question asked most frequently by both the whites
and the blacks. The answers to this question I shall state as simply
as possible.

1. We want freedom. We want a full and complete freedom.
2. We want justice. Equal justice under the law. We want justice applied equally to all regardless of creed, class or color.
3. We want equality of opportunity. We want equal membership in society with the best in civilized society.
4. We want our people in America whose parents or grand-
parents were descendants from slaves to be allowed to establish a
separate state or territory of their own—either on this continent or
elsewhere. We believe that our former slave-masters are obligated
to provide such land and that our area must be fertile and miner-
ally rich. We believe that our former slave-masters are obligated to
maintain and supply our needs in this separate territory for the

*Source:* Elijah Muhammad, *Message to the Blackman in America* (Chicago: Muhammad Mosque of Islam No. 2, 1965).

next 20 or 25 years until we are able to produce and supply our own needs.

Since we cannot get along with them in peace and equality after giving them 400 years of our sweat and blood and receiving in return some of the worst treatment human beings have ever experienced, we believe our contributions to this land and the suffering forced upon us by white America justifies our demand for complete separation in a state or territory of our own.

5. We want freedom for all Believers of Islam now held in federal prisons. We want freedom for all black men and women now under death sentence in innumerable prisons in the North as well as the South.

We want every black man and woman to have the freedom to accept or reject being separated from the slave-masters' children and establish a land of their own.

We know that the above plan for the solution of the black and white conflict is the best and only answer to the problem between two people.

6. We want an immediate end to the police brutality and mob attacks against the so-called Negro throughout the United States.

We believe that the Federal government should intercede to see that black men and women tried in white courts receive justice in accordance with the laws of the land, or allow us to build a new nation for ourselves, dedicated to justice, freedom and liberty.

7. As long as we are not allowed to establish a state or territory of our own, we demand not only equal justice under the laws of the United States but equal employment opportunities—NOW!

We do not believe that after 400 years of free or nearly free labor, sweat and blood, which has helped America become rich and powerful, so many thousands of black people should have to subsist on relief or charity or live in poor houses.

8. We want the government of the United States to exempt our people from ALL taxation as long as we are deprived of equal justice under the laws of the land.

9. We want equal education—but separate schools up to 16 for boys and 18 for girls on the conditions that the girls be sent to women's colleges and universities. We want all black children educated, taught and trained by their own teacher.

Under such school system we believe we will make a better nation of people. The United States government should provide free all necessary text books and equipment, schools and college buildings. The Muslim teachers shall be left free to teach and train their people in the ways of righteousness, decency and self respect.

10. We believe that <u>intermarriage or race mixing</u> should be prohibited. We want the religion of Islam taught without hindrance or suppression.

These are some of the things that we, the Muslims, want for our people in North America.

1. We believe in the One God Whose proper name is Allah.

2. We believe in the Holy Qur-an and in the Scriptures of all the Prophets of God.

3. We believe in the truth of the Bible, but we believe that it has been tampered with and must be reinterpreted so that mankind will not be snared by the falsehoods that have been added to it.

4. We believe in Allah's Prophets and the Scriptures they brought to the people.

5. We believe in the resurrection of the dead—not in physical resurrection but mental resurrection. We believe that the so-called Negroes are most in need of mental resurrection; therefore, they will be resurrected first.

Furthermore, we believe we are the <u>people of God's</u> choice as it has been written that God would <u>choose the rejected and the despised. We can find no other persons fitting this description</u> in these last days more than the so-called Negroes in America. We believe in the resurrection of the righteous.

6. We further believe in the judgment. We believe this first judgment will take place, as God revealed, in America.

7. We believe this is the time in history for the separation of the so-called Negroes and the so-called white Americans. We believe the black man should be freed in name as well as in fact. By this we mean that he should be freed from names imposed upon him by his former slave-masters. Names which identified him as being the slave of a slave-master. We believe that if we are free indeed, we should go in our own people's names—the black peoples of the earth.

8. We believe in justice for all whether in God or not. We believe as others that we are due equal justice as human beings. We believe in equality—as a nation—of equals. We do not believe that we are equal with our slave-masters in the status of "Freed slaves."

We recognize and respect American citizens as independent peoples, and we respect their laws which govern this nation.

9. We believe that the offer of integration is hypocritical and is made by those who are trying to deceive the black peoples into believing that their 400-year-old open enemies of freedom, justice and equality are, all of a sudden, their "friends." Furthermore, we

believe that such deception is intended to prevent black people from realizing that the time in history has arrived for the separation from the whites of this nation.

If the white people are truthful about their professed friendship toward the so-called Negro, they can prove it by dividing up America with their slaves.

We do not believe that America will ever be able to furnish enough jobs for her own millions of unemployed in addition to jobs for the 20,000,000 black people.

10. We believe that we who declared ourselves to be righteous Muslims should not participate in wars which take the lives of humans. We do not believe this nation should force us to take part in such wars, for we have nothing to gain from it unless America agrees to give us the necessary territory wherein we may have something to fight for.

11. We believe our women should be respected and protected as the women of other nationalities are respected and protected.

12. We believe that Allah (God) appeared in the Person of Master W. Fard Muhammad, July, 1930—the long awaited "Messiah" of the Christians and the "Mahdi" of the Muslims.

We believe further and lastly that Allah is God and besides HIM there is no God and He will bring about a universal government of peace wherein we can live in peace together.

**Malcolm X.** Rejecting the nonviolent, integrationist civil rights movement, militant black nationalist Malcolm X for a time urged African Americans to get their freedom "by any means necessary."

# Malcolm X
## (El Hajj Malik El Shabazz)

### A Nationalist Alternative to Elijah Muhammad

*Converted in prison to the teachings of Elijah Muhammad, Malcolm X (raised Malcolm Little) was for years a major spokesman for the sect. After a rupture with the leader, he planned for a practical social and economic organization of black people. A journey to Mecca revealed to him that the Moslem faith reaches to all races, and he turned from his earlier repudiation of all association with whites. He still advocated separate organizations for black people, and to that end he founded the Organization of Afro-American Unity. On February 21, 1965, he was murdered.*

I'll tell you something. The whole stream of Western philosophy has now wound up in a cul-de-sac. The white man has perpetrated upon himself, as well as upon the black man, so gigantic a fraud that he has put himself into a crack. He did it through his elaborate, neurotic necessity to hide the black man's true role in history.

And today the white man is faced head on with what is happening on the Black Continent, Africa. Look at the artifacts being discovered there, that are proving over and over again, how the black man had great, fine, sensitive civilizations before the white man was out of the caves. Below the Sahara, in the places where most of America's Negroes' foreparents were kidnapped, there is being unearthed some of the finest craftsmanship, sculpture and other objects, that has ever been seen by modern man. Some of these things now are on view in such places as New York City's Museum of Modern Art. Gold work of such fine tolerance and workmanship that it has no rival. Ancient objects produced by black

*Source:* Malcolm X, *The Autobiography of Malcolm X*, with the assistance of Alex Haley; introduction by M. S. Handler; epilogue by Alex Haley (1964, 1965; New York: Ballantine Books, 1973). Reprinted by permission.

hands . . . refined by those black hands with results that no human hand today can equal.

History has been so "whitened" by the white man that even the black professors have known little more than the most ignorant black man about the talents and rich civilizations and cultures of the black man of millenniums ago. I have lectured in Negro colleges and some of these brain-washed black Ph.D.'s, with their suspenders dragging the ground with degrees, have run to the white man's newspapers calling me a "black fanatic." Why, a lot of them are fifty years behind the times. If I were president of one of these black colleges, I'd hock the campus if I had to, to send a bunch of black students off digging in Africa for more, more and more proof of the black race's historical greatness. The white man now is in Africa digging and searching. An African elephant can't stumble without falling on some white man with a shovel. Practically every week, we read about some great new find from Africa's lost civilizations. All that's new is white science's attitude. The ancient civilizations of the black man have been buried on the Black Continent all the time. . . .

It was a big order—the organization I was creating in my mind, one which would help to challenge the American black man to gain his human rights, and to cure his mental, spiritual, economic, and political sicknesses. But if you ever intend to do anything worthwhile, you have to start with a worthwhile plan.

Substantially, as I saw it, the organization I hoped to build would differ from the Nation of Islam in that it would embrace all faiths of black men, and it would carry into practice what the Nation of Islam had only preached.

Rumors were swirling, particularly in East Coast cities—what was I going to do? Well, the first thing I was going to have to do was to attract far more willing heads and hands than my own. Each day, more militant, action brothers who had been with me in Mosque Seven announced their break from the Nation of Islam to come with me. And each day, I learned, in one or another way, of more support from non-Muslim Negroes, including a surprising lot of the "middle" and "upper class" black bourgeoisie, who were sick of the status-symbol charade. There was a growing clamor: "When are you going to call a meeting, to get organized?"

To hold a first meeting, I arranged to rent the Carver Ballroom of the Hotel Theresa, which is at the corner of 125th Street and Seventh Avenue, which might be called one of Harlem's fusebox locations.

The *Amsterdam News* reported the planned meeting and many readers inferred that we were establishing our beginning mosque in the Theresa. Telegrams and letters and telephone calls came to the hotel for me, from across the country. Their general tone was that this was a move that people had waited for. People I'd never heard of expressed confidence in me in moving ways. Numerous people said that the Nation of Islam's stringent moral restrictions had repelled them—and they wanted to join me.

A doctor who owned a small hospital telephoned long-distance to join. Many others sent contributions—even before our policies had been publicly stated. Muslims wrote from other cities that they would join me, their remarks being generally along the lines that "Islam is too inactive" ... "The Nation is moving too slow."

Astonishing numbers of white people called, and wrote, offering contributions, or asking could *they* join? The answer was, no, they couldn't join; our membership was all black—but if their consciences dictated, they could financially help our constructive approach to America's race problems.

Speaking-engagement requests came in—twenty-two of them in one particular Monday morning's mail. It was startling to me that an unusual number of the requests came from groups of white Christian ministers.

I called a press conference. The microphones stuck up before me. The flashbulbs popped. The reporters, men and women, white and black, representing media that reached around the world, sat looking at me with their pencils and open notebooks.

I made the announcement: "I am going to organize and head a new mosque in New York City known as the Muslim Mosque, Inc. This will give us a religious base, and the spiritual force necessary to rid our people of the vices that destroy the moral fiber of our community.

"Muslim Mosque, Inc. will have its temporary headquarters in the Hotel Theresa in Harlem. It will be the working base for an action program designed to eliminate the political oppression, the economic exploitation, and the social degradation suffered daily by twenty-two million Afro-Americans." ...

The *color-blindness* of the Muslim world's religious society and the *color-blindness* of the Muslim world's human society, these two influences had each day been making a greater impact, and an increasing persuasion against my previous way of thinking. ...

I kept having all kinds of troubles trying to develop the kind of Black Nationalist organization I wanted to build for the American Negro. Why Black Nationalism? Well, in the competitive American society, how can there ever be any white-black solidarity before there is first some black solidarity? If you will remember, in my childhood I had been exposed to the Black Nationalist teachings of Marcus Garvey—which, in fact, I had been told had led to my father's murder. Even when I was a follower of Elijah Muhammad I had been strongly aware of how the Black Nationalist political, economic and social philosophies had the ability to instill within black men the racial dignity, the incentive, and the confidence that the black race needs today to get up off its knees, and to get on its feet, and get rid of its scars, and to take a stand for itself.

One of the major troubles that I was having in building the organization that I wanted—an all-black organization whose ultimate objective was to help create a society in which there could exist honest white-black brotherhood—was that my earlier public image, my old so-called "Black Muslim" image, kept blocking me. I was trying to gradually reshape that image. I was trying to turn a corner, into a new regard by the public, especially Negroes; I was no less angry than I had been, but at the same time the true brotherhood I had seen in the Holy World had influenced me to recognize that anger can blind human vision.

Every free moment I could find, I did a lot of talking to key people whom I knew around Harlem, and I made a lot of speeches, saying: "True Islam taught me that it takes *all* of the religious, political, economic, psychological, and racial ingredients, or characteristics, to make the Human Family and the Human Society complete.

"Since I learned the *truth* in Mecca, my dearest friends have come to include *all* kinds—some Christians, Jews, Buddhists, Hindus, agnostics, and even atheists! I have friends who are called capitalists, Socialists, and Communists! Some of my friends are moderates, conservatives, extremists—some are even Uncle Toms! My friends today are black, brown, red, yellow, and *white!*"

I said to Harlem street audiences that only when mankind would submit to the One God who created all—only then would mankind even approach the "peace" of which so much *talk* could be heard . . . but toward which so little *action* was seen.

I said that on the American racial level, we had to approach the black man's struggle against the white man's racism as a human problem, that we had to forget hypocritical politics and propaganda. I said that both races, as human beings, had the obligation, the responsibility, of helping to correct America's human problem. The well-meaning white people, I said, had to combat, actively and directly, the racism in other white people. And the black people had to build within themselves much greater awareness that along with equal rights there had to be the bearing of equal responsibilities.

I knew, better than most Negroes, how many white people truly wanted to see American racial problems solved. I knew that many whites were as frustrated as Negroes. I'll bet I got fifty letters some days from white people. The white people in meeting audiences would throng around me, asking me, after I had addressed them somewhere, "What *can* a sincere white person do?"

When I say that here now, it makes me think about that little co-ed I told you about, the one who flew from her New England college down to New York and came up to me in the Nation of Islam's restaurant in Harlem, and I told her that there was "nothing" she could do. I regret that I told her that. I wish that now I knew her name, or where I could telephone her, or write to her, and tell her what I tell white people now when they present themselves as being sincere, and ask me, one way or another, the same thing that she asked.

The first thing I tell them is that at least where my own particular Black Nationalist organization, the Organization of Afro-American Unity, is concerned, they can't *join* us. I have these very deep feelings that white people who want to join black organizations are really just taking the escapist way to salve their consciences. By visibly hovering near us, they are "proving" that they are "with us." But the hard truth is this *isn't* helping to solve America's racist problem. The Negroes aren't the racists. Where the really sincere white people have got to do their "proving" of themselves is not among the black *victims*, but out on the battle lines of where America's racism really *is*—and that's in their own home communities; America's racism is among their own fellow whites. That's where the sincere whites who really mean to accomplish something have got to work.

\*      \*      \*

... [D]espite their differences, [the African leaders] were able to sit down and form what was known as the Organization of African Unity, which has formed a coalition and is working in conjunction with each other to fight a common enemy.

Once we saw what they were able to do, we determined to try and do the same thing here in America among Afro-Americans who have been divided by our enemies. So we have formed an organization known as the Organization of Afro-American Unity which

*Source:* Malcolm X at the founding rally of the Organization of Afro-American Unity, in *By Any Means Necessary: Speeches, Interviews and a Letter by Malcolm X,* edited by George Breitman (A Merit Book; New York: Pathfinder Press, 1970). The speech was delivered in New York City on June 28, 1964.

has the same aim and objective—to fight whoever gets in our way, to bring about the complete independence of people of African descent here in the Western Hemisphere, and first here in the United States, and bring about the freedom of these people by any means necessary.

That's our motto. We want freedom by any means necessary. We want justice by any means necessary. We want equality by any means necessary. We don't feel that in 1964, living in a country that is supposedly based upon freedom, and supposedly the leader of the free world, we don't think that we should have to sit around and wait for some segregationist congressmen and senators and a President from Texas in Washington, D.C., to make up their minds that our people are due now some degree of civil rights. No, we want it now or we don't think anybody should have it.

The purpose of our organization is to start right here in Harlem, which has the largest concentration of people of African descent that exists anywhere on this earth. There are more Africans in Harlem than exist in any city on the African continent. Because that's what you and I are—Africans. You catch any white man off guard in here right now, you catch him off guard and ask him what he is, he doesn't say he's an American. He either tells you he's Irish, or he's Italian, or he's German, if you catch him off guard and he doesn't know what you're up to. And even though he was born here, he'll tell you he's Italian. Well, if he's Italian, you and I are African—even though we were born here.

So we start in New York City first. We start in Harlem—and by Harlem we mean Bedford-Stuyvesant, any place in this area where you and I live, that's Harlem—with the intention of spreading throughout the state, and from the state throughout the country, and from the country throughout the Western Hemisphere. Because when we say Afro-American, we include everyone in the Western Hemisphere of African descent. South America is America. Central America is America. South America has many people in it of African descent. And everyone in South America of African descent is an Afro-American. Everyone in the Caribbean, whether it's the West Indies or Cuba or Mexico, if they have African blood, they are Afro-Americans. If they're in Canada and they have African blood, they're Afro-Americans. If they're in Alaska though they might call themselves Eskimos, if they have African blood, they're Afro-Americans.

So the purpose of the Organization of Afro-American Unity is to unite everyone in the Western Hemisphere of African descent into one united force. And then, once we are united among ourselves in the Western Hemisphere, we will unite with our brothers on the motherland, on the continent of Africa. . . .

"We assert that in those areas where the government is either unable or unwilling to protect the lives and property of our people, that our people are within our rights to protect themselves by whatever means necessary." I repeat, because to me this is the most important thing you need to know. I already know it. "We assert that in those areas where the government is either unable or unwilling to protect the lives and property of our people, that our people are within our rights to protect themselves by whatever means necessary. . . .

"We propose to support and organize political clubs, to run independent candidates for office, and to support any Afro-American already in office who answers to and is responsible to the Afro-American community." We don't support any black man who is controlled by the white power structure. We will start not only a voter registration drive, but a voter education drive to let our people have an understanding of the science of politics so they will be able to see what part the politician plays in the scheme of things; so they will be able to understand when the politician is doing his job and when he is not doing his job. And any time the politician is not doing his job, we remove him whether he's white, black, green, blue, yellow or whatever other color they might invent. . . .

"The Afro-American community must accept the responsibility for regaining our people who have lost their place in society. We must declare an all-out war on organized crime in our community; a vice that is controlled by policemen who accept bribes and graft must be exposed. We must establish a clinic, whereby one can get aid and cure for drug addiction. . . .

"Armed with the knowledge of our past, we can with confidence charter a course for our future. Culture is an indispensable weapon in the freedom struggle. We must take hold of it and forge the future with the past."

And to quote a passage from *Then We Heard the Thunder* by John Killens, it says: " 'He was a dedicated patriot: Dignity was his country, Manhood was his government, and Freedom was his land.' " Old John Killens.

This is our aim. It's rough, we have to smooth it up some. But we're not trying to put something together that's smooth. We don't care how rough it is. We don't care how tough it is. We don't care how backward it may sound. In essense it only means we want one thing. We declare our right on this earth to be a man, to be a human being, to be respected as a human being, to be given the rights of a human being in this society, on this earth, in this day, which we intend to bring into existence by any means necessary. . . .

Now, if white people want to help, they can help. But they can't join. They can help in the white community, but they can't join. We accept their help. They can form the White Friends of the Organization of Afro-American Unity and work in the white community on white people and change their attitude toward us. They don't ever need to come among us and change our attitude. We've had enough of them working around us trying to change our attitude. That's what got us all messed up.

So we don't question their sincerity, we don't question their motives, we don't question their integrity. We just encourage them to use it somewhere else—in the white community. If they can use all of this sincerity in the white community to make the white community act better toward us, then we'll say, "Those are good white folks."

This is the only known photograph of both the Reverend Martin Luther King, Jr., and Malcolm X. Toward the end of his life, Malcolm was moderating his views on black separatism, but many of his followers held to his earlier statements. *(Courtesy, AP/Wide World Photos)*

# Ella Baker

## Organization Without Dictatorship

*Ella Baker, a central figure in the foundation of the Student
Nonviolent Coordinating Committee, is known both for her
own independence and for her commitment to free forms of
organization and community.*

New York City, December 27, 1966.

[Ella Baker is a middle-aged woman, a graduate of Shaw University in Raleigh, North Carolina. She has worked for the NAACP
and SCLC and it was she who called the conference at which SNCC
was founded. She was a strong influence over it in its early years.]

Q. What is the basic goal of SNCC?

A. To change society so that the have-nots can share in it.

Q. Could you discuss in detail SNCC's move from the sit-ins
to other things?

A. In the early days, there was little communication, except
on a highly personal basis, as between friends and relatives, in
the sit-in movement. I had originally thought of pulling together
120–125 sit-in leaders for a leadership training conference—but
the rate of speed of the sit-ins was so rapid and the response so
electrifying, both North and South, that the meeting ended up
with 300 people. Many colleges sent representatives; there was a
great thrust of human desire and effort. The first sit-in took place
February 1, 1960; the meeting in Raleigh was around April 17,
1960, for three days. Nineteen colleges above the Mason-Dixie Line
sent representatives, most of them white. There were so many
Northerners that at the meeting it was decided that Northerners
could not participate in decision-making. This decision was made
sort of by mutual agreement after discussion, because the North-

*Source:* Emily Stoper, *The Student Nonviolent Coordinating Committee: The Growth
of Radicalism in a Civil Rights Organization*, preface by David J. Garrow (Brooklyn:
Carlson Publishing, 1989). Reprinted by permission.

erners recognized that the thrust of the action came from the South. They had been drawn magnetically to the movement because of their great admiration for the wonderful, brave Southerners. The Southerners wanted it that way, at that meeting, because of the divergent levels of political thinking both within the Northern group and between the North and the politically unsophisticated Deep South. (There were many representatives from Georgia, Louisiana, Alabama, although only token representation from Mississippi.) There was an outstanding leadership group from Nashville. It was a basic insecurity that caused the South to keep the North out of decision-making. The North and South used different terminology, had trouble communicating. This has cropped up again in SNCC. It became more subdued in the summer of '64 when there was a real program to be carried out.

Q. What else was decided on at the meeting?

A. That the coordinating group (SNCC) was not to be part of any other organization. Some tried to make it the student arm of SCLC, which had put up the few dollars to hold the meeting. They decided that it was too early to fix the structure of the organization, but the feeling was that it ought to be independent from adults.

Moreover, some of those who took part (I realize in retrospect) saw a basic difference in the role of leadership in the two organizations. In SCLC, the organization revolved around King; in SNCC, the leadership was group-centered (although I may have had some influence). Southern members of the movement were somewhat in awe of each other. There was a feeling that it was the "dawn of a new era," that something new and great was happening and that only they could chart the course of history. A strong equalitarian philosophy prevailed. There was a belief you could just go into an area and organize if you had had no leadership experience. SNCC rejected the idea of a God-sent leader. A basic goal was to make it unnecessary for the people to depend on a leader, for them to be strong themselves. SNCC hoped to spread into a big movement, to develop leadership from among the people. . . .

Q. What is SNCC's basic goal, that makes it unique?

A. The NAACP, Urban League, etc., do not *change* society, they want to get in. It's a combination of concern with the black goal for itself and, beyond that, with the whole society, because this is the acid test of whether the outs can get in and share in equality and worth. By worth, I mean creativity, a contribution to society. SNCC defines itself in terms of the blacks but is concerned with all excluded people.

Q. Has there been a change in SNCC's goal over time?

A. During the sit-in movement, we were concerned with seg-regation of public accommodations. But even then we recognized that that was only a surface goal. These obvious "irritants" had to be removed first; this was natural. Some people probably thought this in itself would change race relations; others saw deeper.

Q. Would you tell in detail how SNCC's policy changed after the sit-ins?

A. From the start, there were those who knew sitting-in would not bring basic changes. Youngsters who had not thought it through had not bargained with the intractable resistance of the power structure. The notion of "appeals to the conscience" as-sumed that there is a conscience, and after a while the question began to be raised, *is* there a conscience? Students, because they were most out front in the movement, began to see this and its political connotations. People began asking who *really* controlled things. The realization arose in Georgia that the rural areas had control because of the county unit system and that change had to be in the direction of political action. The NAACP had long been conducting voter action through the courts. In the process of in-ternal communications, the question of the vote arose. SNCC peo-ple began to go to Washington to talk to the attorney general, at first about Interstate Commerce [Commission rulings]. Kennedy [Attorney General] tried to sell them on the idea of voter registra-tion. . . .

Some people in SNCC thought voter registration was it; others liked the nonviolent resistance effort and feared that it would be sacrificed to voter registration. It was later decided that you couldn't possibly have voter registration without demon-strations. . . .

Q. How were whites in SNCC dealt with before the summer of '64?

A. It was not a major problem. Anybody who wanted to help was welcomed. After '64 the problem arose not in terms of whites but in terms of the right of the individual to make his own deci-sions in SNCC (this was Freedom High).

At a staff meeting in November '64, the issue of structure ver-sus non-structure arose. Some wanted structure; others thought the real genius of SNCC was in the scope given to the original or-ganizer. Some people said nobody should ever be fired. I thought this was unrealistic, that people were thinking in terms of a small closed society. It was a tragedy . . . people finding their personal need was not SNCC's purpose.

Old radicals have a saying: "You can't make the new world

and live in it too." The young people in SNCC wanted to live in it too. This was all part of a general thing about young people not conforming. At first we dressed in work clothes in order to identify with those with whom we were working, but later this became a part of our *right* to identity.

Q. Was the Freedom High connected with the white-black problem?

A. I'm not sure. I think maybe it was—because there were more whites in Freedom High, especially whites who felt their talents hadn't been well used, for reasons of their philosophy or their psychological problems. In those days, resentment against whites came not from black nationalism but from a feeling that it was the whites who brought in these ideas (Freedom High) and who perhaps had trouble accepting leadership.

Freedom High was an effort to develop a nucleus of the "pure" in which you could disregard the outside world.

*       *       *

The sense of community was pervasive in the black community as a whole, I mean especially the community that had a sense of roots. This community had been composed to a large extent by relatives. Over the hill was my grandfather's sister who was married to my Uncle Carter, and up the grove was another relative who had a place. So it was a deep sense of community. I think these are the things that helped to strengthen my concept about the need for people to have a sense of their own value, and *their* strengths, and it became accentuated when I began to travel in the forties for the National Association for the Advancement of Colored People. Because during that period, in the forties, racial segregation and discrimination were very harsh. As people moved to towns and cities, the sense of community diminished. A given area was made up of people from various and sundry other areas. They didn't come from the same place. So they had to *learn* each other, and they came into patterns of living that they had not been accustomed to. And so whatever deep sense of community that may have been developed in that little place that I spoke of, didn't always carry over to the city when they migrated. They lost their roots. When you lose that, what will you do next. You *hope* that you begin to think in terms of the *wider* brotherhood. . . .

*Source:* Ellen Cantarow with Susan Gushee O'Malley and Sharon Hartman Strom, *Moving the Mountain: Women Working for Social Change* (Old Westbury, NY: The Feminist Press, 1980). Reprinted with permission.

I guess revolutionary is relative to the situations that people find themselves in, and whatever their goals are, and how many people are in agreement that this is a desired goal. The original four kids who sat down in Greensboro, North Carolina, I'm confident that they had little or no knowledge of the revolutionary background that people talk about when they speak of changing the society by way of socialism or communism. They were youngsters who had a very simple reaction to an inequity. When you're a student with no money, and you go buy what you need like your paper or your pencils, where do you go? The five-and-ten-cent-store. At least you could then, because the prices were not quite as disproportionate as they are now. These two had been talking with a dentist, a black dentist who apparently had some experience with the earlier days of the formation of the Congress of Racial Equality (CORE). They were able to talk with him about their frustrations, going in there, spending all their little money, and yet not being able to sit and buy a five-cent Coke. That was a rather simple challenge as you look back. They decided they were going to do something about it, and so they sat down. Then some others followed their actions. A sister who had a brother in school in another town, her town had already sat in. She might call and ask, why doesn't his school sit in? This was the communication link, plus the media. They sat, and the others came and sat, and it spread. I guess one of the reasons it spread was because it was simple, and it struck home to a lot of young people who were in school.

It hadn't gone on so long before I suggested that we call a conference of the sit-inners to be held in Raleigh. It was very obvious to the Southern Christian Leadership Conference that there was little or no communication between those who sat in, say, in Charlotte, North Carolina, and those who eventually sat in at some other place in Virginia or Alabama. They were motivated by what the North Carolina four had started, but they were not in contact with each other, which meant that you couldn't build a sustaining force just based on spontaneity.

My estimate was that the conference would bring together a couple hundred of the young leadership. I had not hoped for such large numbers of adults who came. These adults were part and parcel of groups such as the Montgomery bus boycott. They also may have been relating to the organizing first steps of SCLC, which had been officially established but had not expanded very much.

We ended up with about three hundred people. We had insisted that the young people be left to make their own decisions. Also, we provided for those who came from outside the South to meet separately from those who came from the sit-in areas, because the persons who came from say, New York, frequently had had wider experience in organizing and were too articulate. In the initial portion of the conference, the southern students had the right to meet, to discuss, and to determine where they wanted to go. It wasn't my idea to separate the northern and southern students. I hesitated to project ideas as pointedly as that, but those who had worked closely with me knew that I believed very firmly in the right of the people who were under the heel to be the ones to decide what action they were going to take to get from under their oppression. As a group, basically, they were the black students from the South. The heritage of the South was theirs, and it was one of oppression. Those who came from the other nineteen schools and colleges and universities up North didn't have the same oppression, and they were white. They were much more erudite and articulate, farther advanced in the theoretical concepts of social change. This can become overwhelming for those who don't even understand what you're talking about and feel put down.

The Southern Christian Leadership Conference felt that they could influence how things went. They were interested in having the students become an arm of SCLC. They were most confident that this would be their baby, because I was their functionary and I had called the meeting. At a discussion called by the Reverend Dr. King, the SCLC leadership made decisions who would speak to whom to influence the students to become part of SCLC. Well, I disagreed. There was no student at Dr. King's meeting. I was the nearest thing to a student, being the advocate, you see. I also knew from the beginning that having a woman be an executive of SCLC was not something that would go over with the male-dominated leadership. And then, of course, my personality wasn't right, in the sense I was not afraid to disagree with the higher authorities. I wasn't one to say, yes, because it came from the Reverend King. So when it was proposed that the leadership could influence the direction by speaking to, let's say, the man from Virginia, he could speak to the leadership óf the Virginia student group, and the assumption was that having spoken to so-and-so, so-and-so would do what they wanted done, I was outraged. I walked out.

# Gloria Richardson

## The Struggle for Power in Cambridge

*Gloria Richardson was a leader in the civil rights move-
ment in Cambridge, Maryland. The economic conditions
for African Americans in Cambridge were especially bad
and black unemployment rates high. During the spring of
1963 demonstrations against segregation increasingly
turned to violent forms of protest driven by black poverty.
In June 1963 martial law was declared, and troops
remained in the city until May 1965.*

On October 2, 1963, Negro voters in Cambridge rejected the
proposed Charter Amendment which would have made discrimination on the basis of race illegal in restaurants, hotels and motels
in this city. This plebiscite followed a period of violence and tension initiated and perpetuated by white mobs in retaliation to non-
violent street demonstrations—directed by the Cambridge Non-
violent Action Committee. This fight, which intensified last
summer, had been going on for two years with the support of the
overwhelming majority of the Negro people here, who believed in,
or were persuaded to believe in, the tactics of nonviolence.

When the October 2nd referendum was called, CNAC took the
position that the referendum was unconstitutional, illegal and
immoral. We called for Negroes to boycott the polls in an expression of passive resistance in the face of an illegal hoax being perpetrated against the people. At that time I was generally credited
with irresponsible leadership, although since that time much of
the press and people have begun to agree with our position.

There were several facts to be considered here, and who is to
say which is the most important. In the first place those Negroes
who have fought for America, who have paid direct and indirect
taxes were not inclined to vote on something which no other citi-

*Source:* Gloria Richardson, "Focus on Cambridge," *Freedomways,* 4 (Winter 1964).

zen or alien in America had to vote upon. These same Negro citizens were not permitted to vote as to whether they should fight for this country or pay taxes or any of the other responsibilities imposed on United States citizens. We were being asked to tuck our dignity in our pockets and crawl to the polls to prove in a stacked vote that once again we were going to let the whites in control say what we would be permitted to do in a "free, democratic country." Negro leadership at many levels was saying "we know the principle involved but it is expedient to do it this way." One Negro woman leader in the state said it was time that I learn to make deals. No one was ready to take a temporary loss and assume responsibility for the thousands of black people across the south who, once we submitted, would be subject to the same tactic although they would not even have the advantage of a swing-vote. They would be forced, in the *name* of democracy, to submit to the biased whims of a majority, and in the name of the democratic process be bound by it. In the name of all the black and white people in America this type of precedent would have laid people bare to the whims of dishonest, big business politicians who would piously use "the referendum" as a tool to shove down the throats of an unsuspecting and unwary racial or economic minority any type of racially punitive or economically punitive legislation, on a local, state or federal level. (As a matter of fact it is now used against voters not exposed to a voter education program.)

Finally, and specifically, in reference to this referendum, it was clearly unconstitutional. Equal accommodations in public places is a right inherent to citizens, and should not be subject to the wishes and prejudices of any individual or group. Two years ago the Supreme Court of the United States, in reversing the convictions of Negro students arrested for "sitting-in" made this quite clear. In its decision the Court stated unequivocally that any facility or establishment that is public, that is to say, that operates on the basis of a franchise or license to "serve the public" granted by any unit of government, be it local, state or federal, is operating in contract with that government, and consequently with its constituents, the people. The Court pointed out that any discrimination against any group of citizens was a breach of that contract.

The referendum was an attempt to make the constitutional rights of the Negro people, as citizens of Cambridge, subject to the possible prejudices of the white majority. It was further an attempt by the city commissioners to rewrite the constitution at the expense of the rights of Cambridge's Negro citizens. Equal accommodation in public places is a right to which we are entitled, and it is as important as any other human right. But it is not the most pressing problem facing Cambridge Negroes. Here Negroes are faced with chronic and widespread unemployment and underemployment, inadequate and substandard housing and living conditions, discrimination in every area of endeavor and what is worse, in the absence of any indication that the power structure of Cambridge is prepared to reform the system, or to effect any real improvement in the forseeable future.

Today the revolt is now ready to go into a new phase. No longer are we primarily interested in public accommodations. The "bread and butter" issues have come to the fore. A one-point program will become more and more obsolete as months wear on. The attack now has to be directed toward the economic and political structure of a community if any real progress is to be made and if tokenism is to be eliminated. The leadership within the movement is moving toward this and the people are moving with them. Always there is this togetherness after confidence in one another has been established. If the leadership ever defaults I am sure that the people for whom we are fighting will continue their own battle. For example, in Cambridge we have become very sophisticated in the technique of the boycott. Without even calling for one, the majority of the community will spontaneously put a boycott into effect.

This brings me to another facet of the Negro revolt: it is incumbent on every civil rights worker to educate the community as well as to articulate its desires. This does not mean educate in terms of books or schools. Many so-called educated people today do not understand what we mean when we say the first step is to educate the people, and a serious mistake can be made here. Education in this context simply means that a community has to become familiar with what it wants to achieve, how it can be achieved and how to apply techniques so that they become second nature, a part of one's way of life. To learn and believe that they can overcome, to learn that the fight will be hard, that great sacrifices will be demanded but that it will *not* take another hundred years or even ten to gain the victory. To learn that what happens in Danville, Selma, Birmingham, Jackson, Albany happens to us too, in Cambridge, Baltimore, and Washington: to feel the rapport with other Negroes in other parts of the country and to become slowly and surely aware that as long as one of us has a segregationist breathing down our necks all of us are enslaved; that even though we have partial progress within our own locale, we will have to continue to stage sympathy demonstrations or acts of civil disobedience until discrimination and segregation are erased, everywhere.

# Robert Parris Moses

## Building Power and Community in Mississippi

*This account by Bob Moses gives an idea of both the danger and the drudgery that attended breaking through the material and psychological barriers to black community power in Mississippi. Moses was a black New Yorker who came to the state in 1961 to encourage voter registration on the part of blacks. He remained at work there for four years.*

... I accompanied about three people down to Liberty in Amite County to begin our first registration attempt there. One was a very old man, and then two ladies, middle-aged. We left early morning of August 15, it was a Tuesday, we arrived at the courthouse at about 10 o'clock. The registrar came out, I waited by the side for the man or one of the ladies to say something to the registrar. He asked them what did they want, what were they here for in a very rough tone of voice. They didn't say anything, they were literally paralyzed with fear. So, after a while, I spoke up and said that they would like to come to register to vote. So, he asked, "Well, who are you? What do you have to do with them? Are you here to register?" So I told him who I was and that we were conducting a school in McComb and that these people had attended the school and they wanted an opportunity to register. Well, he said that I'd have to wait "cuz there was someone there filling out the form." Well, there was a young white lady there with her husband and she was sitting down completing the registration form. When she finished, then our people started to register one at a time. In the meantime, a procession of people began moving in and out of the registration office. The sheriff, a couple of his deputies, people from the tax office, people who do the drivers' license, looking in, staring, moving back out, muttering. A highway patrolman finally came in and sat down in the office. And we stayed that way

*Source:* Bob Moses, "Mississippi: 1961–1962," *Liberation,* 14 (January 1970).

in sort of uneasy tension all morning. The first person who filled out the form took a long time to do it and it was noontime before he was finished. When we came back, I was not permitted to sit in the office, but was told to sit on the front porch, which I did. We finally finished the whole process at about 4:30; all of the three people had had a chance to register, at least to fill out the form. This was victory, because they had been down a few times before and had not had a chance to even fill out the forms.

On the way home we were followed by the highway patrolman who had spent the day in the registrar's office, Officer Carlyle. He tailed us about ten miles, about 25 or 30 feet behind us, all the way back towards McComb. At one point we pulled off, and he passed us, circled around us and we pulled off as he was passing us in the opposite direction, and then he turned around and followed us again. Finally he flagged us down and I got out of the car to ask him what the trouble was because the people in the car were very, very frightened. He asked me who I was, what my business was, and told me that I was interfering in what he was doing. I said I simply wanted to find out what the problem was and what we were being stopped for. He told me to get back in the car. As I did so, I jotted his name down. He then opened the car door, shoved me in and said, "Get in the car, nigger," slamming the door after me. He then told us to follow him and took us over to McComb where I was told that I was placed under arrest. He called up the prosecuting attorney; he came down, and then he and the highway patrolman sat down and looked through the law books to find a charge. They first charged me with interfering with an officer in the process of arresting somebody. Then he found out that the only person arrested was myself and they changed the charge to interfering with an officer in the discharge of his duties. The county attorney asked me if I was ready for trial and I said, could I make a phone call. He said yeah, so I picked up the phone and called Washington, D.C. and the Justice Department, because I had been in communication with some members of the Justice Department and particularly John Doar and had received letters delineating those sections of the Civil Rights Act of 1957 and 1960 which guaranteed protection to those people who are trying to register and anyone who is aiding people who are trying to register. And he also indicated that if we had any trouble we were to call Washington or the nearest office of the FBI. So I called them, collect; the people in the office were rather astonished that the call went through and then they began to get figity. Well, as to the call, I explained to Mr. Doar exactly what happened in their presence and told him that I thought the people were being intimidated simply because they had gone down to register.

Well, we had the trial right after that. I was found guilty of this charge of interfering with an officer, and the judge and the county prosecutor went out, consulted, and came back and I was given a suspended sentence, 90 days suspended sentence, and fined $5 for the cost of court. I refused to pay the $5 cost of court and argued that I shouldn't be given anything at all and should be set free since I was obviously not guilty. I was taken to jail then, and this was my first introduction to Mississippi jails. I spent a couple days in jail and was finally bailed out when the bondsman came through, supplied by the NAACP. We decided at that point to appeal the case, though later the appeal was dropped. Well, that was our first introduction to Amite county. . . .

Characteristic of the Mississippi jails is that you sit and rot. There's no program if you're not working, which they wouldn't let us do because they weren't going to have those "uppity niggers" out there on the line with a chance for causing trouble. Nothing to do inside. They give you your meals two or three times a day; they give you your shower one or two times a week; they give you silence or nasty words otherwise. We played chess quite a bit; Hollis and Curtis and I were in the same cell. I taught Hollis and Curtis how to play and we wrote home and got a couple of books. People would come by and they treated us very well, the Negro people in McComb, while we were in jail: they baked chicken and pies, and they would come down, at first, everyday with something to give us. And they finally cut that out and would only let them down once or twice a week. When they came they would smuggle in letters and we would smuggle out letters, and we had a little underground of information passing back and forth between us and the people in town.

Well, we spent most of the month of November and on into December in jail; we were finally released and the high school kids who were seniors went onto Campbell to school and the rest of us then regrouped to decide what could be done and what projects we needed to carry out next, how we could pick up the pieces. We had, to put it mildly, got our feet wet. We now knew something of what it took to run a voter registration campaign in Mississippi; we knew some of the obstacles we would have to face; we had some general idea of what had to be done to get such a campaign started. First there were very few agencies available in the Negro community that could act as a vehicle for any sort of campaign. The Negro churches could not in general be counted on; the Negro business leaders could also not in general be counted on except for under-the-cover help; and, in general, anybody who had a specific economic tie-in with the white community could not be counted on when the pressure got hot. Therefore, our feeling was that the only way to run this campaign was to begin to build a group of young people who would not be responsible economically to any sector of the white community and who would be able to act as free agents. And we began to set about doing this. In most cases it was a conjunction between the young people and some indigenous farmers, independent people, or some courageous businessman able to stick his neck out, or willing to stick his neck out, which was the combination which worked in the voter registration drive.

Curtis Hayes and Hollis Watkins were the first two to start such drives. They worked down at Hattiesburg in the spring of 1962 at our first attempt at setting up voter registration drives around the state. Most of the winter was lean, we were just hanging on in Jackson. It is true that we participated in some of the political campaigns involving Reverend Smith and also Reverend Lindsey and Reverend Trumall and it's true that we made many trips back and forth to the areas where we had been and trips around into the southwestern part of Mississippi, Natchez, Port Gibson and Clayborn digging up material, laying foundations, beginning to get ready for the next drive next summer.

Summer came and we outlined the program whereby we would be working in about five or six counties, most of them in the delta area of Mississippi, in Washington where Greenville is located, in Coahoma where Clarksdale is located, in Sunflower where Ruleville and Indianola are, in Bolivar where Cleveland is, in LaFlore where Greenwood is, and in Marshall County where Holly Springs and Rust College are. We began these programs in the summer. We first had a week of orientation and workshops at the Highlander Folk School, and Miles Horton opened up his school for us and gave the benefit of his experience to the kids who were going to work that summer in the voter registration program. When we came back from there, the kids began working, most all of them from Mississippi and most all of them people we had recruited that spring in these various towns. They had some success in some and weren't so successful in others.

The drives can be separated out in those counties where you encountered physical and economic reprisals and those counties where you encountered fear, psychological fear, and a great, great deal of immobility on the part of the Negroes. So that in Greenville and Washington County and in Coahoma and Clarksdale they got some results, they got some people to go down. But the kind of operation there was day-to-day drudgery, going around in the hot sun, talking to people, trying to get them to overcome their fear, trying to convince them that nothing would happen to them if they went down, that their houses wouldn't be bombed, that they would not be shot at, that they would not lose their jobs. In the other counties, we couldn't convince people of these things because for one, it wasn't true. In Sunflower and LaFlore counties which are the center of the core of the problem in Mississippi, indeed, I think, for much of the South, you ran into quite different situations. More like the situations we ran into in Amite and Walthall last summer. These two counties, one where the Citizen's Council first was formed at Sunflower where Indianola is the county seat, and housed the first meeting of the White Citizen's Council. And the other, LaFlore, where Greenwood is the county seat, where the Citizen's Council finds its home and has its mailing address, for the state of Mississippi much of the very racial leadership and much of the very, very conservative and reactionary leadership. Sunflower County is the home of Senator Eastland, and it was this county where we got our first reactions of arrests and then later got shootings and violence.

However, it was in LaFlore County where we got our first real scare. Sam Block was working in LaFlore County. And he began his work there with a voter registration drive organized around a police brutality case. Shortly after he arrived the police had picked up a young fellow, Milton McSwine, 14 years old. Somebody had been peeking into some white lady's house and that somebody had been some young Negro, and the police were out looking and picked up Milton McSwine and accused him of doing it. They took him back to the police station where they stripped him and beat him with their bullwhips until knots and welts were raised on his thighs and until his screams attracted a postal employee working next door, who was a Negro, late at night. The next morning Sam found out about the case when the fellow was released, had his pictures taken, had affidavits made and reported the case to the Justice Department and then to the FBI. It set the tone for the voter registration project in Greenwood; from then on it was Sam vs. the police. Sam had some success in carrying people down. He took down about 20–25 people, I think, in his first two weeks. And then finally one day when we carried people down, the newspapers gave us a big play. We took about 25 people down that day. And the CBS people were down taking pictures; they had some kind of station wagon set up with a hidden camera, and they were trying to photograph the voter registration operation in practice. That night it appeared in the local papers, big headlines saying, "Voter Registration Drive in Progress" and letting the white citizens in town know that there was actually a voter registration drive being organized in Greenwood, that they were holding their offices at 616 Avenue I, and that young students, "outside agitators," as they say, even though Sam comes from Cleveland, Mississippi, which is about 30 miles away, were in Greenwood stirring up their niggers. The next night I got a phone call about 12 o'clock. The operator said it was a collect call from Greenwood, Mississippi. When I took it, I found out it was Sam Block on the line. Sam said that there was some people outside, police cars, about 12 o'clock at night, he didn't know what they were there for. Said that there was also white people riding up and down the street, and that they felt something was going to happen. I told him to keep in touch with us, hung up, called the Justice Department. We had to track down a member of the Justice Department or staff of the Justice Department at his home and explained to him what was happening. He told us to try and keep in touch with Sam; we gave him Sam's number and he had some instructions about calling the local FBI. Sam called back again: the police were gone and white people had come in their cars, were standing outside the office. He was crouched in the office looking out the window, talking on the phone in a very hushed voice, describing people downstairs with guns and chains, milling around down outside his office. He had to hang up, said he had to leave. We didn't know what to do then, we were over in Cleveland, Mississippi about an hour's drive away. By that time it was about 1:30 in the morning. Willy Peacock and I then decided to drive over to Greenwood. We got there about 3:30 or 4:00, the office was empty, the door was knocked down, the window was up, Sam was gone, so was Giat and Lavonne. Well, the next morning when they came in, they told us what had happened. People had charged up the back of the stairs, had come into the office, they had escaped out the window across the roof of the adjoining building, down a TV antenna, and on into somebody else's home.

Shortly after that the person they were renting the office from was charged with bigamy, and they had to move. You have to understand that in Mississippi it is probably easier for a Negro to get another wife than it is for him to get a divorce. In the first place, there are only three Negro lawyers in the whole state, and they are all in Jackson. In the second place, the white people probably don't care very much for the Negroes to get divorces, and don't encourage them to get one at all; it fits their conception of the Negro for him to have to live with another wife after he has left his first wife without getting a legal divorce. This was the first case, in any case, that we had heard of a Negro being charged with bigamy. There was no doubt in my mind that it was done so on account of voter registration. However, we couldn't prove this, and his only course was to sever any connection that he had with the voter registration drive and convince the local people that he was clean. This he did, and we moved out of the office.

It took approximately five months to find another office in Greenwood, Mississippi. But now, just a couple of weeks ago, Sam and Willie, who stayed on to work, have an office, and are back in business again. During that time they carried on essentially what I consider holding operations. That is, they stayed in town, they told the white people, in effect, that we were not going to move, they showed up everyday doing their work, that is, going around and visiting people, breaking down the psychological feeling on the part of the Negroes that these boys were just coming in here, that they're going to be here for a short time, and then they are going to leave, and we're going to be left holding the bag. Because it's very important that the Negroes in the community feel that you're coming in there to stay, work with them and live with them, and that you're going to ride through whatever trouble arrives. And in general, the deeper the fear, the deeper the problems in the community, the longer you have to stay to convince them. So far this month, Sam and Willie have been there taking a few down, a couple here, a couple there, done a lot of talking, showing up around the community, and let the people know that the voter registration drive was continuing. And in the past week, the voter registration drive launched under a food relief program, they processed over a thousand applications, which are providing them with people who will eventually be going down and attempting to register to vote.

# Letters Home From Freedom Summer

## A Summer of Discovery

*Part of the army of volunteers heavily represented by north-
ern white students who came to Mississippi in 1964 to aid
in the empowerment of the state's black community, these
writers were in the process of discovering also what powers
they were capable of mustering in themselves.*

Dear folks,                                        Mileston, August 18
One can't move onto a plantation cold; or canvas a plantation in
the same manner as the Negro ghetto in town. It's far too dangerous. Many plantations—homes included—are posted, meaning
that no trespassing is permitted, and the owner feels that he has
the prerogative to shoot us on sight when we are in the house of
one of *his* Negroes.

Before we canvas a plantation, our preparation includes finding out whether the houses are posted, driving through or around
the plantation without stopping, meanwhile making a detailed
map of the plantation.

We're especially concerned with the number of roads in and
out of the plantation. For instance, some houses could be too dangerous to canvas because of their location near the boss man's
house and on a dead end road.

In addition to mapping, we attempt to talk to some of the
tenants when they are off the plantation, and ask them about conditions. The kids often have contacts, and can get on the plantation unnoticed by the boss man, with the pretense of just visiting
friends.

Our canvassing includes not only voter registration, but also
extensive reports on conditions—wages, treatment by the boss
man, condition of the houses, number of acres of cotton, etc. Much
more such work needs to be done. The plantation system is crucial

in Delta politics and economics, and the plantation system must be brought to an end if democracy is to be brought to the Delta. . . .

Love,
Joel

July 18

Four of us went to distribute flyers announcing the meeting. I talked to a woman who had been down to register a week before. She was afraid. Her husband had lost his job. Even before we got there a couple of her sons had been man-handled by the police. She was now full of wild rumors about shootings and beatings, etc. I checked out two of them later. They were groundless. This sort of rumorspreading is quite prevalent when people get really scared.

At 6 P.M. we returned to Drew for the meeting, to be held in front of a church (they wouldn't let us meet inside, but hadn't told us not to meet outside). A number of kids collected and stood around in a circle with about 15 of us to sing freedom songs. Across the street perhaps 100 adults stood watching. Since this was the first meeting in town, we passed out mimeoed song sheets. Fred Miller, Negro from Mobile, stepped out to the edge of the street to give somebody a sheet. The cops nabbed him. I was about to follow suit so he wouldn't be alone, but Mac's policy [Charles McLaurin, SNCC project director] was to ignore the arrest. We sang on mightily "Ain't going to let no jailing turn me around." A group of girls was sort of leaning against the cars on the periphery of the meeting. Mac went over to encourage them to join us. I gave a couple of song sheets to the girls. A cop rushed across the street and told me to come along. I guess I was sort of aware that my actions would get me arrested, but felt that we had to show these girls that we were not afraid. I was also concerned with what might happen to Fred if he was the only one. . . .

The cop at the station was quite scrupulous about letting me make a phone call. I was then driven to a little concrete structure which looked like a power house. I could hear Fred's courageous, off-key rendition of a freedom song from inside and joined him as we approached. He was very happy to see me. Not long thereafter, four more of our group were driven up to make their calls. . . .

The Drew jail consists of three small cells off a wide hall. It was filthy, hot and stuffy. A cop came back to give us some toilet paper. We sang songs for a while, and yelled greetings to Negroes who drove by curiously. One of the staff workers had been in jail 106 times. I asked the cop if he could open another cell as there were not enough beds accessible to us. He mumbled something about how that would be impossible and left. They hadn't confiscated anything and one of the guys had a battered copy of *The Other America*, so we divided up the chapters. I got the dismal one on the problems of the aged. . . . To be old and forgotten is certainly a worse sentence than mine (I wouldn't recommend that book for those planning to do time).

Well, the night was spent swatting mosquitoes. An old Negro couple walked by in front of the jail and asked how we were doing. They said they supported us and the old lady said, "God bless you all." This, in the context of a tense town with a pretty constant stream of whites in cars driving by. . . .

Dear Mom and Dad:                                      Holly Springs
The atmosphere in class is unbelievable. It is what every teacher dreams about—real, honest enthusiasm and desire to learn anything and everything. The girls come to class of their own free will. They respond to everything that is said. They are excited about learning. They drain me of everything that I have to offer so that I go home at night completely exhausted but very happy. . . .

I start out at 10:30 teaching what we call the Core Curriculum, which is Negro History and the History and Philosophy of the Movement, to about fifteen girls ranging from 15 to 25 years of age. I have one girl who is married with four children, another who is 23 and a graduate from a white college in Tennessee, also very poorly educated. The majority go to a Roman Catholic High School in Holly Springs and have therefore received a fairly decent education by Mississippi standards. They can, for the most part, express themselves on paper but their skills in no way compare to juniors and seniors in northern suburban schools.

In one of my first classes, I gave a talk on Haiti and the slave revolt which took place there at the end of the eighteenth century. I told them how the French government (during the French Revolution) abolished slavery all over the French Empire. And then I told them that the English decided to invade the island and take it over for a colony of their own. I watched faces fall all around me. They knew that a small island, run by former slaves, could not defeat England. And then I told them that the people of Haiti succeeded in keeping the English out. I watched a smile spread slowly over a girl's face. And I felt girls sit up and look at me intently. Then I told them that Napoleon came to power, reinstated slavery, and sent an expedition to reconquer Haiti. Their faces began to fall again. They waited for me to tell them that France defeated the former slaves, hoping against hope that I would say that they didn't.

But when I told them that the French generals tricked the Haitian leader Toussaint to come aboard their ship, captured him and sent him back to France to die, they knew that there was no hope. They waited for me to spell out the defeat. And when I told them that Haiti did succeed in keeping out the European powers and was recognized finally as an independent republic, they just looked at me and smiled. The room stirred with a gladness and a pride that this could have happened. And I felt so happy and so humble that I could have told them this little story and it could have meant so much.

We have also talked about what it means to be a Southern white who wants to stand up but who is alone, rejected by other whites and not fully accepted by the Negroes. We have talked about their feelings about Southern whites. One day three little while girls came to our school and I asked them to understand how the three girls felt by remembering how it feels when they are around a lot of whites. We agreed that we would not stare at the girls but try to make them feel as normal as possible. . . .

Every class is beautiful. The girls respond, respond, respond. And they disagree among themselves. I have no doubt that soon they will be disagreeing with me. At least this is one thing that I am working towards. They are a sharp group. But they are under-educated and starved for knowledge. They know that they have been cheated and they want anything and everything that we can give them.

I have a great deal of faith in these students. They are very mature and very concerned about other people. I really think that they will be able to carry on without us. At least this is my dream.

Love,
Pam

Indianola, August 17

I can see the change. The 16-year-old's discovery of poetry, of Whitman and Cummings and above all, the struggle to express thoughts in words, to translate ideas into concrete written words. After two weeks a child finally looks me in the eye, unafraid, acknowledging a bond of trust which 300 years of Mississippians said should never, could never exist. I can feel the growth of self-confidence. . . .

Biloxi, Aug. 16

In the Freedom School one day during poetry writing, a 12-year-old girl handed in this poem to her teacher:

*What Is Wrong?*

What is wrong with me everywhere I go
  No one seems to look at me.
Sometimes I cry.

I walk through woods and sit on a stone.
  I look at the stars and I sometimes wish.

Probably if my wish ever comes true,
  Everyone will look at me.

Then she broke down crying in her sister's arms. The Freedom
School here had given this girl the opportunity of meeting someone she felt she could express her problems to. . . .

To my brother,

                                                    Ruleville
    Last night, I was a long time before sleeping, although I was
extremely tired. Every shadow, every noise—the bark of a dog, the
sound of a car—in my fear and exhaustion was turned into a ter-
rorist's approach. And I believed that I heard the back door open
and a Klansman walk in, until he was close by the bed. Almost paralyzed by the fear, silent, I finally shone my flashlight on the spot
where I thought he was standing. . . . I tried consciously to overcome this fear. To relax, I began to breathe deep, think the words
of a song, pull the sheet up close to my neck . . . still the tension.
Then I rethought why I was here, rethought what could be gained
in view of what could be lost. All this was in rather personal terms,
and then in larger scope of the whole Project. I remembered Bob
Moses saying he had felt justified in asking hundreds of students to
go to Mississippi because he was not asking anyone to do something that he would not do. . . . I became aware of the uselessness of
fear that immobilizes an individual. Then I began to relax.
    "We are not afraid. Oh Lord, deep in my heart, I do believe.
We Shall Overcome Someday" and then I think I began to truly
understand what the words meant. Anyone who comes down here
and is not afraid I think must be crazy as well as dangerous to this
project where security is quite important. But the type of fear that
they mean when they, when we, sing "we are not afraid" is the
type that immobilizes. . . . The songs help to dissipate the fear.
Some of the words in the songs do not hold real meaning on their
own, others become rather monotonous—but when they are sung
in unison, or sung silently by oneself, they take on new meaning
beyond words or rhythm. . . . There is almost a religious quality

about some of these songs, having little to do with the usual concept of a god. It has to do with the miracle that youth has organized to fight hatred and ignorance. It has to do with the holiness of the dignity of man. The god that makes such miracles is the god I do believe in when we sing "God is on our side." I know I am on that god's side. And I do hope he is on ours.

Jon, please be considerate to Mom and Dad. The fear I just expressed, I am sure they feel much more intensely without the relief of being here to know exactly how things are. Please don't go defending me or attacking them if they are critical of the Project. . . .

They said over the phone "Did you know how much it takes to make a child?" and I thought of how much it took to make a Herbert Lee (or many others whose names I do not know). . . . I thought of how much it took to be a Negro in Mississippi twelve months a year for a lifetime. How can such a thing as a life be weighed?

With constant love,
Heather

Greenwood, June 29

We have heard rumors twice to the effect that the three men were found weighted down in that river. Both stories, though the same, were later completely dropped in an hour or so. How do you like that guy Gov. Johnson saying that they might be hiding in the North or maybe in Cuba for all he knew. . . .

Tchula, July 16

Yesterday while the Mississippi River was being dragged looking for the three missing civil rights workers, two bodies of Negores were found————one cut in half and one without a head. Mississippi is the only state where you can drag a river any time and find bodies you were not expecting. Things are really much better for rabbits—there's a closed season on rabbits.

Como, August 3

About three weeks ago there was a flying rumor that they had been found in a rural jail. Tonight it was said that three graves had been found near Philadelphia. How the ghosts of those three shadow all our work! "Did you know them?" I am constantly asked. Did I need to?

Meridian, August 4

Last night Pete Seeger was giving a concert in Meridian. We

sang a lot of freedom songs, and every time a verse like 'No more lynchings' was sung, or 'before I'd be a slave I'd be buried in my grave,' I had the flash of understanding that sometimes comes when you suddenly think about the meaning of a familiar song . . . I wanted to stand up and shout to them, "Think about what you are singing—people really have died to keep us all from being slaves." Most of the people there still did not know that the bodies had been found. Finally just before the singing of "We Shall Overcome," Pete Seeger made the announcement. "We must sing 'We Shall Overcome' now," said Seeger. "The three boys would not have wanted us to weep now, but to sing and understand this song." That seems to me the best way to explain the greatness of this project—that death can have this meaning. Dying is not an ever-present possibility in Meridian, the way some reports may suggest. Nor do any of us want to die. Yet in a moment like last night, we can feel that anyone who did die for the Project would wish to be remembered not by tributes or grief but by understanding and continuation of what he was doing. . . .

As we left the church, we heard on the radio the end of President Johnson's speech announcing the air attacks on Vietnam. . . . I could only think "This must not be the beginning of a war. There is still a freedom fight, and we are winning. We must have time to live and help Mississippi to be alive." Half an hour before, I had understood death in a new way. Now I realized that Mississippi, in spite of itself, has given real meaning to life. In Mississippi you never ask, "What is the meaning of life?" or "Is there any point to it all?" but only that we may have enough life to do all that there is to be done. . . .

Dear Folks,

> Laurel, August 11

. . . The memorial service began around 7:30 with over 120 people filling the small, wooden-pew lined church. David Dennis of CORE, the Assistant Director for the Mississippi Summer Project, spoke for COFO. He talked to the Negro people of Meridian—it was a speech to move people, to end the lethargy, to make people stand up. It went something like this:

"I am not here to memorialize James Chaney, I am not here to pay tribute—I am too sick and tired. Do YOU hear me, I am S-I-C-K and T-I-R-E-D. I have attended too many memorials, too many funerals. This has got to stop. Mack Parker, Medgar Evers, Herbert Lee, Lewis Allen, Emmett Till, four little girls in Birmingham, a 13-year old boy in Birmingham, and the list goes on and on.

I have attended these funerals and memorials and I am SICK and TIRED. But the trouble is that YOU are NOT sick and tired and for that reason YOU, yes YOU, are to blame, Everyone of your damn souls. And if you are going to let this continue now then you are to blame, yes YOU. Just as much as the monsters of hate who pulled the trigger or brought down the club; just as much to blame as the sheriff and the chief of police, as the governor in Jackson who said that he 'did not have time' for Mrs. Schwerner when she went to see him, and just as much to blame as the President and Attorney General in Washington who wouldn't provide protection for Chaney, Goodman and Schwerner when we told them that protection was necessary in Neshoba County.... Yes, I am angry, I AM. And it's high time that you got angry too, angry enough to go up to the courthouse Monday and register—everyone of you. Angry enough to take five and then other people with you. Then and only then can these brutal killings be stopped. Remember it is your sons and your daughters who have been killed all these years and you have done nothing about it, and if you don't do nothing NOW baby, I say God Damn Your Souls....

Dear Blake,

Mileston, August 9

Dave finally broke down and couldn't finish and the Chaney family was moaning and much of the audience and I were also crying. It's such an impossible thing to describe but suddenly again, as I'd first realized when I heard the three men were missing when we were still training up at Oxford, I felt the sacrifice the Negros have been making for so long. How the Negro people are able to accept all the abuses of the whites—all the insults and injustices which make me ashamed to be white—and then turn around and say they want to love us, is beyond me. There are Negros who want to kill whites and many Negros have much bitterness but still the majority seem to have the quality of being able to look for a future in which whites will love the Negroes. Our kids talk very critically of all the whites around here and still they have a dream of freedom in which both races understand and accept each other. There is such an overpowering task ahead of these kids that sometimes I can't do anything but cry for them. I hope they are up to the task, I'm not sure I would be if I were a Mississippi Negro. As a white northerner I can get involved whenever I feel like it and run home whenever I get bored or frustrated or scared. I hate the attitude and position of the Northern whites and despise myself when I think that way. Lately I've been feeling homesick and longing for pleasant old Westport and sailing and swimming and my friends. I don't quite know what to do because I can't ignore my desire to go home and yet I feel I am a much weaker person than I like to think I am because I do have these emotions. I've always tried to avoid situations which aren't so nice, like arguments and dirty houses and now maybe Mississippi. I asked my father if I could stay down here for a whole year and I was almost glad when he said "no" that we couldn't afford it because it would mean supporting me this year in addition to three more years of college. I have a desire to go home and to read a lot and go to Quaker meetings and be by myself so I can think about all this rather than being in the middle of it all the time. But I know if my emotions run like they have in the past, that I can only take that pacific sort of life for a little while and then I get the desire to be active again and get involved with knowing other people. I guess this all sounds crazy and I seem to always think out my problems as I write to you. I am angry because I have a choice as to whether or not to work in the Movement and I am playing upon that choice and leaving here. I wish I could talk with you 'cause I'd like to know if you ever felt this way about anything. I mean have you ever despised yourself for your weak conviction or something. And what is making it worse is that all those damn northerners are thinking of me as a brave hero. . . .

Martha

# Septima P. Clark

## Education and Empowerment

*Septima Clark was director of teacher training in the
citizenship education program of the Southern Christian
Leadership Conference. That education is necessary for the
acquisition of political and social power and for a full discovery of power within the individual was a conviction
common among civil rights activists. The establishment of
informal schooling with the free participation of students
and teachers was itself an act of defiance of local custom, a
taking control by participants over their own lives.*

The teacher wrote "Citizen" on the blackboard. Then she
wrote "Constitution" and "Amendment." Then she turned to her
class of 30 adult students.

"What do these mean, students?" she asked. She received a
variety of answers, and when the discussion died down, the
teacher was able to make a generalization.

"This is the reason we know we are citizens: Because it's written in an amendment to the Constitution."

An elderly Negro minister from Arkansas took notes on a yellow legal pad. A machine operator from Atlanta raised his hand to
ask another question.

This was an opening session in an unusual citizenship education program that is held once each month at Dorchester Center,
McIntosh, Georgia for the purpose of helping adults help educate
themselves.

In a five day course, those three words became the basis of
a new education in citizenship for the Negroes and whites who
attended the training session. Each participant left with a burning desire to start their own Citizenship Education schools among
their own communities.

*Source:* Septima P. Clark, "Literacy and Education," *Freedomways,* 4 (Winter 1964).

The program now being sponsored by the Southern Christian Leadership Conference has resulted in the training of more than eight hundred persons in the best methods to stimulate voter registration back in their home towns. Their home towns comprising eleven southern states from eastern Texas to northern Virginia. The program was transferred to SCLC from The Highlander Folk School in Monteagle, Tennessee.

I learned of Highlander in 1952 but attended my first workshop in 1954. In 1955 I directed my first workshop and did door to door recruiting for the school. Unable to drive myself I found a driver for my car and made three trips from Johns Island, South Carolina to Monteagle, Tennessee. On each trip six islanders attended and were motivated. They became literate and are still working for liberation.

In 1954 in the South, segregation was the main barrier in the way of the realization of democracy and brotherhood. Highlander was an important place because Negroes and whites met on an equal basis and discussed their problems together.

There was a series of workshops on Community Services and Segregation; Registration and Voting; and Community Development. Then it became evident that the South had a great number of functional illiterates who needed additional help to carry out their plans for coping with the problems confronting them. Problems such as the following: Six-year-old Negro boys and girls walking five miles on a muddy road in icy, wet weather to a dilapidated, cold, log cabin school house in most of the rural sections of the south. In cities like Charleston, South Carolina children of that same tender age had to leave home while it was yet dark, 7:00 a.m., to attend an early morning session and vacate that classroom by 12:30 p.m. for another group in that same age bracket which would leave at 5:30 p.m. for home (night time during the winter months). These children would pass white schools that had regular school hours and fewer children enrolled. The Negro parents accepted this for many years. They did not know what to do about it. They had to be trained.

Highlander had always believed in people and the people trusted its judgement and accepted its leadership. It was accepted by Negroes and whites of all religious faiths because it had always accepted them and made them feel at home. The staff at Highlander knew that the great need of the South was to develop more people to take leadership and responsibility for the causes in which they believed. It set out on a program designed to bring out leadership qualities in people from all walks of life.

Adults from all over the South, about forty at a time, went there for the specific purpose of discussing their problems. They lived together in rustic, pleasant, rural surroundings on the top of the Cumberland plateau in a number of simple cabins around a lake, remote from business and other affairs that normally demand so much attention and energy. Though of different races and often of greatly contrasting economic or educational backgrounds, they rarely felt the tension that such differences can cause and if they did, as it occurred sometimes, it was never for long. They soon became conscious of the irrelevance of all such differences. Each person talked with people from communities with problems similar to those of his own. Each discussed both formally and informally the successes and difficulties he had had in his efforts to solve these problems in various ways.

The participants of the workshops included community leaders and civic minded adults affiliated with agencies and organizations. They had a common concern about problems but no one knew easy solutions. The issues then as now were among the most difficult faced by society. The highly practical discussions at the workshops challenged their thinking which in turn helped them to understand the difficulties and in most cases steps were suggested towards a solution. They found out that it was within their power to take the steps necessary to meet with members of school boards. In Charleston County they asked for new schools and buses to transport their children. They staged a boycott to get rid of double sessions. *They won!* The immense value of a willingness to take responsibility and to act becomes clear when one sees what others have done, apparently through this willingness alone.

Prior to the Supreme Court's decision of 1954 the Negro communities of the South would have been characterized as uncoordinated, made up of groups whose interests diverged or conflicted. Today one can say that the school integration issue has served to mobilize and unify the groups. The present psychological health of Negro leaders is good. Such things as an official ballot handed to Negro leaders in Alabama, on which is engraved a rooster crowing "white supremacy," will not weaken their determination nor courage to be free. They have amassed funds, sent men to the Justice Department and took their gerrymandering cases to the courts. Today they are registering to vote. The registrars are not hiding in the bank vaults any more. Literacy means liberation.

# Staughton Lynd

## Education and Empowerment, Continued

*In 1964 Staughton Lynd, a northern college teacher and historian, directed the Freedom School Project in Mississippi.*

People sometimes ask me how to start a Freedom School. This question seems almost funny. Few of us who planned the curriculum and administrative structure of the Mississippi Freedom Schools had any experience in Northern Freedom Schools. And in any case, our approach to curriculum was to have no curriculum and our approach to administrative structure was not to have any (I will explain this in a moment). So my answer to the question: "How do you start a Freedom School?" is, "I don't know." And if people ask, "What were the Freedom Schools like?" again I have to answer, "I don't know." I was an itinerant bureaucrat. I saw a play in Holly Springs, an adult class in Indianola, a preschool mass meeting in McComb, which were exciting. But who can presume to enclose in a few words what happened last summer when 2,500 youngsters from Mississippi and 250 youngsters from the North encountered each other, but not as students and teachers, in a learning experience that was not a school?

There was one educational experience for which I did most of the initial planning and which I took part in personally: the Freedom School Convention at Meridian on the weekend of August 7–9. Perhaps because this was the one "class" which I "taught," the Convention has loomed larger and larger in my mind as I have reflected on the summer. If I were to start a Freedom School now (and we are about to start one in New Haven), I would suggest: Begin with a Freedom School Convention and let that provide your curriculum.

The Freedom School Convention went a step beyond the

*Source:* Staughton Lynd, "The Freedom Schools: Concept and Organization," *Freedomways*, 5 (Spring 1965).

thinking which took place before the summer in its implications for the administration and curriculum of a school "stayed on freedom." Originally, we planned to have two residential schools for high school students who in the judgment of COFO staff had most leadership potential, with a network of twenty day schools feeding into them. Sometime in April it became apparent that sites for residential schools would not be forthcoming, and if they did, there would be no money to rent them. And we realized, after a few painful days, that this was a good thing. It meant that teachers would live within Negro communities rather than on sequestered campuses. It meant that we would have to ask ministers for the use of church basements as schools. In short, it meant we would run a school system without buildings, equipment or money (which we did: less than $2,000 passed through my office in Jackson in the course of the summer, about half of it for film rental).

It meant, too, that each school would be on its own, succeeding or failing by improvisation without much help from a central point. In my own mind the image which kept recurring was that of the guerrilla army which "swims in the sea" of the people among whom it lives. Clearly, whether we swam or drowned depended on the naked reaction of Negro children and their parents. No apparatus of compulsion or material things could shield us from their verdict. At the Oxford orientation, I kept repeating that when the Freedom School teachers got off the bus and found no place to sleep, despite previous assurances, and no place to teach, because the minister had gotten scared; when they were referred to an old lady of the local church for help in finding lodging, and to a youngster hanging around the COFO office for help in finding students— as they did these things, they would be building their school, their teaching would have begun. After about a week we knew that somehow, some way it was working. We had expected 1,000 students at the most; I can remember the night when I wrote on a blackboard in the Jackson COFO office: "1,500 students in Freedom School. *Yippee!*"

# Jack Minnis

## Economics and Race

*In 1965 Jack Minnis was director of the research department of SNCC. His comments reflect an interest in questions of the basis of power that go beyond the emotions of race.*

There has persisted, during the past hundred years and more, the impression that the race problems of the U.S. are largely a matter of prejudice, and that the prejudice is vulnerable to a program of education and information. In other words, this position holds that those who are in power, as well as those whose racial abuses are confined to their everyday acquaintances, act as they do because they sincerely believe that Negroes are inferior to whites. It further holds that if these persons were adequately informed, they would stop their anti-Negro behavior, and—presto—America's race problems would be ended.

This position, for all its orthodoxy, has never made much sense. The logical and physical contradictions in beliefs about racial inferiority are so notorious that they need not be dwelt on here. The point is that much, even, of Negroes' thinking about their problems is tainted with this orthodox position, and much of the civil rights movement is thoroughly committed to that position, though they probably wouldn't admit it.

The political program of the Mississippi Freedom Democratic Party during 1964 and early 1965, and what happened as a result of that program, if sufficiently understood, should lay to rest once and for all this myth about the superficiality of the race question in the U.S.

The term "closed society," referring to Mississippi and that state's race problem, gained much currency during the past two years as a result of the writings of Professor James Silver. Here

*Source:* Jack Minnis, "The Mississippi Freedom Democratic Party: A New Declaration of Independence," *Freedomways*, 5 (Spring 1965).

again there is a tendency, among many, grossly to oversimplify the meaning of the "closed society," and, consciously or not, to ignore the enormous implications of it. Professor Silver himself, I think, is guilty of this. When he supposes that the closed society in Mississippi can be opened by "the country as a whole, backed by the power and authority of the federal government," he ignores the simple fact that Mississippi could not have been what it has been all these years without the consent of "the country as a whole, backed by the power and authority of the federal government."

These two myths fit together perfectly. Mississippi is a "closed society" and what keeps it closed is the prejudice of white Mississippians who are prevented from learning the truth and thus dispelling their misbeliefs about Negroes. The myths are convenient and comfortable. They permit good, sound, solid Americans to put all the blame on a few Bilbos and Barnetts and the ignorant crew of "rednecks" who supposedly keep them in power.

Another myth which grows out of the joining of these two is that the solution to the problem is more federal legislation. In the past hundred years the 13th, 14th and 15th amendments, the several civil rights acts of the post-Civil War period, the civil rights Acts of 1957, 1960 and 1964 have become a part of the law of the land. The shelves of the law libraries are literally groaning under the weight of the laws which guarantee the rights of Negroes. Still Negroes do not have those rights, as a matter of fact.

The liberals, in and out of Congress, have for years lamented the control exercised in both Houses by conservatives, largely Southerners. The Southerners' longevity in office, it is said, coupled with the custom of according powerful positions based upon longevity, is responsible for the conservative bent of the Congress. Liberals offer as a solution the proposal that power be accorded on some basis other than longevity. They say this will make the U.S. Congress more representative of more people. The fact is, of course, that the longevity of the Southerners (who constitute the core of the power bloc in both houses) is based upon the disfranchisement of Negroes and of a large proportion of whites. So the *real* problem is not one of longevity, but of disfranchisement. It is hardly to be supposed that the problem of conservative control can be resolved so long as the disfranchisement remains, because the disfranchisement is the basis of the longevity which breeds the power, whatever the mechanics of organization by which the power is implemented. Now let's examine what this conservative power bloc does.

The South is notoriously lagging in industrial development.

And such development as has occurred has been in the labor-intensive industries such as minerals extraction, textiles, pulp-wood and paper, etc. Yet the Southerners are the darlings of the National Association of Manufacturers, the U.S. Chamber of Commerce, the American Bankers Association, the American Medical Association—in short, the Southerners are clearly representing interests which have little to do with the constituencies from which the Southerners are elected.

On the other hand, the liberals in Congress come from precisely those states in which the interests represented by these organizations are most involved. Thus, industrial development having brought about some degree of effective political mobilization of the people, the conservative interests in those states have sought and obtained disproportionate representation in Congress by trading upon the disfranchisement of Southerners, which guarantees the longevity upon which congressional power is based.

Here, I think, is the answer to that compelling question: Why has no federal administration, Democrat or Republican, enforced existing legislation guaranteeing the right to vote in the South? The enormous cost of winning nomination and election to the Presidency can only be borne by those who control the institutions of corporate wealth in the U.S. I think, in a very real sense, whether consciously or unconsciously, any President and any Vice-President becomes the creature of corporate wealth as a condition of his access to the prerequisites of nomination and election. Indeed, I should suppose that by the time an individual has pursued politics long enough to have become presidential timber, he *is* their creature, whether or not he seeks the presidency.

# Mrs. Fannie Lee Chaney

## Meridian Awakened

*Mrs. Chaney was the mother of James Chaney, the black civil rights worker murdered along with the northern volunteers Andrew Goodman and Michael Schwerner in the Freedom Summer project.*

I am here to tell you about Meridian, Mississippi. That's my home. I have been there all of my days. I know the white man; I know the black man. The white man is not for the black man—we are just there. Everything to be done, to be said, the white man is going to do it; *he* is going to say it, right or wrong. We hadn't, from the time that I know of, been able to vote or register in Meridian. Now, since the civil rights workers have been down in Mississippi working, they have allowed a lot of them to go to register. A lot of our people are scared, afraid. They are still backward. "I can't do that; I never have," they claimed. "I have been here too long. I will lose my job; I won't have any job." So, that is just the way it is. My son, James, when he went out with the civil rights workers around the first of '64 felt it was something he wanted to do, and he enjoyed working in the civil rights Movement. He stayed in Canton, Mississippi, working on voter registration from February through March. When he came home he told me how he worked and lived those few weeks he was there; he said, "Mother, one half of the time, I was out behind houses or churches waiting to get the opportunity to talk to people about what they needed and what they ought to do." He said, "Sometime they shunned me off and some would say, 'I want you all to stay away from here and leave me alone.'" But he would pick his chance and go back again. That is what I say about Mississippi right now. There is one more test I want to do there. I am working with the civil rights Movement, my

*Source:* "An Address by Mrs. Fannie Lee Chaney of Meridian, Mississippi," *Freedom-ways,* 5 (Spring 1965).

whole family is, and my son, Ben, here, he is going to take his big brother's place.

He has been working for civil rights. Everything he can do, he does it. For his activities, he had been jailed twice before he was 12 years old. He told me when he was in jail he wasn't excited. He is not afraid; he would go to jail again! I am too, because we need and we've got to go to jail and we've got to get where the white man is. The white man has got Mississippi and we are just there working for the white man. He is the one getting rich. And when he gets rich, we can be outdoors or in old houses and he is going to knock on the door and get his rent money.

This is not something that has just now started, it has been going on before my time and I imagine before my parents' time. It is not just *now* the white man is doing this; it was borne from generation to generation. So, as I say, Ben is going to take his big brother's place, and I am with him and the rest of the family also. You all read about Mississippi—all parts of Mississippi, but I just wish it was so you could just come down there and be able to see; just try to live there just for one day, and you will know just how it is there.

# Bayard Rustin

## Protest Movement and Social Movement

*Bayard Rustin, a seasoned black civil rights and peace activist—a member of the Fellowship of Reconciliation, he was an early official of CORE—here speaks for a moment when champions of civil rights were learning the distinction between overthrowing formal segregation and winning concrete economic equality. Rustin was among those who, in pursuit of economic justice for black Americans, endorsed not black separatism but political alliance between black and white progressives.*

What is the value of winning access to public accommodations for those who lack money to use them? The minute the movement faced this question, it was compelled to expand its vision beyond race relations to economic relations, including the role of education in modern society. And what also became clear is that all these interrelated problems, by their very nature, are not soluble by private, voluntary efforts but require government action— or politics. Already Southern demonstrators had recognized that the most effective way to strike at the police brutality they suffered from was by getting rid of the local sheriff—and that meant political action, which in turn meant, and still means, political action within the Democratic party where the only meaningful primary contests in the South are fought.

And so, in Mississippi, thanks largely to the leadership of Bob Moses, a turn toward political action has been taken. More than voter registration is involved here. A conscious bid for *political power* is being made, and in the course of that effort a tactical shift is being effected: direct-action techniques are being subordinated to a strategy calling for the building of community institutions or

*Source:* Bayard Rustin, "From Protest to Politics: The Future of the Civil Rights Movement," *Commentary*, 39 (February 1965). Reprinted by permission.

power bases. Clearly, the implications of this shift reach far beyond Mississippi. What began as a protest movement is being challenged to translate itself into a political movement. Is this the
right course? And if it is, can the transformation be accomplished?

The very decade which has witnessed the decline of legal Jim
Crow has also seen the rise of *de facto* segregation in our most fundamental socio-economic institutions. More Negroes are unemployed today than in 1954, and the unemployment gap between
the races is wider. The median income of Negroes has dropped
from 57 per cent to 54 per cent of that of whites. A higher percent-
age of Negro workers is now concentrated in jobs vulnerable to
automation than was the case ten years ago. More Negroes attend
*de facto* segregated schools today than when the Supreme Court
handed down its famous decision; while school integration pro-
ceeds at a snail's pace in the South, the number of Northern
schools with an excessive proportion of minority youth prolifer-
ates. And behind this is the continuing growth of racial slums,
spreading over our central cities and trapping Negro youth in a
milieu which, whatever its legal definition, sows an unimaginable
demoralization. Again, legal niceties aside, a resident of a racial
ghetto lives in segregated housing, and more Negroes fall into this
category than ever before.

These are the facts of life which generate frustration in the
Negro community and challenge the civil rights movement. At
issue, after all, is not *civil rights*, strictly speaking, but social and
economic conditions. Last summer's riots were not race riots; they
were outbursts of class aggression in a society where class and
color definitions are converging disastrously. How can the (perhaps misnamed) civil rights movement deal with this problem? . . .

This matter of economic role brings us to the greater problem—the fact that we are moving into an era in which the natural
functioning of the market does not by itself ensure every man with
will and ambition a place in the productive process. The immigrant who came to this country during the late 19th and early 20th
centuries entered a society which was expanding territorially
and/or economically. It was then possible to start at the bottom,
as an unskilled or semi-skilled worker, and move up the ladder, acquiring new skills along the way. Especially was this true
when industrial unionism was burgeoning, giving new dignity
and higher wages to organized workers. Today the situation has
changed. We are not expanding territorially, the western frontier
is settled, labor organizing has leveled off, our rate of economic
growth has been stagnant for a decade. And we are in the midst of

a technological revolution which is altering the fundamental structure of the labor force, destroying unskilled and semi-skilled jobs—jobs in which Negroes are disproportionately concentrated.

Whatever the pace of this technological revolution may be, the *direction* is clear: the lower rungs of the economic ladder are being lopped off. This means that an individual will no longer be able to start at the bottom and work his way up; he will have to start in the middle or on top, and hold on tight. It will not even be enough to have certain specific skills, for many skilled jobs are also vulnerable to automation. A broad educational background, permitting vocational adaptability and flexibility, seems more imperative than ever. We live in a society where, as Secretary of Labor Willard Wirtz puts it, machines have the equivalent of a high school diploma. Yet the average educational attainment of American Negroes is 8.2 years....

Let me sum up what I have thus far been trying to say: the civil rights movement is evolving from a protest movement into a full-fledged *social movement*—an evolution calling its very name into question. It is now concerned not merely with removing the barriers to full *opportunity* but with achieving the fact of *equality*. From sit-ins and freedom rides we have gone into rent strikes, boycotts, community organization, and political action. As a consequence of this natural evolution, the Negro today finds himself stymied by obstacles of far greater magnitude than the legal barriers he was attacking before: automation, urban decay, *de facto* school segregation. These are problems which, while conditioned by Jim Crow, do not vanish upon its demise. They are more deeply rooted in our socio-economic order; they are the result of the total society's failure to meet not only the Negro's needs, but human needs generally....

The revolutionary character of the Negro's struggle is manifest in the fact that this struggle may have done more to democratize life for whites than for Negroes. Clearly, it was the sit-in movement of young Southern Negroes which, as it galvanized white students, banished the ugliest features of McCarthyism from the American campus and resurrected political debate. It was not until Negroes assaulted *de facto* school segregation in the urban centers that the issue of quality education for *all* children stirred into motion. Finally, it seems reasonably clear that the civil rights movement, directly and through the resurgence of social conscience it kindled, did more to initiate the war on poverty than any other single force....

Neither that movement nor the country's twenty million

black people can win political power alone. We need allies. The
future of the Negro struggle depends on whether the contradictions of this society can be resolved by a coalition of progressive
forces which becomes the *effective* political majority in the United
States. I speak of the coalition which staged the March on Washington, passed the Civil Rights Act, and laid the basis for the Johnson landslide—Negroes, trade unionists, liberals, and religious
groups. . . .

The role of the civil rights movement in the reorganization
of American political life is programmatic as well as strategic.
We are challenged now to broaden our social vision, to develop
functional programs with concrete objectives. We need to propose alternatives to technological unemployment, urban decay,
and the rest. We need to be calling for public works and training,
for national economic planning, for federal aid to education, for
attractive public housing—all this on a sufficiently massive scale
to make a difference. We need to protest the notion that our integration into American life, so long delayed, must now proceed in
an atmosphere of competitive scarcity instead of in the security of
abundance which technology makes possible. We cannot claim to
have answers to all the complex problems of modern society. That
is too much to ask of a movement still battling barbarism in Mississippi. But we can agitate the right questions by probing at the
contradictions which still stand in the way of the "Great Society."
The questions having been asked, motion must begin in the larger
society, for there is a limit to what Negroes can do alone.

# Mrs. Fannie Lou Hamer

## Sustaining the Original Vision of SNCC

*Mrs. Hamer was present at the Democratic Convention of 1964 as part of the Mississippi Freedom Democratic Party delegation. Her plea there for justice and her recounting of the beating she had received for attempting to register for the vote provided the Convention with its most eloquent moments. Despite her disappointment at the failure of the party to provide an adequate place for the MFDP, she did not later follow other black members of SNCC in rejecting cooperation with whites. As the final selection here reveals, her power was interior to her.*

Mr. Chairman, and the Credentials Committee, my name is Mrs. Fannie Lou Hamer, and I live at 626 East Lafayette Street, Ruleville, Mississippi, Sunflower County, the home of Senator James O. Eastland, and Senator Stennis.

It was the 31st of August in 1962 that eighteen of us traveled twenty-six miles to the county courthouse in Indianola to try to register to try to become first-class citizens. We was met in Indianola by Mississippi men, highway patrolmens, and they only allowed two of us in to take the literacy test at the time. After we had taken this test and started back to Ruleville, we was held up by the City Police and the State Highway Patrolmen and carried back to Indianola, where the bus driver was charged that day with driving a bus the wrong color.

After we paid the fine among us, we continued on to Ruleville, and Reverend Jeff Sunny carried me four miles in the rural area where I had worked as a timekeeper and sharecropper for eighteen years. I was met there by my children, who told me the plantation owner was angry because I had gone down to try to register. After

*Source:* Kay Mills, *This Little Light of Mine: The Life of Fannie Lou Hamer* (New York: Dutton, 1993).

they told me, my husband came, and said the plantation owner was raising cain because I had tried to register, and before he quit talking the plantation owner came, and said, "Fannie Lou, do you know—did Pap tell you what I said?"

I said, "Yes, sir."

He said, "I mean that," he said. "If you don't go down and withdraw your registration, you will have to leave," said, "Then if you go down and withdraw," he said. "You will—you might have to go because we are not ready for that in Mississippi."

And I addressed him and told him and said, "I didn't try to register for you. I tried to register for myself." I had to leave that same night.

On the 10th of September, 1962, sixteen bullets was fired into the home of Mr. and Mrs. Robert Tucker for me. That same night two girls were shot in Ruleville, Mississippi. Also Mr. Joe McDonald's house was shot in.

And in June the 9th, 1963, I had attended a voter-registration workshop, was returning back to Mississippi. Ten of us was traveling by the Continental Trailway bus. When we got to Winona, Mississippi, which is Montgomery County, four of the pople got off to use the washroom, and two of the people—to use the restaurant—two of the people wanted to use the washroom. The four people that had gone in to use the restaurant was ordered out. During this time I was on the bus. But when I looked through the window and saw they had rushed out, I got off of the bus to see what had happened, and one of the ladies said, "It was a state highway patrolman and a chief of police ordered us out."

I got back on the bus and one of the persons had used the washroom got back on the bus, too. As soon as I was seated on the bus, I saw when they began to get the four people in a highway patrolman's car. I stepped off the bus to see what was happening and somebody screamed from the car that the four workers was in and said, "Get that one there," and when I went to get in the car, when the man told me I was under arrest, he kicked me.

I was carried to the county jail, and put in the booking room. They left some of the people in the booking room and began to place us in cells. I was placed in a cell with a young woman called Miss Euvester Simpson. After I was placed in the cell I began to hear sounds of licks and screams. I could hear the sounds of licks and horrible screams, and I could hear somebody say, "Can you say, yes sir, nigger? Can you say yes, sir?"

And they would say other horrible names. She would say, "Yes, I can say yes, sir."

"So say it."

She says, "I don't know you well enough."

They beat her, I don't know how long, and after a while she began to pray, and asked God to have mercy on those people.

And it wasn't too long before three white men came to my cell. One of these men was a State Highway Patrolman and he asked me where I was from, and I told him Ruleville. He said, "We are going to check this." And they left my cell and it wasn't too long before they came back. He said, "You are from Ruleville all right," and he used a curse word, and he said, "We are going to make you wish you was dead."

I was carried out of that cell into another cell where they had two Negro prisoners. The State Highway Patrolman ordered the first Negro to take the blackjack. The first Negro prisoner ordered me, by orders from the State Highway Patrolman for me, to lay down on a bunk bed on my face, and I laid on my face. The first Negro began to beat, and I was beat by the first Negro until he was exhausted, and I was holding my hands behind me at that time on my left side because I suffered from polio when I was six years old. After the first Negro had beat until he was exhausted, the State Highway Patrolman ordered the second Negro to take the blackjack.

The second Negro began to beat and I began to work my feet, and the State Highway Patrolman ordered the first Negro who had beat to set on my feet to keep me from working my feet. I began to scream and one white man got up and began to beat me in my head and tell me to hush. One white man—my dress had worked up high, he walked over and pulled my dress down—and he pulled my dress back, back up.

I was in jail when Medgar Evers was murdered. . . .

All of this is on account we want to register, to become first-class citizens, and if the Freedom Democratic Party is not seated now, I question America, is this America, the land of the free and the home of the brave where we have to sleep with our telephones off the hooks because our lives be threatened daily because we want to live as decent human beings, in America?

"Thank you."

*     *     *

[Interview on September 2, 1967, in Ruleville, Mississippi.]

---

*Source:* Emily Stoper, *The Student Nonviolent Coordinating Committee.*

Q. When did you first become involved with SNCC?

A. In 1962. I had never been involved in civil rights before. In fact, I had hardly ever heard about these things. I was too tired from working in the fields to keep up with the news.

My pastor told me about the first mass meeting. James Forman, James Bevel and Reggie Robinson were there. They talked about how it was our constitutional right to register to vote, to be a first-class citizen. [Mrs. Blackwell reported same.]

Q. Did they give other reasons for registering?

A. [hesitates] Well, yes, they said you could vote people out of office if you weren't satisfied with them. Then they asked for volunteers to try to register. I was one of eighteen volunteers. The same day I tried to register, I was fired from my job. The landlord told me straight out it was because I had tried to register.

Q. What was SNCC trying to do that was different from what the NAACP was trying to do?

A. The NAACP talked big, but they weren't doing anything. They just weren't going out in the local areas and getting people to do things. I had never even heard of the NAACP before SNCC came on the scene. Since then, I've also worked with CORE and SCLC.

Q. Were you ever on SNCC staff?

A. Yes, I was put on staff in '63. I worked on voter registration. I hoped and I still hope to use the ballot to get our share of the control. We [Negroes] are 60% of Sunflower County [where Ruleville is]. I think the white man respects power and would change his ways if we had power.

Q. Do you remember how the FDP was founded?

A. In '64, after we had tried to go to the Democratic Party precinct meetings and been barred from them, we held our own precinct meetings. Then, on April 26, 1964, the MFDP was officially organized in Jackson. It was organized because we could not get into the regular party. I have learned a great deal through it.

Both the people in SNCC and the local people wanted to go to Atlantic City. I didn't actually expect to be seated, but I believed we'd get *something*, and that compromise they offered us was nothing. After the convention, some people became bitter, some became disillusioned, some became discouraged. I myself was shocked by what happened. I was educated by what I had to fight. I found out there was no trick too low that a man wouldn't stoop to it for power.

But I think blacks and whites still got to work together. I'd like to see democracy work—I haven't given up yet. I'm not one of those who go around hating all the time. If I was like that, I'd be a miserable person. I keep remembering that righteousness exalts a nation; hate just makes people miserable.

I remained a member of SNCC until last December. I wouldn't work even with FDP if it didn't function for people. The races have got to try to understand each other. I feel sorry for the suffering of the poor whites too.

\*       \*       \*

Well, one time, I asked my mother why wasn't we white; and she really had a fit when I said that to her. . . . [W]e would work all the summer and we would work until it get so cold that you would have to tie rags around our feet and sacks . . . to keep our feet warm while we would get out and scrap cotton. Well, then we wouldn't have anything; we wouldn't have anything to eat; sometime we wouldn't have anything but water and bread. And I asked her why wasn't we white, because they were the people that wasn't working, they were the people that had food because when we will go to their house to wash they clothes, I would notice they would have very good food, and they wasn't doing anything.

So, I said then, to make it you had to be white, and I wanted to be white; and she told me, she said, no that's not it, don't ever let me say that word again. Said, be grateful that you are black, because if God had wanted you to be white, you would have been white, so you accept yourself for what you are. And says, one thing I want you to get in your head and she began to tell me things, over and over, and it wasn't many weeks passed that she wouldn't . . . say, you respect yourself as a black child, and when you get grown, if I'm dead and gone, you respect yourself as a black woman; and other people will respect you. . . . But as time pass, and as I got older, I used to watch my mother with tears in my eyes. . . . I used to see my mother cut those same trees with an axe just like a man; she would carry us out . . . in these different areas, where they were cleaning up new grounds and we would have to rake up brush you know, and burn it. The same land thats in cultivation now, that they got closed to us that we can't own, my parent helped to make this ground what it is. So then I watched her. As I got older, it was a time just to give us a decent meal then her clothes would be heavy with patches, just mended over and over, where she would mend it and that mend would break, and she would mend it with

*Source:* Transcript of Mrs. Fannie Lou Hamer, oral history interview, Moorland-Spingarn Research Center, Howard University. Interview on August 20, 1968; Robert Wright, interviewer.

something else. Her clothes would become very heavy. So, I promised myself if I ever got grown, I would never see her wear a patched piece; I didn't want her to wear it. And I began to see the suffering that she had gone through. At night she would sing ... songs that would really sank down in me, you know, and some of the songs was like, "I would not be a white man, I'll tell you the reason why, I'm afraid my lord might would call me and I wouldn't be ready to die." You know because she knowed, she would say in songs what was really happening to us. And then, I think it was 1954, or '55, '54 I think it was, she moved with us moved in the house with me and my husband; because she had got very old and, you know, she was just beaten down by what the oppressor had done to us.

# Stokely Carmichael
# (Kwame Ture)

## Definitions of Black Power

*In the first of the two selections here, Stokely Carmichael
works toward a reasoned definition of the purposes of black
power. In the other, he affects a more belligerent rhetoric.
Together, the two reveal the elusiveness of the phrase and
the ease with which differing meanings and emotions
could fix themselves to it. Carmichael eventually took the
African name.*

Traditionally, for each new ethnic group, the route to social
and political integration into America's pluralistic society has
been through the organization of their own institutions with which
to represent their communal needs within the larger society. This
is simply stating what the advocates of black power are saying.
The strident outcry, *particularly* from the liberal community, that
has been evoked by this proposal can only be understood by exam-
ining the historic relationship between Negro and White power in
this country.

Negroes are defined by two forces, their blackness and their
powerlessness. There have been traditionally two communities in
America. The White community, which controlled and defined the
forms that all institutions within the society would take, and the
Negro community which has been excluded from participation in
the power decisions that shaped the society, and has traditionally
been dependent upon, and subservient to the White community.

This has not been accidental. The history of every institution
of this society indicates that a major concern in the ordering and
structuring of the society has been the maintaining of the Negro
community in its condition of dependence and oppression. This
has not been on the level of individual acts of discrimination
between individual whites against individual Negroes, but as total

---

*Source:* Stokely Carmichael, "Toward Black Liberation," *The Massachusetts Review*, 7 (Autumn 1966). Reprinted by permission.

acts by the White community against the Negro community. This fact cannot be too strongly emphasized—that racist assumptions of white superiority have been so deeply ingrained in the structure of the society that it infuses its entire functioning, and is so much a part of the national subconscious that it is taken for granted and is frequently not even recognized.

Let me give an example of the difference between individual racism and institutionalized racism, and the society's response to both. When unidentified white terrorists bomb a Negro Church and kill five children, that is an act of individual racism, widely deplored by most segments of the society. But when in that same city, Birmingham, Alabama, not five but 500 Negro babies die each year because of a lack of proper food, shelter and medical facilities, and thousands more are destroyed and maimed physically, emotionally and intellectually because of conditions of poverty and deprivation in the ghetto, that is a function of institutionalized racism. But the society either pretends it doesn't know of this situation, or is incapable of doing anything meaningful about it. And this resistance to doing anything meaningful about conditions in that ghetto comes from the fact that the ghetto is itself a product of a combination of forces and special interests in the white community, and the groups that have access to the resources and power to change that situation benefit, politically and economically, from the existence of that ghetto.

It is more than a figure of speech to say that the Negro community in America is the victim of white imperialism and colonial exploitation. This is in practical economic and political terms true. There are over 20 million black people comprising ten percent of this nation. They for the most part live in well-defined areas of the country—in the shanty-towns and rural black belt areas of the South, and increasingly in the slums of northern and western industrial cities. If one goes into any Negro community, whether it be in Jackson, Miss., Cambridge, Md. or Harlem, N.Y., one will find that the same combination of political, economic, and social forces are at work. The people in the Negro community do not control the resources of that community, its political decisions, its law enforcement, its housing standards; and even the physical ownership of the land, houses, and stores *lie outside that community.* . . .

In recent years the answer to these questions which has been given by most articulate groups of Negroes and their white allies, the "liberals" of all stripes, has been in terms of something called "integration." According to the advocates of integration, social justice will be accomplished by "integrating the Negro into the

mainstream institutions of the society from which he has been traditionally excluded." It is very significant that each time I have
heard this formulation it has been in terms of "the Negro," the
individual Negro, rather than in terms of the community.

This concept of integration had to be based on the assumption that there was nothing of value in the Negro community and
that little of value could be created among Negroes, so the thing to
do was to siphon off the "acceptable" Negroes into the surrounding middle-class white community. Thus the goal of the movement
for integration was simply to loosen up the restrictions barring
the entry of Negroes into the white community. Goals around
which the struggle took place, such as public accommodation,
open housing, job opportunity on the executive level (which is easier to deal with than the problem of semi-skilled and blue collar
jobs which involve more far-reaching economic adjustments), are
quite simply middle-class goals, articulated by a tiny group of
Negroes who had middle-class aspirations. It is true that the student demonstrations in the South during the early sixties, out of
which SNCC came, had a similar orientation. But while it is hardly
a concern of a black sharecropper, dishwasher, or welfare recipient
whether a certain fifteen-dollar-a-day motel offers accommodations to Negroes, the overt symbols of white superiority and the
imposed limitations on the Negro community had to be destroyed.
Now, black people must look beyond these goals, to the issues of
collective power.

Such a limited class orientation was reflected not only in the
program and goals of the civil rights movement, but in its tactics
and organization. It is very significant that the two oldest and
most "respectable" civil rights organizations have constitutions
which *specifically* prohibit partisan political activity. CORE once
did, but changed that clause when it changed its orientation
toward black power. But this is perfectly understandable in terms
of the strategy and goals of the older organizations. The civil rights
movement saw its role as a kind of liaison between the powerful white community and the dependent Negro one. The dependent status of the black community apparently was unimportant
since—if the movement were successful—it was going to blend
into the white community anyway. We made no pretense of organizing and developing institutions of community power in the
Negro community, but appealed to the conscience of white institutions of power. The posture of the civil rights movement was that
of the dependent, the suppliant. The theory was that without
attempting to create any organized base of political strength itself,
the civil rights movement could, by forming coalitions with vari-

ous "liberal" pressure organizations in the white community—liberal reform clubs, labor unions, church groups, progressive civic groups—and at times one or other of the major political parties—influence national legislation and national social patterns.

I think we all have seen the limitations of this approach. We have repeatedly seen that political alliances based on appeals to conscience and decency are chancy things, simply because institutions and political organizations have no consciences outside their own special interests. The political and social rights of Negroes have been and always will be negotiable and expendable the moment they conflict with the interests of our "allies." If we do not learn from history, we are doomed to repeat it, and that is precisely the lesson of the Reconstruction. Black people were allowed to register, vote and participate in politics because it was to the advantage of powerful white allies to promote this. But this was the result of white decision, and it was ended by other white men's decision before any political base powerful enough to challenge that decision could be established in the southern Negro community. (Thus at this point in the struggle Negroes have no assurance—save a kind of idiot optimism and faith in a society whose history is one of racism—that if it were to become necessary, even the painfully limited gains thrown to the civil rights movement by the Congress will not be revoked as soon as a shift in political sentiments should occur.)

The major limitation of this approach was that it tended to maintain the traditional dependence of Negroes, and of the movement. We depended upon the good-will and support of various groups within the white community whose interests were not always compatible with ours. To the extent that we depended on the financial support of other groups, we were vulnerable to their influence and domination.

\*       \*       \*

Now we've got to talk about this thing called the serious coalition. You know what that's all about? That says that black folks and their white liberal friends can get together and overcome. We have to examine our white liberal friends. And I'm going to call names this time around. We've got to examine our white liberal friends who come to Mississippi and march with us, and can afford to march because our mothers, who are their maids, are taking care of their house and their children; we got to examine them

*Source:* Robert L. Scott and Wayne Brockriede, comps., *The Rhetoric of Black Power* (New York and Evanston: Harper and Row, 1969).

[applause]. Yeah; I'm going to speak the truth tonight. I'm going to tell you what a white liberal is. You talking about a white college kid joining hands with a black man in the ghetto, that college kid is fighting for the right to wear a beard and smoke pot, and we fighting for our lives [cheers and applause]. We fighting for our lives [continued applause].

That missionary comes to the ghetto one summer, and the next summer he's in Europe, and he's our ally. That missionary has a black mammy, and he stole our black mammy from us. Because while she was home taking care of them, she couldn't take care of us. That's not our ally [applause]. Now I met some of those white liberals on the march, and I asked one man, I said, look here brother. I said, you make what, about twenty-five thousand dollars a year? He mumbled. I said, well dig. Look here. Here are four black Mississippians. They make three dollars a day picking cotton. See they have to march; you can afford to march. I say, here's what we do. Take your twenty-five thousand dollars a year divide it up evenly. Let all five of you make five thousand dollars a year. He was for everybody working hard by the sweat of their brow [laughter and shouts]. That's a white liberal, ladies and gentlemen. That's a white liberal. You can't form a coalition with people who are economically secure. College students are economically secure; they've already got their wealth; we fighting to get ours. And for us to get it is going to mean tearing down their system, and they are not willing to work for their own destruction. Get that into your own minds now [applause]. Get that into your own minds now [continued applause]. . . .

When I talk about Black Power, it is presumptuous for any white man to talk about it, because I'm talking to black people [applause]. And I've got news for our liberal friend Bobby Kennedy. I got news for that white man. When he talks about his Irish Catholic power that made him to the position where he is that he now uses black votes in New York City to run for the presidency in 1972, he ought to not say a word about Black Power. Now the Kennedys built a system of purely Irish Catholic power with Irish Nationalism interwoven into it. Did you know that? And that's how come they run, rule, own Boston lock stock and barrel including all the black people inside it. That's Irish power. And that man going to get up and tell you-all; well he shouldn't talk about Black Power. He ran and won in New York City on Black Power; his brother became president because Black Power made him president [shouts and applause]. Black Power made his brother president [continued applause]. And he's got the white nerve to talk about Black Power [continued applause]. . . .

# Charles Hamilton

## Another Definition

*Charles Hamilton, who had been coauthor with Carmichael of a book on black power, here describes the phenomenon in a way that invites cooperation with whites. The essay is dated April 14, 1968*

Black Power has many definitions and connotations in the rhetoric of race relations today. To some people, it is synonymous with premeditated acts of violence to destroy the political and economic institutions of this country. Others equate Black Power with plans to rid the civil-rights movement of whites who have been in it for years. The concept is understood by many to mean hatred of and separation from whites; it is associated with calling whites "honkies" and with shouts of "Burn, baby, burn!" Some understand it to be the use of pressure-group tactics in the accepted tradition of the American political process. And still others say that Black Power must be seen first of all as an attempt to instill a sense of identity and pride in black people.

Ultimately, I suspect, we have to accept the fact that, in this highly charged atmosphere, it is virtually impossible to come up with a single definition satisfactory to all.

Even as some of us try to articulate our idea of Black Power and the way we relate to it and advocate it, we are categorized as "moderate" or "militant" or "reasonable" or "extremist." "I can accept your definition of Black Power," a listener will say to me. "But how does your position compare with what Stokely Carmichael said in Cuba or with what H. Rap Brown said in Cambridge, Md.?" Or, just as frequently, some young white New Left advocate will come up to me and proudly announce: "You're not radical enough. Watts, Newark, Detroit—that's what's happening, man! You're nothing but a reformist. We've got to blow up this society.

*Source: The New York Times Magazine* (April 14, 1968).

Read Ché or Debray or Mao." All I can do is shrug and conclude that some people believe that making a revolution in this country involves rhetoric, Molotov cocktails and being under 30.

To have Black Power equated with calculated acts of violence would be very unfortunate. First, if black people have learned anything over the years, it is that he who shouts revolution the loudest is one of the first to run when the action starts. Second, open calls to violence are a sure way to have one's ranks immediately infiltrated. Third—and this is as important as any reason—violent revolution in this country would fail; it would be met with the kind of repression used in Sharpeville, South Africa, in 1960, when 67 Africans were killed and 186 wounded during a demonstration against apartheid. It is clear that America is not above this. There are many white bigots who would like nothing better than to embark on a program of black genocide, even though the imposition of such repressive measures would destroy civil liberties for whites as well as for blacks. Some whites are so panicky, irrational and filled with racial hatred that they would welcome the opportunity to annihilate the black community. This was clearly shown in the senseless murder of Dr. Martin Luther King, Jr., which understandably—but nonetheless irrationally—prompted some black militants to advocate violent retaliation. Such cries for revenge intensify racial fear and animosity when the need—now more than ever—is to establish solid, stable organizations and action programs.

Many whites will take comfort in these words of caution against violence. But they should not. The truth is that the black ghettos are going to continue to blow up out of sheer frustration and rage, and no amount of rhetoric from professors writing articles in magazines (which most black people in the ghettos do not read anyway) will affect that. There comes a point beyond which people cannot be expected to endure prejudice, oppression and deprivation, and they *will* explode. . . .

Black Power rejects the lessons of slavery and segregation that caused black people to look upon themselves with hatred and disdain. To be "integrated" it was necessary to deny one's heritage, one's own culture, to be ashamed of one's black skin, thick lips and kinky hair. In their book, "Racial Crisis in America," two Florida State University sociologists, Lewis M. Killian and Charles M. Grigg, wrote: "At the present time, integration as a solution to the race problem demands that the Negro foreswear his identity as a Negro. But for a lasting solution, the meaning of 'American' must lose its implicit racial modifier, 'white.' " The black man must change his demeaning conception of himself; he must develop a sense of pride and self-respect. Then, if integration comes, it will deal with people who are psychologically and mentally healthy, with people who have a sense of their history and of themselves as whole human beings. . . .

This brings us to a consideration of the external problems of the black community. It is clear that black people will need the help of whites at many places along the line. There simply are not sufficient economic resources—actual or potential—in the black community for a total, unilateral, boot-strap operation. Why should there be? Black people have been the target of deliberate denial for centuries, and racist America has done its job well. This is a serious problem that must be faced by Black Power advocates. On the one hand, they recognize the need to be independent of "the white power structure." And on the other, they must frequently turn to that structure for help—technical and financial. Thus, the rhetoric and the reality often clash.

Resolution probably lies in the realization by white America that it is in her interest not to have a weak, dependent, alienated black community inhabiting the inner cities and blowing them up periodically. Society needs stability, and as long as there is a sizable powerless, restless group within it which considers the society illegitimate, stability is not possible. However it is calculated, the situation calls for a black-white rapprochement, which may well come only through additional confrontations and crises. More frequently than not, the self-interest of the dominant society is not clearly perceived until the brink is reached.

# James Forman

## The Black Manifesto

*James Forman, an official of SNCC during its transition from its interracial phase, here presents to the National Black Economic Development Conference in Detroit a statement that the Conference adopted on April 26, 1969. The demands were a momentarily sensational event in the black power movement. Forman was among the leading activists during the angriest days of the 1960s but also one of the most reflective.*

To the White Christian Churches and the Synagogues in the United States of America and to All Other Racist Institutions: . . .

We are an African people. We sit back and watch the Jews in this country make Israel a powerful conservative state in the Middle East, but we are not concerned actively about the plight of our brothers in Africa. We are the most advanced technological group of black people in the world, and there are many skills that could be offered in Africa. At the same time, it must be publicly stated that many African leaders are in disarray themselves, having been duped into following the lines as laid out by the western imperialist governments. Africans themselves succumbed to and are victims of the power of the United States. For instance, during the summer of 1967, as the representatives of SNCC, Howard Moore and I traveled extensively in Tanzania and Zambia. We talked to high, very high, government officials. We told them there were many black people in the United States who were willing to come and work in Africa. All these government officials, who were part of the leadership in their respective governments, said they wanted us to send as many skilled people as we could contact. But this program never came into fruition, and we do not know

*Source: Black Manifesto: Religion, Racism, and Reparations,* edited by Robert S. Lecky and H. Elliott Wright (New York: Sheed and Ward, 1969). Reprinted by permission.

the exact reasons, for I assure you that we talked and were committed to making this a successful program. It is our guess that the United States put the squeeze on these countries, for such a program directed by SNCC would have been too dangerous to the international prestige of the United States. It is also possible that some of the wild statements by some black leader frightened the Africans. . . .

Our fight is against racism, capitalism and imperialism, and we are dedicated to building a socialist society inside the United States where the total means of production and distribution are in the hands of the State, and that must be led by black people, by revolutionary blacks who are concerned about the total humanity of this world. And, therefore, we obviously are different from some of those who seek a black nation in the United States, for there is no way for that nation to be viable if in fact the United States remains in the hands of white racists. Then too, let us deal with some arguments that we should share power with whites. We say that there must be a revolutionary black vanguard, and that white people in this country must be willing to accept black leadership, for that is the only protection that black people have to protect ourselves from racism rising again in this country. . . .

We the black people assembled in Detroit, Michigan, for the National Black Economic Development Conference are fully aware that we have been forced to come together because racist white America has exploited our resources, our minds, our bodies, our labor. For centuries we have been forced to live as colonized people inside the United States, victimized by the most vicious, racist system in the world. We have helped to build the most industrialized country in the world.

We are therefore demanding of the white Christian churches and Jewish synagogues, which are part and parcel of the system of capitalism, that they begin to pay reparations to black people in this country. We are demanding $500,000,000 from the Christian white churches and the Jewish synagogues. This total comes to fifteen dollars per nigger. This is a low estimate, for we maintain there are probably more than 30,000,000 black people in this country. Fifteen dollars a nigger is not a large sum of money, and we know that the churches and synagogues have a tremendous wealth and its membership, white America, has profited and still exploits black people. We are also not unaware that the exploitation of colored peoples around the world is aided and abetted by the white Christian churches and synagogues. This demand for $500,000,000 is not an idle resolution or empty words. Fifteen dollars for every black brother and sister in the United States is only a beginning of the reparations due us as people who have been exploited and degraded, brutalized, killed and persecuted. Underneath all of this exploitation, the racism of this country has produced a psychological effect upon us that we are beginning to shake off. We are no longer afraid to demand our full rights as a people in this decadent society. . . .

We call upon all delegates to find within the white community those forces which will work under the leadership of blacks to implement these demands by whatever means necessary. By taking such actions, white Americans will demonstrate concretely that they are willing to fight the white skin privilege and the white supremacy and racism which has forced us as black people to make these demands.

We call upon all white Christians and Jews to practice patience, tolerance, understanding and nonviolence as they have encouraged, advised and demanded that we as black people should do throughout our entire enforced slavery in the United States. The true test of their faith and belief in the Cross and the words of the prophets will certainly be put to a test as we seek legitimate and extremely modest reparations for our role in developing the industrial base of the western world through our slave labor. But we are no longer slaves, we are men and women, proud of our African heritage, determined to have our dignity.

# The Black Panther Manifesto

*This manifesto, drafted in 1966, was a leading statement of the ideology of the Black Panther Party.*

1. **We want freedom. We want power to determine the destiny of our Black Community.**

We believe that black people will not be free until we are able to determine our destiny.

2. **We want full employment for our people.**

We believe that the federal government is responsible and obligated to give every man employment or a guaranteed income. We believe that if the white American businessman will not give full employment, then the means of production should be taken from the businessmen and placed in the community so that the people of the community can organize and employ all of its people and give a high standard of living.

3. **We want an end to the robbery by the CAPITALIST of our Black Community.**

We believe that this racist government has robbed us and now we are demanding the overdue debt of forty acres and two mules. Forty acres and two mules was promised 100 years ago as restitution for slave labor and mass murder of black people. We will accept the payment in currency which will be distributed to our many communities. The Germans are now aiding the Jews in Israel for the genocide of the Jewish people. The Germans murdered six million Jews. The American racist has taken part in the slaughter of over fifty million black people, therefore, we feel that this is a modest demand that we make.

Source: *The Negro Almanac: A Reference Work on the African American*, compiled and edited by Harry A. Ploski and James Williams, fifth edition (Detroit: Gale Research, 1989).

**4. We want decent housing, fit for shelter of human beings.**
We believe that if the white landlords will not give decent housing to our black community, then the housing and the land should be made into cooperatives so that our community, with government aid, can build and make decent housing for its people.

**5. We want education for our people that exposes the true nature of this decadent American society. We want education that teaches us our true history and our role in the present-day society.**
We believe in an educational system that will give to our people a knowledge of self. If a man does not have knowledge of himself and his position in society and the world, then he has little chance to relate to anything else.

**6. We want all black men to be exempt from military service.**
We believe that Black people should not be forced to fight in the military service to defend a racist government that does not protect us. We will not fight and kill other people of color in the world who, like black people, are being victimized by the white racist government of America. We will protect ourselves from the force and violence of the racist police and the racist military, by whatever means necessary.

**7. We want an immediate end to POLICE BRUTALITY and MURDER of black people.**
We believe we can end police brutality in our black community by organizing black self-defense groups that are dedicated to defending our black community from racist police oppression and brutality. The Second Amendment to the Constitution of the United States gives a right to bear arms. We therefore believe that all black people should arm themselves for self-defense.

**8. We want freedom for all black men held in federal, state, county and city prisons and jails.**
We believe that all black people should be released from the many jails and prisons because they have not received a fair and impartial trial.

**9. We want all black people when brought to trial to be tried in court by a jury of their peer group or people from their black communities, as defined by the constitution of the United States.**
We believe that the courts should follow the United States Constitution so that black people will receive fair trials. The 14th Amendment of the U.S. Constitution gives a man a right to be tried by his

peer group. A peer is a person from a similar economic, social, religious, geographical, environmental, historical and racial background. To do this the court will be forced to select a jury from the black community from which the black defendant came. We have been, and are being tried by all-white juries that have no understanding of the "average reasoning man" of the black community.

10. **We want land, bread, housing, education, clothing, justice and peace. And as our major political objective, a United Nations-supervised plebiscite to be held throughout the black colony in which only black colonial subjects will be allowed to participate, for the purpose of determining the will of black people as to their national destiny.**

When, in the course of human events, it becomes necessary for one people to dissolve the political bands which have connected them with another, and to assume, among the powers of the earth, the separate and equal station to which the laws of nature and nature's God entitle them, a decent respect to the opinions of mankind requires that they should declare the causes which impel them to the separation.

We hold these truths to be self-evident, that all men are created equal; that they are endowed by their Creator with certain inalienable rights; that among these are life, liberty, and the pursuit of happiness. **That, to secure these rights, governments are instituted among men, deriving their just powers from the consent of the governed; that, whenever any form of government becomes destructive of these ends, it is the right of the people to alter or to abolish it, and to institute a new government, laying its foundation on such principles, and organizing its powers in such form, as to them shall seem most likely to effect their safety and happiness.** Prudence, indeed, will dictate that governments long established should not be changed for light and transient causes; and, accordingly, all experience hath shown, that mankind are more disposed to suffer, while evils are sufferable, than to right themselves by abolishing the forms to which they are accustomed. **But, when a long train of abuses and usurpations, pursuing invariably the same object, evinces a design to reduce them under absolute despotism, it is their right, it is their duty, to throw off such government, and to provide new guards for their future security.**

# Black Panthers

## The Rhetoric of Revolution

*Among the most militant of black organizations during the
1960s, the Panthers spoke a language of revolution. Like
others in the time of black power, they insisted on the distinctiveness of the black race. Yet numbers of Panther
statements indicate a concentration not on black separatism but on revolutionary cooperation between blacks and
whites.*

In an interview with a representative of *The Movement* Bobby
Seale made the following comments in answer to a question concerning criticism of the BPP by "cultural nationalists": "The cultural nationalists have accused the Black Panther party of being
. . . a front for white radicals and of course we are not a front for
white radicals. We are an organization that represents black people and many white radicals relate to this and understand that the
Black Panther Party is a righteous revolutionary front against this
racist decadent, capitalistic system. Our organization doesn't have
any white people as members. If a white man in a radical group
wants to give me some guns, I'll take them. I'm not going to refuse
them because he's white" (*The Black Panther*, March 3, 1969: 10,
11). . . .

The following statement was attributed to Bobby Seale, and
BPP members George Sams and Cleveland Brooks. The statement,
which appeared in an article entitled "Reactionary Paper Tigers,"
is as follows: "This is a class struggle. To all those lackeys, oppor-
tunists, rotten ferocious, diseased mother fuckers, we will not stop
until we have destroyed and committed destruction on capitalism.
You must understand that the revolutionary struggle has yet to

*Source: The Black Panther Leaders Speak: Huey P. Newton, Bobby Seale, Eldridge
Cleaver and Company Speak Out Through the Black Panther Party's Official Newspaper*, edited by G. Louis Heath (Metuchen, NJ: The Scarecrow Press, 1976). Reprinted by permission.

**256**

continue. So let there be bloodshed because these racists fuckers have to go check it out in Vietnam ... So you see, people, as brother Mao Tse-tung puts it, 'We are the advocates of the abolition of war, we do not want war, but war can only be abolished through war. And in order to get rid of the gun, it is necessary to take up the gun' " (*The Black Panther*, May 25, 1969:4). ...

Seale is quoted as having stated: "When we say revolution we mean changing the system ... We mean changing it for real and very concrete ... And we prefer nonantagonistic contradictions, you see." In response to a question concerning carrying weapons, Seale stated: "We don't carry guns unless we are authorized to, and we would only authorize it in a matter that's related to self defense. Where somebody is being unjustly attacked, brutalized, murdered or killed by fascists, racists, or racist bigots, and even racist policemen who're trying to murder us." ...

Seale also denied that the Black Panther Party is a "separatist movement."

"We're not Black separatists, we don't believe in abstract notions of integration and abstract notions of separation" (*The Black Panther*, Feb. 7, 1970:3). ...

A race war, [Eldridge] Cleaver stated, "will mean the end of our dreams for the Class War which America needs and the beginning of the Race War which America cannot endure. This is the political consequence which America faces because of the unspeakably evil attempt to murder Chairman Bobby Seale in the Electric Chair" (*The Black Panther*, March 7, 1970:10, 11). ...

"There must be a revolution in the white mother country, led by white radicals and poor whites, and national liberation in the black and third world colony here in America. We can't triumph in the colony alone because that is just like cutting one finger off a hand. It still functions, you dig it. No, when we deal with a monster we just deal with it totally. ..."

# Huey P. Newton

## Revolution as Liberation

*These excerpts from an essay by Newton, a Black Panther leader, are notable in combining a concept of black revolution with a traditional left idea of revolution as liberating the creative and productive capacities of every individual.*

The Black Panther Party is the people's party. We are fundamentally interested in one thing, that is, freeing all people from all forms of slavery in order that every man will be his own master.

At present men are engaged in a struggle for self-determination on both an ethnic and an international level. People everywhere want to eliminate the slave-master in order to gain sacred freedom. People must be involved in this struggle so as to control the decisions that effect them. A basic tenet of this struggle and its object also, is the principle that things we all commonly use and commonly need should be commonly owned. In other words, the people should collectively decide exactly what they need and they should share fully in the wealth they produce. To this end the whole administration of the government should be subject to the dictates of the people, something that doesn't occur in present capitalistic society....

The Black Panther Party feels that the present government and its subsidiary institutions are illegitimate because they fail to relate to the people and they fail to meet the needs of the people. Therefore, they have no right to exist. The Black Panther Party feels that in the interest of the people, new institutions, both political and economic, should be established, and that the old institutions should disappear.

*Source:* Huey P. Newton, "The Black Panthers," *The Black Revolution: An Ebony Special Issue* (Chicago: Johnson Publishing Company, 1970). Reprinted by permission.

There is no excuse in our modern times, with the technology that exists in America, for people to be without the basic necessities of life, to say nothing of the psychological state man needs for day to day living.

Black people have been oppressed for so long that we have forgotten how to make decisions. We suffer from what psychology calls "fixation." We have done the same things over and over again. Even if no gratification whatsoever results from that activity, we still go along with the outmoded values, which are in strict contradiction to our very existence simply because we have been programmed, indoctrinated and totally stripped of our dignity. In America the true basis of creativity is suppressed. Returning to my basic premise, the value of man, the purpose of man is to be free and to engage in productive creativity. This is the freedom we are talking about; this is the freedom that makes life worth living.

The time has come for black people to start making decisions that affect their lives. While this may seem like an easy thing to do, it isn't. A man living in modern society is affected both by his relationship to production (and consumption), and his relationship to other men. Black people have largely been excluded from a significant relationship to production and have suffered from inadequate participation in consumption.

In addition, their relationship to other men has resulted in social, as well as economic, oppression. These external conditions have produced internal states. That is, the explanations offered by society for the external conditions have become internalized, thus preventing black people from exercising both physical and mental mobility. Freud realized that men become ill when they feel they have no control over their lives. So, to free man from these forces, he evolved psychoanalysis which attempts to make man aware of those internal states which influence his behavior. The assumption of psychoanalysis is that once man is aware of these subconscious forces, he can take the first steps toward controlling them, and these steps are the initial steps toward freedom. And it is this type of freedom the Black Panther Party is seeking.

The truth, the hard truth which all people, whether black or white, must understand is that the capitalistic system functions for the benefit of the owners of production, whether it be classical capitalism, state capitalism or monopoly capitalism. The function of production is to produce controlled distribution that produces profits. Whatever good comes from production is coincidental. In other words, production does not exist for the benefit of the people, but only for the producers. Thus, man is a tool; he is used to produce and he is used to dispose of the products of production. When he fails to produce or dispose, he is considered a counterproductive member of society. But a stigma attaches to those on welfare. It is as if they were enemies of the state. . . .

There are divisions in the black community that impede the path to self-determination and freedom. One of these divisions is between cultural nationalists and revolutionary nationalists.

The cultural nationalist seeks refuge by retreating to some ancient African behavior and culture, and he refuses to take into consideration those forces that are acting both on his own group and on the world as a whole. The revolutionary nationalist sees that there is no hope for cultural or individual expression, or even hope that his people can exist as a unique entity in a complex whole as long as the bureaucratic capitalist is in control.

The Black Panthers are revolutionary nationalists. We do not believe that it is necessary to go back to the culture of eleventh century Africa. In reality, we must deal with the dynamic present in order to forge a progressive future. We feel no need to retreat to the past, although we respect our African heritage. The things that are useful in the African heritage we will use to deal with the forces that are working on us today. Those things that are out-dated, that are antique, we will look upon with respect, as a fact of our heritage, but not as the basis for a pattern of behavior to follow in the present time.

The revolutionary nationalist respects people, particularly the oppressed people, everywhere and he realizes all men's common struggle for freedom. And this is what the Black Panther Party is primarily interested in. . . .

We are not alone in our struggle for freedom. Young whites are beginning to realize more and more each day that they are not free. They have become very angry because the ideas with which they have been indoctrinated have turned out to be lies. They are told that they are free, yet when they try to create and manifest a new form of decision-making on the college campuses they are arrested and some are even shot down. . . .

Today in some white communities people are suffering from the same repression that we in the black community suffer. The same forces are there—the police, the National Guard and sometimes even the Regular Army. This will continue to happen time and again in the coming years, thus forming a basis for unity between the peoples of both the black and white communities. Not only are we coming together in unity in this country, we are all part of the international brotherhood of oppressed people.

# SUGGESTED READINGS

The history of the civil rights movement is an area rich with sources from the times, reminiscences, reflections, and firsthand accounts. Many of the participants have left written or oral records of their involvement and a sizable number of rights activists continue to be engaged in the cause of justice for African Americans. In abundance too is a visual record of the modern civil rights campaign. The camera, especially the television camera, had a vital role in the success of the rights workers.

The civil rights movement was the nation's first televised reform movement. The March on Washington on August 28, 1963, the Alabama police riot at the Pettus Bridge in 1965: such events came to Americans in their comfortable living rooms and troubled their consciences as black protestors and their white allies marched or rode or sang only about their determination to have for black Americans the same rights, the same opportunities, and the same dignity accorded white citizens: to be judged, in the eloquent simplicity of Dr. King's phrase, not "by the color of their skin but by the content of their character." Over television news programs, in what in the 1950s and sixties was rapidly becoming the nation's public forum, people observed close up the tactics of white supremacy. Suddenly, through television and the other media, places like Birmingham and Selma, Little Rock and Nashville became familiar neighborhoods. What victories rights activists won they achieved by displaying before a national audience a stoic resignation and courage as they met violence with nonviolence and answered racial epithets with hymns of faith. The nation looked at what was happening in the South and it was ashamed.

But what the media giveth, the media taketh away. Americans learned the names of southern cities by viewing the peaceful struggle of black demonstrators against the customs of Jim Crow and the institutions of racial segregation. Later they watched on their home screens as another kind of black assertion, a power of rage and frustration expressed in fire and violence, swept through places like the Watts district of Los Angeles and the ghettos of Detroit and Newark and other northern cities. This time television was no friend to African Americans. Television could not capture the complex circumstances of economic deprivation and joblessness and the despair they bred that had triggered the urban riots. Television is not good at dealing with complexity; it lacks the capacity for deep analysis—nor, perhaps, has it the interest. It deals in images that appeal largely to the emotions.

The emotions that the pictures of the early movement activities stirred were those of guilt and sympathy. How could a moral society deny African Americans when they asked nothing more than to share a lunch counter or a school or when they sought the ballot, especially as they made those demands while employing the tactics of nonviolence? When the pictures changed, so did many of the feelings. The images conveyed from the northern cities were of burned-out businesses and looted shops and angry mobs of black teenagers running through the streets hurling clubs and bricks. The problems behind the cries of the urban demonstrators for economic justice and the sudden aggressiveness of the black power movement were more difficult to fathom than the earlier campaigns for social and political equity. White Americans looked at what was happening in the cities of the North and they were confused and afraid and many were angry. How could the same movement that had begun with the extraordinary self-control required of nonviolence end in what appeared to be the senseless violence, the chaos, of the urban North?

Television could not answer that question. When the issue of the place of black Americans in the life of the nation became complicated, television failed. In the images it presented, however, and in ways unlike the ways of any other form of communication, it became the means by which blacks brought that issue to the center of the country's attention. And here historians and other scholars have found their task: going behind the visuals to examine the movement in detail for its many and occasionally conflicting interests; to assess the variety of tactics and strategies it displayed; to describe its many goals and sift through the unplanned consequences of its work; and to observe the subtle play of gender and class as well as race within and across the many layers of activity that were part of the country's civil rights era.

The study of the civil rights years in the United States might properly begin with the visual and oral record of the movement. To recall some of the images and words that pushed and pulled at the moral temperament of the nation see the excellent video series *Eyes on the Prize, I and II: History of the American Civil Rights Movement* (Boston: Henry Hampton and Blackside, Inc., 1986). Journalist Juan Williams is the author of a crisply written companion volume to the series, *Eyes on the Prize: America's Civil Rights Years, 1954–1965* (New York: Viking, 1987). Interviews with many of the prominent figures of the civil rights campaign and with many of the ordinary men and women whose lives were affected by the freedom struggle are gathered at the Ralph J. Bunche Oral History Collection, Moreland-Spingarn Research Center, Howard University. Available at the Research Center is an expertly organized guide to the collection compiled and edited by Avril J. Madison, librarian of the collection. The editors of *To Redeem A Nation* are grateful to Ms. Madison for her able assistance and sound advice as they examined transcripts for inclusion in this volume. There are also strong oral histories of the movement at the University of Southern Mississippi and at Duke. Howell Raines, a Pulitzer prize-winning newspaperman, has compiled a published collection of oral histories in *My Soul Is Rested: Movement Days in the Deep South Re-*

*membered* (New York: G. P. Putnam's Sons, 1977). Oral histories present extraordinary opportunities for understanding the personal dimensions of the movement; they exhibit also, however, some unique problems. Kim Lacy Rogers discusses the promise and problems of using oral history collections in "Oral History and the History of the Civil Rights Movement," *Journal of American History*, 75 (1988): 567–76.

Written records and histories remain, of course, the largest source of material on black America and the civil rights era. It is always necessary to get events in their proper sequence and locale; Alton Hornsby, Jr., ed., *Chronology of African-American History: Significant Events and People from 1619 to the Present* (Detroit, MI: Gale Research, 1991) is indispensable in this regard. Chapters 8 through 11 deal with the civil rights era. And Charles D. Lowery and John F. Marszolek, eds., *Encyclopedia of African-American Civil Rights: From Emancipation to the Present* (Westport, CT: Greenwood Press, 1992) is a useful reference for identifying important individuals, organizations, and occasions in African American civil rights history.

A number of other reference works identify sources in the history of the civil rights movement. See, for example, Steven F. Lawson, "Freedom Then, Freedom Now: The Historiography of the Civil Rights Movement," *American Historical Review*, 96 (April 1991): 456–71 and Robert L. Zangrando, "Manuscript Sources for Twentieth-Century Civil Rights Research," *Journal of American History*, 74 (1987): 243–51. The *Kaiser Index to Black Resources, 1948–1986: From the Schomburg Center for Research in Black Culture of the New York Public Library*, 5 volumes (Brooklyn, NY: Carlson Publishing, 1992) is a guide to one of the nation's richest collections of materials on African American history. Debra L. Newman, comp., *Black History: A Guide to Civilian Records in the National Archives* (Washington, DC: National Archives Trust Fund, General Services Administration, 1984) provides a listing of items dealing with black America assembled by the United States government. In a category of its own both as a guide to important sources of civil rights history and as a record of the civil rights movement is the journal *Freedomways: A Quarterly Review of the Negro Freedom Movement*. Founded and edited by Shirley Graham, wife of W. E. B. Du Bois, the journal, which began publication with a Spring 1961 issue, documents most of the important events of the civil rights campaign and contains essays by many of the movement's leaders and collections of letters by those involved in the movement and interviews with many rights activists. Included too are materials that reflect the culture of black Americans and in particular the culture of the civil rights movement: poems, songs of protest and struggle, prose pieces, and art work. The journal ceased publication in 1985 after producing many volumes dealing with the black freedom movement in the United States and abroad.

The civil rights movement was a broad movement for social and economic change and yet it was made of the countless details of the lives of many Americans, the many individual acts of courage and resolution in the cause of justice. A number of studies have tried to preserve the detail of the rights movement even as they endeavor to give a portrait of the origins and general sweep and direction of the movement. Among the best of the general studies of the civil rights era are Taylor Branch, *Parting the Waters: America in the King Years, 1964–63* (New York: Simon and Schuster, 1988); Robert Weisbrot, *Freedom Bound: A History of America's Civil Rights Movement* (New York: Norton, 1990); Harvard Sitkoff, *The Struggle for Black Equality, 1954–1992* (New York: Hill and Wang, rev. ed., 1993); Aldon D. Morris, *The Origins of the Civil Rights Movement: Black Communities Organizing for Change* (New York: Free Press, 1984); and Fred Powledge, *Free At Last? The Civil Rights Movement and the People Who Made It* (Boston: Little, Brown, 1991). Other works which take a wide look at civil rights activities include Sean Dennis Cashman, *African-Americans and the Quest for Civil Rights, 1900–1990* (New York: New York University Press, 1991); Thomas R. Brooks, *Walls Come Tumbling Down: A History of the Civil Rights Movement, 1940–1970* (Englewood Cliffs, NJ: Prentice-Hall, 1974); Manning Marable, *Race, Reform and Rebellion: The Second Reconstruction in Black America, 1945–1982*, 2nd ed. (Jackson: University Press of Mississippi, 1991); and Vincent Harding, *The Other American Revolution* (Los Angeles: UCLA Center for Afro-American Studies, 1980). Rhoda Lois Blumberg, *Civil Rights: The 1960s Freedom Struggle*, 2nd ed. (Boston: Twayne Publishers, 1991) looks at a critical decade in the history of the movement. There are also several fine collections of essays: David J. Garrow, ed., *We Shall Overcome: The Civil Rights Movement in the United States in the 1950s and 1960s*, 3 volumes (Brooklyn, NY: Carlson Publishing, 1989); Charles Eagles, ed., *The Civil Rights Movement in America: Essays* (Jackson: University of Mississippi Press, 1986); Armstead Robinson and Patricia Sullivan, eds., *New Directions in Civil Rights Studies* (Charlottesville: Carter G. Woodson Institute Series in Black Studies, University of Virginia Press, 1991); and Herbert Hill and James E. Jones, Jr., eds., *Race in America: The Struggle for Equality* (Madison: University of Wisconsin Press, 1993). The culture of the freedom movement along with some of its images is captured in Guy and Candie Carawan, eds., *Freedom is a Constant Struggle: Songs of the Freedom Movement With Documentary Photographs* (New York: Oak Publications, 1968). An important recent study by Richard H. King, *Civil Rights and the Idea of Freedom* (New York: Oxford University Press, 1992) offers an intellectual history of the civil rights era that focuses on the different and contested ways in which the idea of "freedom" was invested with meaning. Cultural historian Scott A. Sandage, "A Marble House Divided: The Lincoln Memorial, the Civil Rights Movement, and the Politics of Memory, 1939–1963," *Journal of American History*, 80 (June 1993): 135–67, examines the symbolic and ritualistic importance of the Lincoln Memorial, the site of more than one hundred civil rights demonstrations between 1939 and 1963.

It is a convention of current scholarship to use 1954, the year of the *Brown* decision, as the date of the beginning of the modern civil rights era. Black activism and protest, however, have a history much longer than that and many of the ideas held by civil rights campaigners and the tactics and programs they embraced were anticipated in the work of their ancestors. For background, see Vincent Harding's *There Is a River: The Black Struggle for Freedom in America* (New York: Vintage, 1983). It documents the history of rebellion by African Americans against the curtailment of their freedoms from the early days of their enslavement through to the Civil War and the adoption of the Thirteenth Amendment in 1865, "the year of jubilee." Also see John Hope Franklin and Alfred A. Moss, Jr., *From Slavery to Freedom: A History of Negro Americans*, 6th ed. (New York: Alfred A. Knopf, 1988), which carries the story of the freedom struggle to the present.

Two figures dominate the history of black leadership in the early twentieth century: Booker T. Washington and W. E. B. Du Bois. More complex and subtle in his thinking than has generally been recognized, Washington is perhaps best to be understood in his own words in Louis R. Harlan, ed., *The Booker T. Washington Papers*, 14 volumes (Urbana: University of Illinois Press, 1972–1989). Harlan has given us his own assessment of Washington in two fine volumes of biography, *Booker T. Washington: The Making of a Black Leader, 1856–1901* (New York: Oxford University Press, 1972) and *Booker T. Washington: The Wizard of Tuskegee, 1901–1915* (New York: Oxford University Press, 1983). The major works of W. E. B. Du Bois are conveniently collected in *Writings* (New York: The Library of America, 1986). Biographer Marable Manning's *W. E. B. Du Bois: Black Radical Democrat* (Boston: Twayne, 1986) is a sympathetic treatment of its subject; David Levering Lewis' *W. E. B. Du Bois, 1868–1919: Biography of a Race* (New York: Holt, 1993), the first of a two-volume history, promises to be more critical.

Although Marcus Mosiah Garvey never produced writings with the emotional appeal of Washington's *Up from Slavery* (1901) or with the elegant intellectual sophistication of Du Bois' *The Souls of Black of Black Folk* (1903), during the early 1920s he was one of the most popular figures among the African American leadership. His ideas about pride of race and uniting the peoples of African descent for their collective benefit inspired a devoted following. Echoes of Garvey's talk of black pride and black nationalism can be heard in the writings and speeches of the leaders of the civil rights era. Garvey's works are in Robert A. Hill, ed., *The Marcus Garvey and Universal Negro Improvement Association Papers* (Berkeley: University of California Press, 1983–1990) and his life and ideas are explored by E. David Cronon, *Black Moses: The Story of Marcus Garvey and the Universal Negro Improvement Association* (Madison: University of Wisconsin Press, 1969), and, more recently, by Judith Stein, *The World of Marcus Garvey: Race and Class in Modern Society* (Baton Rouge: Louisiana State University Press, 1986). On the literary and artistic movement of the 1920s and 1930s known as the Harlem Renaissance, which gave cultural expression to black protest, four works are helpful: Nathan Irvin Huggins, *Harlem Renaissance* (New York: Oxford University Press, 1971); Cary D. Wintz, *Black Culture and the Harlem Renaissance* (Houston, Texas: Rice

University Press, 1968); Jervis Anderson, *This Was Harlem: A Cultural Portrait, 1900–1950* (New York: Noonday Press, a division of Farrar, Straus and Giroux, 1982); and Arnold Rampersad, *The Life of Langston Hughes* (New York: Oxford University Press, 1986). A provocative essay by Robert Korstad and Nelson Lichtenstein, "Opportunities Found and Lost: Labor, Radicals, and the Early Civil Rights Movement," *Journal of American History*, 75 (December 1988): 786–811, argues that many of the economic and political issues that drove the civil rights movement were first elaborated in the radical camp of the labor movement. Labor radicals shared an ideology with early civil rights activists and provided their campaign with tactical advice, models of organization and personnel.

Much of the story of the civil rights era is that of memory, the recollections, in memoirs or autobiographies, of those who participated in the movement. The experiences documented by the activists, local workers and national leaders, often furnish the best view of the day-to-day reality of the movement, the numbing fear of challenging authority and the joys of even small successes. To these accounts historians and journalists have added biographies of some of the prominent figures in the freedom struggle.

Paula F. Pfeffer, *A. Philip Randolph, Pioneer of the Civil Rights Movement* (Baton Rouge: Louisiana State University Press, 1990), assesses the life and thinking of the man who founded the Brotherhood of Sleeping Car Porters and Maids in 1925 and organized the March on Washington Movement to achieve fair hiring practices in government. Randolph's career spanned the entire civil rights era during which he was active in most of its major crusades. Another excellent biography of Randolph is William H. Harris, *Keeping the Faith: A. Philip Randolph, Milton P. Webster, and the Brotherhood of Sleeping Car Porters* (New York: Oxford University Press, 1982). Roy Wilkins, who succeeded W. E. B. Du Bois in 1934 as editor of the *Crisis* and was executive director of the National Association for the Advancement of Colored People (NAACP) from 1955 until he retired in 1977, recalls campaigning for rights in a work written with the assistance of Tom Mathews, *Standing Fast: The Autobiography of Roy Wilkins* (New York: Viking Press, 1982). Wilkins always spoke against the use of violence by activists and, after the successful defeat of legal segregation, opposed the programs of black nationalists as schemes for reintroducing segregation. In two books, *Freedom—When?* (New York: Random House, 1965) and *Lay Bare the Heart: An Autobiography of the Civil Rights Movement* (New York: Arbor House, 1986), James Farmer recounts some of the history of the Congress of Racial Equality (CORE), which he helped organize in 1942, and of the Freedom Ride project he initiated in 1961 into the deep South. Lawyer and minister Floyd B. McKissick, *Three-Fifths of a Man* (New York: Macmillan, 1969), succeeded Farmer as national director of CORE in 1961 and as an advocate of black power urged the organization to assume a more aggressive position.

Whitney Young, Jr., head of the moderate research-oriented National Urban League, in *To Be Equal* (New York: McGraw-Hill, 1964), tells the story of his participation in an organization that believed it necessary to arm the movement with the sorry statistics of the social and economic consequences of racial discrimination as a weapon to gain a moral advantage in the battle for equality. See too, Nancy J. Weiss, *Whitney M. Young, Jr., and the Struggle for Civil Rights* (Princeton, NJ: Princeton University Press, 1989). Roger Wilkins, *A Man's Life: An Autobiography* (New York: Simon and Schuster, 1982), offers the unique perspective of a black attorney working in Lyndon Johnson's Justice Department at the time of the passage of the 1964 Civil Rights Act and the 1965 Voting Rights Act. Ralph David Abernathy, *And the Walls Came Tumbling Down: An Autobiography* (New York: Harper and Row, 1989), is the autobiography of the friend and associate who succeeded Martin Luther King, Jr., as president of the Southern Christian Leadership Conference (SCLC). Brian Urquhart, *Ralph Bunche: An American Life* (New York: W. W. Norton and Company, 1993), covers Bunche's civil rights activity but concentrates mostly on his years in diplomacy as the chief troubleshooter for the United Nations in the two decades following World War II. Others who recall the movement days include Pat Watters, *Down to Now: Reflections on the Southern Civil Rights Movement* (New York: Pantheon Books, 1971), and Danny Lyon, *Memories of the Southern Civil Rights Movement* (Chapel Hill: University of North Carolina Press for the Center of Documentary Studies, Duke University, 1992), a collection of the photographs and commentary by the author who was the staff photographer for the Student Nonviolent Coordinating Committee (SNCC). Although not easy to categorize, the writer James Baldwin exercised a profound influence on black and white students and intellectuals. Drawing upon his personal experiences, especially his religious upbringing, Baldwin made the case in *The Fire Next Time* (New York: Dial Press, 1963) of the need for African Americans to draw strength from their suffering and warned white Americans to attend to the complaints of blacks or suffer the consequences. Baldwin's voice was among the most powerful and uncompromising in the black protest movement.

In the pursuit of racial justice, however, no voice was stronger and no one more influential than Dr. Martin Luther King, Jr. He is the towering figure of the civil rights era and the symbol of the black freedom movement. Not surprisingly, there is a large body of scholarship concerned with Dr. King and various aspects of his career only some of the most recent and best of which is sampled here. The historian Clayborne Carson has organized a thorough bibliography of materials dealing with King, *A Guide to Research on Martin Luther King, Jr., and the Modern Black Freedom Struggle* (Stanford, CA: Stanford University Libraries, 1989). Carson is also the general editor of *The Papers of Martin Luther King, Jr.*, a compilation of writings and documents which will add importantly to our knowledge and understanding of King. The first volume of the papers, *Called to Serve, January 1929–June 1951* (Berkeley: University of California Press, 1992), is edited by Carson, Ralph E. Luker, Penny A. Russell, and Louis R. Harlan. Dr. King's views are available to us in his own words in *Stride Toward Freedom: The Montgomery Story* (New York: Harper, 1958), which in addition to describing the 1955–56 Montgomery bus boycott also discusses King's intellectual development and the influence on his thought, and especially his philosophy of nonviolence, of the work of Karl Marx, Henry David Thoreau, Walter Rauschenbusch, and Mohandas Gandhi, among others. *Strength to Love* (New York: Viking Press, 1982; 1st ed., New York: Harper and Row, 1963) is a collection of Dr. King's sermons. Biographies, in addition to that by Taylor Branch, include Stephen B. Oates, *Let the Trumpet Sound: The Life of Martin Luther King, Jr.* (New York: Harper and Row, 1982), and David Levering Lewis, *King: A Critical Biography* (New York: Praeger, 1970). John J. Anshoro, *Martin Luther King, Jr.: The Making of a Mind* (Maryknoll, NY: Orbis Books, 1982), describes the origins and development of many of King's ideas. Ira G. Zepp, Jr., *The Social Vision of Martin Luther King, Jr.* (Brooklyn, NY: Carlson Publishing, 1989), also looks at the philosophical roots of King's thinking. James A. Colaiaco, *Martin Luther King, Jr.: Apostle of Militant Nonviolence* (New York: St. Martin's Press, 1993), looks at the way King employed the strategy of nonviolent direct action in various campaigns. There are two important collections of essays: David J. Garrow, ed., *Martin Luther King, Jr.: Civil Rights Leader, Theologian, and Orator*, 3 volumes (Brooklyn, NY: Carlson Publishing, 1989), and Peter J. Albert and Ronald Hoffman, eds., *We Shall Overcome: Martin Luther King, Jr., and the Black Freedom Struggle* (New York: Pantheon Books, 1990). Keith D. Miller, *Voice of Deliverance: The Language of Martin Luther King, Jr., and Its Sources* (New York: Free Press, 1992), examines the roots of King's oratory and how he used language to frame the civil rights demand for racial equality. And Richard Lentz, *Symbols, the News Magazines, and Martin Luther King* (Baton Rouge: Louisiana State University Press, 1990), looks at King as the symbol of the civil rights movement and how that symbol was perceived and presented by the media, especially the news magazines, *Time, Newsweek* and *U. S. News & World Report*.

The beginnings of the modern civil rights movement in the 1950s and early 1960s are usually associated with the agitation to end racial segregation at lunch counters, in areas of public accommodation and, most importantly, in the schools. For background on segregationist customs and policies one work remains unsurpassed: C. Vann Woodward, 3d ed., *The Strange Career of Jim Crow* (New York: Oxford University Press, 1974). W. Fitzhugh Brundage, *Lynching in the New South: Georgia and Virginia, 1880–1930* (Urbana and Chicago, IL: University of Illinois Press, 1993), describes the ruthlessness with which the codes of racial etiquette were enforced in the South.

School desegregation began with the May 17, 1954, Supreme Court decision in *Oliver Brown* v. *Board of Education of Topeka, Kansas*, sometimes referred to as *Brown I*, which reversed the longstanding doctrine, established by the *Plessy* decision of 1896, that allowed separate educational facilities for the races by declaring that "in the field of public education the doctrine of 'Separate but equal' has no place." *Brown II*, decided in 1955, which many viewed as a step back from the aggressively egalitarian position of *Brown I*, addressed the issue of implementation and held that federal judges would determine the pace of integration as local conditions warranted. Joseph Tussman, ed., *The Supreme Court on Racial Discrimination* (New York: Oxford University Press, 1963), gives the full texts of Supreme Court decisions dealing with matters of race. The best history of the *Brown* case is Richard Kluger, *Simple Justice: The History of Brown v. Board of Education and Black America's Struggle for Equality* (New York: Alfred Knopf, 1975). The legal scholar Mark V. Tushnet analyzes the work of the NAACP's Legal Defense and Educational Fund lawyers in challenging the *Plessy* principle in *The NAACP's Legal Strategy against Segregated Education, 1925–1950* (Chapel Hill: University of North Carolina Press, 1987). J. Harvie Wilkinson, III, *From Brown to Bakke: The Supreme Court and School Integration, 1954–1978* (New York: Oxford University Press, 1979), carries the story of the Court and desegregation forward through the 1970s and its decisions in the 1978 case of the *University of California Regents v. Bakke*, a case in which the issue of "reverse discrimination" was raised and affirmative action programs for minorities and minority quotas were challenged. Local studies of the response to *Brown* include Robert C. Smith, *They Closed Their Schools: Prince Edward County, Virginia, 1951–1964* (Chapel Hill: University of North Carolina Press, 1965), and Robert A. Pratt, *The Color of Their Skin: Education and Race in Richmond, Virginia, 1954–89* (Charlottesville: University Press of Virginia, 1992). I. A. Newby, *Challenge to the Court: Social Scientists and the Defense of Segregation, 1954–1966* (Baton Rouge: Louisiana State University Press, 1969), discusses the quarrel surrounding the use of sociological evidence in the desegregation cases. Most scholars who have written about *Brown* have been supportive; Raymond Wolters, *The Burden of Brown: Thirty Years of School Desegregation* (Knoxville: University of Tennessee Press, 1984), is more critical.

School integration was fiercely resisted by many white southerners, and just as tenaciously pursued by many black southerners and their allies. The events at Little Rock, Arkansas, where in September 1957 nine black children attempted to attend the previously all white Central High, showed just how determined each side was. Ultimately, federal troops were sent in to screen the children from angry mobs and to enforce court-ordered school desegregation. Daisy Bates, official of the local chapter of the NAACP, recalls the desegregation crisis in *The Long Shadow of Little Rock: A Memoir* (New York: David McKay, 1962; Fayetteville: University of Arkansas Press, 1987). Also see Corinne Silverman, *The Little Rock Story* (Tuscaloosa, University of Alabama: Published for the Inter-University Case Program, 1958) and Tony Freyer, *The Little Rock Crisis: A Constitutional Interpretation* (Westport, CT: Greenwood Press, 1984). Desegregation of the South's universities is a topic for James Meredith, who in 1962 was the first black to gain admission to the University of Mississippi, *Three Years in Mississippi* (Bloomington: Indiana University Press, 1966); Russell H. Barrett, *Integration at Ole Miss* (Chicago: Quadrangle Books, 1965); Charlayne Hunter-Gault, who as Charlayne Hunter integrated the University of Georgia in January 1961, *In My Place* (New York: Farrar, Straus and Giroux, 1992); Calvin Trillin, *An Education in Georgia: Charlayne Hunter, Hamilton Holmes, and the Integration of the University of Georgia* (Athens: University of Georgia Press, Brown Thrasher Book, 1991; first published by Viking Press, 1964); and E. Culpepper Clark, *The Schoolhouse Door: Segregation's Last Stand at the University of Alabama* (New York: Oxford University Press, 1993).

The attack on racial separation in the schools was part of a broader movement to end racial discrimination in the workplace, at the polling booth, in eating places and at places of public accommodation, anywhere a black person was denied access solely on the basis of the color of his or her skin. To achieve that purpose African Americans often borrowed and refined tactics from other movements of protest when needed and in other instances created new ones. Among the techniques they employed were boycotts, sit-ins, and freedom rides. On the boycott of public transportation in Montgomery, Alabama, that began when rights activist Rosa Parks refused to move to the back of the bus, see David J. Garrow, ed., *The Montgomery Bus Boycott and the Women Who Started It: The Memoir of Jo Ann Gibson Robinson* (Knoxville: University of Tennessee Press, 1987), and the essays in *The Walking City: The Montgomery Bus Boycott, 1955–1956* (Brooklyn, NY: Carlson Publishing, 1989), also edited by Garrow. Also see Roberta H. Wright, *The Birth of the Montgomery Bus Boycott* (Southfield, MS: Charro Books, forthcoming). William Chafe, *Civilities and Civil Rights: Greensboro, North Carolina, and the Black Struggle for Freedom* (New York: Oxford University Press, 1980), is a local history of the civil rights movement focusing on the city that on February 1, 1960, was the site of the famous sit-in demonstration at the Woolworth lunch counter. The events of that day, and subsequent days in Greensboro, are recounted in Miles Wolff, *Lunch at the Five and Ten: The Greensboro Sit-ins, a Contemporary History* (New York: Stein and Day, 1970). The sit-in campaign spread rapidly to other southern cities: Merrill Proudfoot, *Diary of a Sit-In* (Chapel Hill: University of North Carolina Press, 1962), examines the efforts to desegregate the restaurants and lunch rooms of Knoxville, Tennessee; the essays in David J. Garrow, ed., *Atlanta, Georgia, 1960–1961: Sit-Ins and Student Activism* (Brooklyn, NY: Carlson Publishing, 1989), look at the events in one of the South's major cities. For a sociologist's assessment of the sit-ins, see Martin Oppenheimer, *The Sit-In Movement of 1960* (Brooklyn, NY: Carlson Publishing, 1989). James H. Laue, *Direct Action and Desegregation, 1960–1962* (Brooklyn, NY: Carlson Publishing, 1989), also takes a sociological approach to the tactics of the desegregationists. Two works by rights workers provide firsthand accounts of the sit-ins and freedom rides: Diane Nash, "Inside the Sit-Ins and Freedom Rides," in Matthew Agman, ed., *The New Negro* (Notre Dame, Indiana: Fides Publishers, 1962), and James Peck, *Freedom Ride* (New York: Simon and Schuster, 1962). Diane Nash was one of the founders of the Nashville Student Movement, a well-organized group which conducted a number of successful nonviolent demonstrations in Nashville, Tennessee, in the early 1960s.

James Peck was an official with CORE. Also see August Meier and Elliott Rudwick, "The First Freedom Ride," *Phylon*, 30 (Fall 1969): 213–22 and Catherine A. Barnes, *Journey from Jim Crow: The Desegregation of Southern Transit* (New York: Columbia University Press, 1983).

Although many of the events that make up of the civil rights era arose out of individual and spontaneous acts of courage or frustration, the civil rights movement was a remarkably well disciplined crusade for social justice. A number of organizations worked to harness the energies of rights activists and organize them in carefully planned operations to achieve the expansion of rights for African Americans. Several fine institutional studies of the civil rights movement exist. Though there is no comprehensive treatment of the NAACP, founded in 1910 and among the first of the modern rights organizations, some older works are very informative. See especially Charles Kellogg Flint, *NAACP: A History of the National Association for the Advancement of Colored People* (Baltimore, MD: Johns Hopkins Press, 1967), and Barbara Joyce Ross, *J. E. Spingarn and the Rise of the NAACP, 1911–1939* (New York: Atheneum, 1972). Genna Rae McNeil, *Groundwork: Charles Hamilton Houston and the Struggle for Civil Rights* (Philadelphia: University of Pennsylvania Press, 1983), and Gilbert Ware, *William Hastie: Grace under Pressure* (New York: Oxford University Press, 1984), examine the lives of men who served as legal counsel for the NAACP. Robert L. Zangrando, *The NAACP Crusade against Lynching, 1909–1950* (Philadelphia: Temple University Press, 1980), deals with the issue that was the chief concern of the NAACP, the focus of its first effort to publicize racial problems, before the desegregation campaign. The history of CORE, which was formed in 1942 out of the membership of the Fellowship of Reconciliation, a pacifist group, is documented in "All About CORE," 1963, CORE Papers and in a thoroughly researched work by August Meier and Elliot Rudwick, *CORE: A Study in the Civil Rights Movement, 1942–1968* (New York: Oxford University Press, 1975). Created in 1957 by a group composed mostly of ministers, the Southern Christian Leadership Conference conducted campaigns of civil disobedience and nonviolence to win public support for racial justice. SCLC's story is told in David J. Garrow, *Bearing the Cross: Martin Luther King, Jr. and the Southern Christian Leadership Conference* (New York: William Morrow, 1986); Thomas R. Peake, *Keeping the Dream Alive: A History of the Southern Christian Leadership Conference from King to the 1980s* (New York: P. Lang, 1967); and Adam Fairclough, *"To Redeem the Soul of America": The Southern Christian Leadership Conference and Martin Luther King, Jr.* (Athens: University of Georgia Press, 1987). The Student Nonviolent Coordinating Committee developed out of a conference held at Shaw University in Raleigh, North Carolina, in April 1960 to discuss strategies for better organizing the various student protests that followed in the wake of the Greensboro sit-in. SNCC waged a campaign of direct action nonviolent protest against segregation but achieved perhaps its greatest success in the voter registration drives it conducted in Mississippi and other southern states. There are several good studies of SNCC, the best of which is

Clayborne Carson, *In Struggle: SNCC and the Black Awakening of the 1960s* (Cambridge, MA: Harvard University Press, 1981). Also consult: Emily Stoper, *The Student Nonviolent Coordinating Committee: The Growth of Radicalism in a Civil Rights Organization* (Brooklyn, NY: Carlson Publishing, 1989); Howard Zinn, 2nd ed., *SNCC: The New Abolitionists* (Boston: Beacon, 1965); and Clayborne Carson, ed., *"The Student Voice," 1960–1965: Periodical of the Student Nonviolent Coordinating Committee* (Westport, CT: Greenwood Press, 1990). Cleveland Sellers with Robert Terrell, *The River of No Return: The Autobiography of a Black Militant and the Life and Death of SNCC* (New York: William Morrow, 1973), and James Forman, *The Making of Black Revolutionaries: A Personal Account* (New York: Macmillan, 1972), are works by members of SNCC, one of whom, James Forman, served as executive secretary of the organization for five years, 1961–1966. The two books discuss the activities and ideas of the student group and SNCC's drift in its later years toward greater militancy.

Some other institutions had an important influence on the civil rights movement. Many of the men and women who emerged as leaders in the civil rights movement, among them James Bevel, Rosa Parks, and several SNCC activists, trained at the Highlander Folk School in Monteagle, Tennessee. Founded in 1932 by Myles Horton and Don West, Highlander taught a philosophy of community empowerment and employed training methods aimed at assisting community representatives to organize on behalf of their own interests. The voter education programs and Freedom Schools established by SNCC owed much to the inspiration of Highlander. The school's history is told in three works: Frank Adams with Myles Horton, *Unearthing Seeds of Fire: The Idea of Highlander* (Winston-Salem, NC: John F. Blair, 1975); Aimee Isgrig Horton, *The Highlander Folk School: A History of Its Major Programs, 1932–1961* (Brooklyn, NY: Carlson Publishing, 1989); and John M. Glen, *Highlander: No Ordinary School, 1932–1962* (Lexington: University of Kentucky, 1988). Irwin Klibaner, *Conscience of a Troubled South: The Southern Conference Educational Fund, 1946–1966* (Brooklyn, NY: Carlson Publishing, 1989), is a stimulating study that endeavors to connect the civil rights movement with earlier radical organizations. Sudarshan Kapur, *Raising Up a Prophet: The African-American Encounter with Gandhi* (Boston: Beacon, 1992), is an intellectual history that looks at the ways various civil rights leaders and groups understood and used the theories of nonviolence and direct action of Mohandas K. Gandhi.

The drama of the civil rights movement was played out in the demonstrations and campaigns individual rights organizations or groups of organizations conducted in the South. Much of that drama was captured by the media. On the one hand was the organizational skill the movement had developed over time and the ability of its leaders to mount mass protest rallies or parades. There was also the talent shown by CORE and SCLC and SNCC and others for publicity; rights people were learning to use the media as a pulpit for addressing the nation. On the other hand were the southern white supremacists determined to defend their racial customs even with force and turn back the demonstrators. Without the beatings and burnings, the mass arrests and the murders, the brutal opposition of southern supremacists to racial equality, it is doubtful the media would have deemed worthy of coverage the African American struggle for justice. Working from opposite intentions, engaged in what amounted to unwitting collusion, publicity-seeking rights workers disciplined to nonviolence and southern defenders of racial separation, many of them angry beyond control, together precipitated an outcome neither alone might have excited: they put the race problem on the national agenda.

Nowhere was the struggle for the soul of America more bitterly contested than in Mississippi. For background on the conditions of black life in Mississippi, see Neil R. McMillen, *Dark Journey: Black Mississippians in the Age of Jim Crow* (Urbana: University of Illinois Press, 1989); James W. Silver, 2nd ed., *Mississippi: The Closed Society* (New York: Harcourt, Brace and World, 1966); and Stephen J. Whitfield, *A Death in the Delta: The Story of Emmett Till* (New York: Free Press, 1988). The murder of the fourteen-year-old Till on August 24, 1955, for allegedly wolf-whistling at a white woman and touching her, and the subsequent acquittal of his killers, brought attention to the special viciousness of Mississippi racism. The movement in Mississippi and the important voter registration campaign waged by SNCC and other groups, and the famous Freedom Summer of 1964 that aimed at building the populist Mississippi Freedom Democratic Party, are discussed in several works. See Anne Moody's poignant recollections of movement days in the deep South in *Coming of Age in Mississippi* (New York: Dell Publishers, 1968). Also see Len Holt, *The Summer That Didn't End* (New York: William Morrow, 1965); William McCord, *Mississippi: The Long Hot Summer* (New York: Norton, 1965); Sally Balfrage, *Freedom Summer* (Charlottesville: University Press of Virginia and Curtis Brown, Ltd., 1965); and Doug McAdam, *Freedom Summer* (New York: Oxford University Press, 1988). Mary Aiken Rothschild, *A Case of Black and White: Northern Volunteers and the Southern Freedom Summer, 1964–1965* (Westport, CT: Greenwood Press, 1982), discusses the relations between the almost one thousand college students, most of them white, who went south during Freedom Summer and the black rights workers and Mississippians they worked alongside in 1964–65. Elizabeth Sutherland Martinez, ed., *Letters from Mississippi* (New York: McGraw-Hill, 1965), has collected some of the writings of those young freedom fighters who tried to communicate their experiences. John R. Salter, Jr., *Jackson, Mississippi: An American Chronicle of Struggle and Schism* (Hicksville, New York: Exposition Press, 1979), recalls rights activity, and some of the tensions and divisions among black activists, in the Mississippi city with the largest concentration of black residents. Salter was an associate of Medgar W. Evers, one of the most influential voices in the Jackson movement, who was assassinated on June 11, 1963. The violence of southern racism is further explored in two works dealing with the murder of three Freedom Summer volunteers in Philadelphia, Mississippi, in June 1964: William Bradford Huie, *Three Lives for Mississippi* (New York: New American Library, 1968; originally published, New York: WCC Books, 1965), and Seth Cagin and Philip Dray, *We Are Not Afraid: The Story of Goodman, Schwerner, and Chaney and the Civil Rights Campaign in Mississippi* (New York: Macmillan, 1988). One of the most courageous and enigmatic figures of the civil rights era, Robert Moses, SNCC leader and chief strategist of the Mississippi voter registration drive of 1964, did perhaps more than any other rights crusader to stress the principles of community self-determination and participatory democracy. Some of his views are available in Bob Moses, "Mississippi: 1961–1962," *Liberation*, 14 (January 1970): 7–17, and Eric Burner, *And Gently He Shall Lead Them: Robert Parris Moses and Mississippi SNCC* (New York: New York University Press, 1993), which provides a more complete history of Moses and a better appreciation of the texture of his thought.

A sizable body of work examines other campaigns. The freedom struggle in Selma, Alabama, is recalled in Amelia Boynton Robinson, 2nd ed., *Bridge Across Jordan, The Story of the Civil Rights Struggle in Selma* (Washington, D.C.: Schiller Institute, 1991; 1st ed., as Amelia Platts Boynton, New York: Carlton Press, 1979) and Sheyann Webb and Rachel West Nelson, *Selma, Lord, Selma: Girlhood Memories of the Civil Rights Days* (University of Alabama: University of Alabama Press, 1980). Also see J. L. Chestnut, Jr. and Julie Cass, *Black in Selma: The Uncommon Life of J. L. Chestnut, Jr.* (New York: Farrar, Straus and Giroux, 1990), and David J. Garrow, *Protest at Selma: Martin Luther King, Jr., and the Voting Rights Act of 1965* (New Haven, CT: Yale University Press, 1978). Stephen L. Longenecker, *Selma's Peacemaker: Ralph Smeltzer and Civil Rights Mediation* (Philadelphia: Temple University Press, 1987), analyzes the response of southern white moderates to the political and economic challenges of the campaign for racial equity. Along similar lines, Hollinger F. Barnard, ed., *Outside the Magic Circle: The Autobiography of Virginia Foster Durr* (University of Alabama: University of Alabama Press, 1985), describes the part of progressive southern whites in some of the black civil liberties campaigns. Virginia Durr and her husband Clifford Durr, white Alabama liberals, supported the Montgomery bus boycott. Clifford Durr helped secure the release of Rosa Parks after her arrest and Virginia Durr organized alternative transportation for black workers during the boycott. The essays in David J. Garrow, ed., *Birmingham, Alabama, 1956–1963: The Black Struggle for Civil Rights* (Brooklyn, NY: Carlson Publishing, 1989), deal with events in a southern city in which the response of many whites to black demonstrations was especially brutal. In Birmingham police, led by Public Safety Commissioner "Bull" Connor, set attack dogs on protest marches and turned fire hoses on black school children, capturing national attention. Paul Good, *The Trouble I've Seen: White Journalist/ Black Movement* (Washington, DC: Howard University Press, 1974), describes how one newspaperman covered the events in the South. Robert J. Norrell, *Reaping the Whirlwind: The Civil Rights Movement in Tuskegee* (New York: Alfred Knopf, 1985), deals with protests in another Alabama city, home of Booker T. Washington's Tuskegee Institute. In 1968 the civil rights movement turned its attention to Memphis, Tennessee, and to the concerns of striking black garbage workers. It was Martin Luther King's last crusade. He was murdered in Memphis on April 4, 1968. The Memphis campaign is examined in Michael K. Honey, *Southern Labor and Black Civil Rights: Organizing Memphis Workers* (Champaign: University of Illinois Press, 1993), and Joan Turner Beifuss, *At the River I Stand: Memphis, the 1968 Strike and Martin Luther King* (Brooklyn, NY: Carlson Publishing, 1989). Three works deal with the resistance and frustration Dr. King and the movement encountered in its first major effort, the Chicago Campaign, 1965–1966, to desegregate to a northern city: Alan B. Anderson and George W. Pickering, *Confronting the Color Line, The Broken Promise of the Civil Rights Movement in Chicago* (Athens: University of Georgia Press, 1986); James Ralph, *Northern Protest: Martin Luther King, Jr., Chicago, and the Civil Rights Movement* (Cambridge, MA: Harvard University Press, 1993); and the essays in David J. Garrow, ed., *Chicago 1966 Open-Housing Marches, Summit Negotiations and Operation Breadbasket* (Brooklyn, NY: Carlson Publishing, 1989).

The purpose of the civil rights movement was revolutionary: to improve the social and economic conditions of life for millions of African Americans and consequently to transform the nation. One important means of securing that end was to effect changes in politics, government and public policy. In the years before the *Brown* decision civil rights advocates had been especially successful in altering the regulations affecting blacks in the military. Two works discuss the setting for the integration of the armed forces: Morris J. MacGregor and Bernard C. Nalty, eds., *Blacks in the United States Armed Forces: Basic Documents*, 13 volumes (Wilmington, DE: Scholarly Resources, 1977), and Richard Dalfiume, *Desegregation of the U.S. Armed Forces: Fighting on Two Fronts, 1939–53* (Columbia: University of Missouri Press, 1969). The relationship between the civil rights campaigners and the American Presidents often has been richly rewarding for both sides; and just as often it has proven a source of dissatisfaction to both parties. On blacks and presidential politics in the era of Franklin D. Roosevelt, see Harvard Sitkoff, *A New Deal for Blacks: The Emergence of Civil Rights as a National Issue, The Depression Decade* (New York: Oxford University Press, 1978). William C. Berman, *The Politics of Civil Rights in the Truman Administration* (Columbus: Ohio State University Press, 1970), is very critical of Truman and his handling of civil rights issues; Donald R. McCoy and Richard T. Reuten, *Quest and Response: Minority Rights and the Truman Administration* (Lawrence: University of Kansas Press, 1973), describe the Truman presidency and its politics with more sympathy. In 1946 President Truman appointed a biracial committee of prominent Americans to investigate race relations in the United States and to make policy recommendations for enhancing black civil rights and improving interracial harmony. The President's panel issued its report the following year, President's Committee on Civil Rights, *To Secure These Rights: The Report of the President's Committee on Civil Rights* (Washington, DC: U.S. Government Printing Office, 1947). The presidential politics and programs of the 1950s are the subject of Robert Fredrick Burk, *The Eisenhower Administration and Black Civil Rights* (Knoxville: University of Tennessee Press, 1984), which, among other concerns, assesses Eisenhower's response to the early activities of the integrationists.

The 1960s were the most important decade of the modern civil rights era. During the decade, especially within the presidencies of John Kennedy and Lyndon Johnson, the national government, at the urging of those within the movement, instituted programs and adopted important legislation protecting and expanding minority rights. Allen J. Matusow, *The Unraveling of America: A History of Liberalism in the 1960s* (New York: Harper and Row, 1984), provides an overview of the decade and takes a critical look at Kennedy's "New Frontier" and the social and economic projects of Johnson's "Great Society." Two works deal broadly with the presidency and civil rights during the 1960s: Steven A. Shull, *The President and Civil Rights Policy: Leadership and Change* (New York: Greenwood Press, 1989), and Allan Wolk, *The Presidency and Black Civil Rights: Eisenhower to Nixon* (Rutherford, NJ: Fairleigh Dickinson University Press, 1971). Books on the Kennedy years include: David Burner, *John F. Kennedy and a New Generation* (Boston: Little, Brown, 1988); Carl M. Brauer, *John F. Kennedy and the Second Reconstruction* (New York: Columbia University Press, 1977); James C. Harvey, *Civil Rights During the Kennedy Administration* (Hattiesburg: University and College Press of Mississippi, 1971); and John Walton Cotman, *Birmingham, JFK, and the Civil Rights Act of 1963: Implications for Elite Theory* (New York: P. Long, 1989). In addition to dealing with JFK, David Burner and Thomas R. West, *The Torch is Passed: The Kennedy Brothers and American Liberalism* (New York: Atheneum, 1984), catalogue Robert Kennedy's increasing interest and commitment to African American civil rights. Mark Stern, *Calculating Vision: Kennedy, Johnson, and Civil Rights* (New Brunswick, NJ: Rutgers University Press, 1992), suggests that in addition to being concerned for racial justice, the civil rights Presidents were sharp politicians with a keen eye for public image. On LBJ and the rights of African Americans, see James C. Harvey, *Black Civil Rights During the Johnson Administration* (Jackson: University and College Press of Mississippi, 1973), and Benjamin Muse, *The American Negro Revolution: From Nonviolence to Black Power, 1963–1967* (Bloomington: Indiana University Press, 1968). Norman C. Amaker, *Civil Rights and the Reagan Administration* (Washington, DC: Urban Institute Press, 1988), and Steven A. Shull, *A Kinder, Gentler Racism? The Reagan–Bush Civil Rights Legacy* (Armonk, NY: M.E. Sharpe, 1993), carry the history of the presidency and race issues through the 1980s.

The legislative history of the civil rights movement and the processes whereby it reshaped public policy are explored in these books: Charles Whalen and Barbara Whalen, *The Long Debate: A Legislative History of the 1964 Civil Rights Act* (New York: New American Library, 1985), a history of the comprehensive legislation whose provisions, among others, prohibited discrimination in employment and places of business providing public service; Benjamin Muse, *Ten Years of Prelude: The Story of Integration Since the Supreme Court's 1954 Decision* (New York: Viking Press, 1964); and Hugh Davis Graham, *The Civil Rights Era: Origins and Development of a National Policy, 1960–1965* (New York: Oxford University Press, 1990). Donald G. Nieman, *Promises to Keep, African-Americans and the Constitutional Order, 1776 to the Present* (New York: Oxford University Press, 1991), takes a long look at the relationship between blacks struggling for equal rights and the courts. Journalist Nicholas Lemann, in an excellent and moving book, *The Promised Land: The Black Migration and How It Changed America* (New York: Alfred A. Knopf, 1991), studies the migration of five million southern African Americans into the northern cities that began in the 1940s and continued until the 1960s—there had been large movements of blacks north earlier in the century, during World War I and the 1920s—and the response of politicians and others to that momentous demographic transformation that fixed the nature of the race question through to the present.

The history of the black struggle for political recognition is also, like so much of African American life, a history of the South and southern politics and the interaction between black and white southerners within the political arena. Works on these themes include Earl Black and Merle Black, *Politics and Society in the South* (Cambridge, MA: Harvard University Press, 1987); Numan V. Bartley and Hugh D. Graham, *Southern Politics and the Second Reconstruction* (Baltimore, MD: Johns Hopkins Press, 1975); Earl Black, *Southern Governors and Civil Rights; Racial Segregation as a Campaign Issue in the Second Reconstruction* (Cambridge, MA: Harvard University Press, 1976); and Pat Watters and Reese Cleghorn, *Climbing Jacob's Ladder: The Arrival of Negroes in Southern Politics* (New York: Harcourt, Brace and World, 1967). David Goldfield, *Black, White, and Southern: Race Relations and Southern Culture 1940 to the Present* (Baton Rouge: Louisiana State University Press, 1990), identifies the common elements in the culture of southern blacks and whites that ultimately made possible the settlement of political and social differences.

The drive for political recognition and voting rights by black Americans not only transformed the nature of politics in the United States but ushered in the age of a distinctive African American political culture. Three works by Steven F. Lawson assess the impact of African American voting rights on regional and national politics: *Black Ballots: Voting Rights in the South, 1944–1969* (New York: Columbia University Press, 1976); *In Pursuit of Power, Southern Blacks and Electoral Politics, 1965–1982* (New York: Columbia University Press, 1985); and *Running for Freedom: Civil Rights and Black Politics in America since 1941* (New York: McGraw-Hill, 1991). Frank Parker, *Black Votes Count: Political Empowerment in Mississippi after 1965* (Chapel Hill: University of North Carolina Press, 1990), measures the consequences of the 1965 Voting Rights Act on one deep South state. James W. Button, 2nd ed., *Blacks and Social Change: Impact of the Civil Rights Movement in Southern Communities* (Princeton, NJ: Princeton University Press, 1993), measures the consequences of black participation in the political life of six Florida cities. Doug McAdam, *Political Process and the Development of Black Insurgency, 1930–1970* (Chicago: University of Chicago Press, 1982), gives a long history of the black campaign to seize political responsibility. Denton L. Watson, *Lion in the Lobby: Clarence Mitchell, Jr.'s Struggle for the Passage of Civil Rights Laws* (New York: Morrow, 1990), is a biography of the NAACP's chief lobbyist and the story of the most visible and powerful, and flamboyant, elected black official in the nation before the 1960s is told in Neil Hickey and Ed Edwin, *Adam Clayton Powell and the Politics of Race* (New York: Fleet Publishing, 1965). Also see Charles V. Hamilton, *Adam Clay Powell, Jr.: The Political Biography of an American Dilemma* (New York: Atheneum, 1991).

As broad and insistent as was the movement for black equal rights, so too was the reaction and resistance of whites to that movement. Segregationists organized, formally and informally, to deny African Americans access to white schools; southern state governments developed the political fiction of interposition to invalidate the judgments of the Supreme Court and the policies of the national government; and federal officials often looked with suspicion and distrust on the activities and political views of black leaders and their associates. And many of those forms of resistance were violent or had the potential for violence. For general studies of the white opposition, see Michal R. Belknap, *Federal Law and Southern Order: Racial Violence and Constitutional Conflict in the Post-Brown South* (Athens: University of Georgia Press, 1987); Jack Bloom, *Class, Race, and the Civil Rights Movement: The Political Economy of Southern Racism* (Bloomington: Indiana University Press, 1987); David M. Chalmers, 3d ed., *Hooded Americanism: The History of the Ku Klux Klan* (Durham, NC: Duke University Press, 1987); and Herbert Shapiro, *White Violence and Black Response: From Reconstruction to Montgomery* (Amherst: University of Massachusetts Press, 1988). The southern white campaign against desegregation was centered in the well-organized institution of the Citizens' Council, which at least publicly professed nonviolence, and the policy of massive resistance. The origins and implementation of the policy and the work of the various citizens leagues is discussed in Numan V. Bartley, *The Rise of Massive Resistance: Race and Politics in the South During the 1950's* (Baton Rouge: Louisiana State University Press, 1969); Neil R. McMillen, *The Citizens' Council: Organized Resistance to the Second Reconstruction, 1954–1964* (Urbana: University of Illinois Press, 1971); and Francis M. Wilhoit, *The Politics of Massive Resistance* (New York: Braziller, 1973). State and local studies include Benjamin Muse, *Virginia's Massive Resistance* (Bloomington: Indiana University Press, 1961); Robbins L. Gates, *The Making of Massive Resistance: Virginia's Politics of Public School Desegregation, 1954–56* (Chapel Hill: University of North Carolina Press, 1964); and David R. Colburn, *Racial Change and Community Crisis: St. Augustine, Florida, 1877–1980* (New York: Columbia University Press, 1985). Journalist James Jackson Kilpatrick, now a news commentator of national reputation but during the heady days of the civil rights campaign editor of the pro-segregation *Richmond News Leader*, defended massive resistance, advocated state interposition against federal law, and argued for the advantages to keeping the races separate in *The Southern Case for School Segregation* (New York: Crowell-Collier Press, 1962). Three studies examine federal interference with the black freedom movement and the effort by the FBI to identify some black leaders with radical or communist organizations as a means of discrediting their work: David J. Garrow, *The FBI and Martin Luther King Jr.* (New York: Norton, 1981; also, New York: Penguin, 1983); Kenneth O'Reilly, *"Racial Matters": The FBI's Secret File on Black America, 1960–1972* (New York: Free Press, 1989); and Clayborne Carson, *Malcolm X: The FBI File* (New York: Carroll and Graf Publishers, 1991). Elizabeth Jacoway and David R. Colburn in *Southern Businessmen and Desegregation* (Baton Rouge: Louisiana State University Press, 1982) discuss an important and little acknowledged group of southerners, the shopkeepers, merchants, bankers, and other businessmen, who tried to steer a middle course and mediated between their white clients and customers who supported segregation and black southerners, also clients and customers, determined to bring segregation to an end.

Most of the leaders of the civil rights movement were men. Yet even a casual inspection of the filmed accounts of the movement indicates that the audiences those leaders addressed, the marches they led, the boycotts they initiated and the protests they conducted were staffed by women. Often as much as half the participants at any rights event were women, and frequently more than half. Thanks largely to the influence of professional women in the academic disciplines of history, sociology, and political science, among others, current scholarship has undertaken the task of recovering the work of women in modern social movements. Studies of women in the civil rights campaign identify women not only as followers within the movement but as members who set the agenda and determined the goals of the movement and the special processes by which those goals were to be attained. African American females, unlike black males, faced a dual form of oppression: discriminated against as members of a racial minority, they also faced discrimination based on gender. Dual oppression meant not only struggling across racial lines with white tormentors but contending with the predominately male leadership of the movement.

Works analyzing the participation and influence of women in the civil rights movement—in addition to books already mentioned earlier in this essay—include: two reference collections edited by Darlene Clark Hine, *Black Women in American History: The Twentieth Century*, 4 volumes (Brooklyn, NY: Carlson Publishing, Inc., 1990) and *Black Women in America: An Historical Encyclopedia*, 2 volumes, (Brooklyn, NY: Carlson Publishing, 1993); Jessie Carney Smith, ed., *Notable Black American Women* (Detroit, MI: Gale Research Inc., 1992); and the collection of scholarly essays in Vicki L. Crawford, Jacqueline Rouse, and Barbara Woods, ed., *Women in the Civil Rights Movement: Trailblazers and Torchbearers* (Brooklyn, NY: Carlson Publishing, 1990), volume 16 of Darlene Clark Hine, ed., *Black Women in the United States*. Also see Rhoda Lois Blumberg, "Rediscovering Women Leaders of the Civil Rights Movement," in Jeannine

Swift, ed., *Dream and Reality: The Modern Black Struggle for Freedom and Equality* (Westport, CT: Greenwood Press, 1991), and Paula Giddings, *When and Where I Enter: The Impact of Black Women on Race and Sex in America* (New York: Morrow, 1984). Sara Evans, *Personal Politics: The Roots of Women's Liberation in the Civil Rights Movement and the New Left* (New York: Alfred Knopf, 1979), argues that the women's liberation movement developed out of the experience of white female activists in the civil rights organizations, especially membership in SNCC, where they came in touch with strong black women in local communities throughout the deep South. And Pearl Cleage, *Deals With the Devil, and Other Reasons to Riot* (New York: Ballantine Books, 1993), is a new work certain to provoke debate as an activist black woman reflects on the struggle for black freedom and offers her views on racism and sexism across the color line and within the African American community.

The women of the civil rights era have told their stories, and many have registered in personal histories their anger at race oppression and sex oppression, or they have had their lives examined in some carefully wrought biographies. Mrs. Fannie Lou Hamer, from a desperately poor family in Ruleville, Mississippi, became a member of SNCC in 1962 and was one of the founding members of the Mississippi Freedom Democratic Party. She was one of the most powerful voices of complaint heard—in the stories she recounted of discrimination and the songs of protest she sang. She talks of her part in the freedom movement in *To Praise Our Bridges: An Autobiography of Mrs. Fanny [sic] Lou Hamer* (Jackson, MS: KIPCO, 1967 [reprinted as Fannie Lou Hamer, "To Praise Our Bridges," *Mississippi Writers: Reflections on Childhood and Youth*, ed. Dorothy Abbott (Jackson: University Press of Mississippi, 1986)]). Kay Mills, *This Little Light of Mine: The Life of Fannie Lou Hamer* (New York: Dutton, 1993), is an excellent history of the life and times of Mrs. Hamer. The Fannie Lou Hamer Papers are at the Amistad Research Center, Tulane University. Ella Jo Baker, a member of Martin Luther King's SCLC, helped arrange the Shaw University conference in April 1960 that led to the creation of SNCC. A tireless campaigner, she favored SNCC's grass-roots democracy style of organization, which promised to treat men and women the same, and grew increasingly critical of the male- and minister-led SCLC. She labored to keep the student movement independent of SCLC. A complete biography of Baker has yet to appear—several are in progress—but two essays and a documentary film deal with her life and thought: Ellen Cantarow and Susan Gushee O'Malley, "Ella Baker: Organizing for Civil Rights," in Ellen Cantarow with Susan Gushee O'Malley and Sharon Hartman Strom, *Moving the Mountain: Women Working for Social Change* (Old Westbury, NY: Feminist Press, 1980); Charles Payne, "Ella Baker and Models of Social Change," *Signs*, 14 (1989); 885–99; and film maker Joanne Grant, *"Fundi": The Story of Ella Baker* (New York: First Run Films, 1981). The woman who became a symbol of the struggle for dignity for African Americans, Rosa Parks, describes the event that led to the Montgomery bus boycott and her life of rights activism in *Rosa Parks: My*

*Story* (New York: Dial Books, 1992), with Jim Haskins. Two books, Septima Poinsette Clark with LeGette Blythe, *Echo in My Soul* (New York: E. P. Dutton and Co., 1962), and Septima Poinsette Clark with Cynthia Stokes Brown, *Ready from Within: Septima Clark and the Civil Rights Movement* (Trenton, NJ: Africa World Press, 1990; originally published, Navarro, CA: Wild Trees Press, 1986), describe the work of Septima Clark, one of the founders of the Highlander program and an organizer of southern "citizenship schools" that aimed at qualifying blacks to register to vote. Mary King, *Freedom Song: A Personal Story of the 1960s Civil Rights Movement* (New York: Quill Books, a division of William Morrow, 1987), is a chronicle of SNCC's movement from reform to revolution by a SNCC staffer; it is a study that has been seen as critical of the student organization's treatment of women. A recent work of autobiography, Sarah and A. Elizabeth Delany with Amy Hill Hearth, *Having Our Say, The Delany Sisters' First 100 Years* (New York: Kodansha International, 1993), recounts the history of two black women who challenged the race and gender customs of their time, pursued education and their own lives. And in *Pushed Back to Strength: A Black Woman's Journey Home* (Boston: Beacon, 1993), Gloria Wade-Gayles, now a college professor, recalls what it was like for a young woman to come to maturity in the South in an age when the racial and sexual customs that had stood for centuries were being challenged.

During the 1960s the demands made by many African Americans suddenly seemed more unrelenting and aggressive—more militant. A new phrase, "Black Power," was being used, and although it could be used to describe any number of attitudes and philosophies—from an angrily anti-white insistence on black separatism or black nationalism to the more peaceable encouragements to African Americans to be more aware of their heritage and to cultivate within themselves a greater appreciation of their culture (black pride)—the appearance of Black Power movements divided many former civil rights allies and had a chilling effect on white America. General studies of Black Power include: William L. Van Deburg, *New Day in Babylon: The Black Power Movement and American Culture, 1965–1975* (Chicago: University of Chicago Press, 1992); Herbert Haines, *Black Radicals and the Civil Rights Mainstream, 1954–1970* (Knoxville: University of Tennessee Press, 1988); and E. U. Essien-Udom, *Black Nationalism: A Search for and Identity in America* (Chicago: University of Chicago Press, 1962). Julius Lester, *Look Out, Whitey! Black Power's Gon' Get Your Mama* (New York: Dial Press, 1968), provides an example of the literature and rhetoric of Black Power by an author who both supported the Black Power movement and could be among its harshest critics. As one of the moving forces in SNCC, Stokely Carmichael was responsible for turning that organization from nonviolence and peaceful demonstration to aggressive black self-determination—Carmichael wanted whites excluded from SNCC. It is generally believed that Carmichael's speech in Greenwood, Mississippi, on June 17, 1966, in which he demanded Black Power, drove a wedge in the civil rights movement and set one segment of the movement along a more revolutionary path. Carmichael's views are available in two of his essays, "Toward Black Liberation," *Massachusetts Review*, vol. 7 (Autumn 1966): 639–51, and "What We Want," *New York Review of Books* (September 26, 1966), and in a tamer book with co-author Charles V. Hamilton, *Black Power: The Politics of Liberation in America* (New York: Random House, 1967).

Though Carmichael was the first to popularize the phrase Black Power and to initiate the Black Power movement, the individual who came to symbolize that movement, to be inseparably identified with black militancy in the minds of blacks and whites, was Malcolm X. Interest in Malcolm X recently has been revitalized thanks to a feature film directed by Spike Lee, *Malcolm X* (screenplay by James Baldwin, Arnold Perl, and Spike Lee). The complex and controversial Malcolm X relates his personal history and his views in his own words in Malcolm X, *The Autobiography of Malcolm X* (New York: Ballantine Books, 1992; originally published, New York: Grove Press, 1965) with the assistance of Alex Haley; George Breitman, ed., *Malcolm X Speaks: Selected Speeches and Statements* (New York: Merit Publishers, 1965); and George Breitman, ed., *By Any Means Necessary: Speeches, Interviews and a Letter by Malcolm X* (New York: Pathfinder Press, 1970). Malcolm X's relationship with Elijah Muhammad's Lost-Found Nation of Islam (Black Muslims), from which he resigned in 1964, is discussed in C. Eric Lincoln, *The Black Muslims in America*, 2nd ed. (Boston: Beacon Press, 1973). Biographies include: Bruce Perry, *Malcolm: The Life of a Man Who Changed Black America* (Barrytown, NY: Station Hill Press, 1991), and Peter Goldman, *The Death and Life of Malcolm X*, 2nd ed. (Urbana: University of Illinois Press, 1979). Joe Wood, ed., *Malcolm X: In Our Own Image* (New York: St. Martin's Press, 1992), and James Gwynne, ed., *Malcolm X—Justice Seeker* (New York: Steppingstones Press, 1993), contain scholarly essays. James H. Cone, *Martin and Malcolm and America: A Dream or A Nightmare* (Maryknoll, NY: Orbis Books, 1991), compares the religious thought and philosophy of Malcolm X with that of Martin Luther King, Jr. Journalist Karl Evanzz, *The Judas Factor: The Plot to Kill Malcolm X* (New York: Thunders Mouth Press, Emoryville, CA, distributed by Publishers Group West, 1992), investigates the assassination of Malcolm, during a speech in New York on February 21, 1965. Two essays assess the historical reliability and the influence of Spike Lee's movie: Neil Irvin Painter, "Malcolm X across the Genres," *American Historical Review*, 98 (April 1993): 432–39, and Gerald Horne, " 'Myth' and the Making of 'Malcolm X,' " *American Historical Review*, 98 (April 1993): 440–50.

If Malcolm X was the individual most closely associated with Black Power in the public mind, the Black Panthers, organized in Oakland, California, in October 1966, was the group identified with black radicalism, violence and revolutionary politics. Although the rhetoric of the Panthers could be confrontational and crude, they made intelligent demands for economic reform and initiated economic programs—a successful one included free breakfast for school children—to strengthen local black communities and politically empower their residents. Still the aggressiveness of the Panthers caused them to be the focus of white fear and often made them the target of police attacks. Many of the organizers of the Panther party have provided written records of their activities and beliefs: Bobby Seale, *Seize the Time: The Story of the Black Panther Party and Huey P. Newton* (New York: Random House, 1970); Bobby Seale, *A Lonely Rage: The Autobiography of Bobby Seale*, with a foreword by James Baldwin (New York: Times Books, 1978); Huey Newton with J. Herman Blake, *Revolutionary Suicide* (New York: Harcourt, Brace and Jovanovich, 1973); H. Rap Brown, *Die, nigger, die!* (New York: Dial Press, 1969); Eldridge Cleaver, *Soul on Ice* (New York: McGraw-Hill, 1968); and David Hilliard and Lewis Cole, *This Side of Glory: The Autobiography of David Hilliard and the Story of the Black Panther Party* (Boston: Little, Brown and Co., 1993). Earl Anthony describes his time as a member of the Panthers in *Picking Up the Gun: A Report on the Black Panthers* (New York: Dial Press, 1970). Also see G. Louis Heath, *Off the Pigs! The History and Literature of the Black Panther Party* (Metuchen, NJ: Scarecrow Press, 1976); John Hulett, *The Black Panther Party* (New York: Merit Publishers, 1966); and Gene Marine, *The Black Panthers* (New York: New American Library, 1969).

Three works describe the place of women in the black revolutionary movement: Angela Davis, *Angela Davis: An Autobiography* (New York: Random House, 1974; and New York: International Press, 1988); J. A. Parker, *Angela Davis: The Making of a Revolutionary* (New Rochelle, NY: Arlington House, 1973); and Elaine Brown, *A Taste of Power: A Black Woman's Story* (New York: Pantheon Books, 1992). And the essays in Clyde Taylor, ed., *Vietnam and Black America: An Anthology of Protest and Resistance* (Garden City, NY: Anchor Press, 1973), assess the influence of the civil rights crusade and the Black Power movement on other forms of social protest.

During the year 1967, 164 cases of racial disturbances were reported in America's cities; forty-three citywide disorders were listed for the previous year. The urban race riots of the mid 1960s—the worst of which occurred in Newark, New Jersey, Detroit, Michigan, and the Watts neighborhood of south-central Los Angeles—which many whites incorrectly attributed to the work of Black Power agitators, caused contention among the ranks of civil rights advocates and had an adverse effect on the entire civil rights movement. The major urban disorders were broadcast nationally by television journalists. Works that examine the riots and their consequences include Fred R. Harris and Tom Wicker, eds., *The Kerner Report: The 1968 Report of the National Advisory Commission on Civil Disorders* (New York: Pantheon, 1988); Sidney Fine, *Violence in the Model City: The Cavanaugh Administration, Race Relations and The Detroit Riot of 1967* (Ann Arbor: University of Michigan Press, 1989); Tom Hayden, *Rebellion in Newark: Official Violence and Ghetto Response* (New York: Random House, 1967); James W. Button, *Black Violence: Political Impact of the 1960s Riots* (Princeton, NJ: Princeton University Press, 1978); Paul Bullock, ed., *Watts: The Aftermath by the People of Watts* (New York: Grove Press, 1969); and the forthcoming Gerald Horne, *Fire This Time: The Watts Uprising and the Meaning of the 1960s*.

# NOTES

# NOTES

# NOTES

# NOTES

# NOTES